Waterfront Revolts

A list of books in the series appears at the end of this book.

Waterfront Revolts

NEW YORK AND LONDON DOCKWORKERS, 1946–61

Colin J. Davis

UNIVERSITY OF ILLINOIS PRESS
URBANA AND CHICAGO

Manufactured in the United States of America
C 5 4 3 2 1

This book is printed on acid-free paper.

Library of Congress Cataloging-in-Publication Data

Davis, Colin J. (Colin John), 1954–
Waterfront revolts : New York and London dockworkers, 1946–61 /
Colin J. Davis.
p. cm. — (The working class in American history)
Includes bibliographical references (p.) and index.
ISBN 0-252-02878-3 (cloth : alk. paper)
1. Strikes and lockouts—Stevedores—New York (State)—New York—
History—20th century. 2. Stevedores—Labor unions—New York (State)—
New York—History—20th century. 3. Strikes and lockouts—Stevedores—
England—London—History—20th century. 4. Stevedores—Labor
unions—England—London—History—20th century. 5. Wildcat strikes—
New York (State)—New York. 6. Wildcat strikes—England—London.
I. Title. II. Series.
HD5325.L6D38 2003
331.892'81387164'0942109045—dc21 2003007100

*To Stella, Ava, Madeleine,
and Brenda*

CONTENTS

ACKNOWLEDGMENTS

One of the pleasurable duties of producing a book is thanking those who helped make it possible. The debts I owe are large and numerous. To the late Debra E. Bernhardt of the Robert F. Wagner Labor Archives at New York University I owe special gratitude. She familiarized me with some of the early archival material, but more important, she introduced me to New York longshoremen who were willing to share their tales of work and struggle. Other archives that gave me a solid research experience included those of the Harry S. Truman Presidential Library, the Kheel Center for Labor-Management Documentation and Archives at Cornell University, the New York State Archive in Albany, New York, and Fordham University. In England the staffs of the Public Record Office and the People's History Museum, Manchester, patiently steered me through the collection process. Joane Burman and her staff at the Modern Records Center at the University of Warwick gave both support and suggestions. The book could not have been completed in a timely manner without the support of the staff at Sterne Library at the University of Alabama at Birmingham. Director Jerry Stephens gave the sort of support and guidance that one usually only dreams about.

Grants and fellowships from the following agencies helped me gather a wide array of material: a Larry J. Hackman Research Residency Grant (New York State Archive), New Jersey Historical Commission, the Irish-American Cultural Exchange, the Harry S. Truman Institute, Phi Alpha Theta, the University of Alabama at Birmingham, and the American Philosophical Society.

The following historians read portions of the manuscript: Peter Weiler, Josh Freeman, Eric Arnesen, and Melvyn Dubofsky. Special thanks to Joe McCartin, who read the entire study and provided invaluable and thought-provoking comments. Special thanks also go to David Montgomery. David did a marvelous critique of the book as series editor and has provided invaluable guidance throughout the project. Other historians who have played a critical role in the development of this book include James Barrett, Rick Halpern, George Fredrickson, Peter Alexander, Alex Lichtenstein, Robert Zieger, David Palmer, Dennis Deslippe, Judith Stein, Gary Fink, Nick Salvatore, Mary J. Hickman, John Laslett, Kathleen Paul, Bruce Nelson, Calvin Winslow, Elizabeth Faue, Frederick Cooper, Diane Frost, Marion Casey, Joe Doyle, William DeFazio, Steve Rosswurm, Natalie Boren, and James Cronin. Ray Mohl, as my chair during most of the writing process, exemplified professionalism and crucial direction. For my British research Neville Kirk, Sam Davies, Dick Geary, Chris Wrigley, and Eric Taplin all delivered the support that a researcher needs. Thanks also to Jimmy Ludwig and Cindi Cobbs for being such gracious London hosts.

A special thanks to the International Institute of Social History in Amsterdam. A conference it sponsored that examined dockworkers around the world did much to shape the book. Thanks to Klaus Weinhauer, Lex Heerma van Voss, Sam Davies, and Lidewij Hesselink. On my many research visits friends gave me not just their living spaces but also their input. Questions asked by Michael Hyman and Tom Coogan have done much to strengthen this study. Thanks also to colleagues in Birmingham who either read portions of the book or just provided a sympathetic ear, specifically, Tom McKenna, Wendy Gunther-Canada, Carolyn Conley, and Charlotte Borst. Joan Lorden, graduate dean and vice president of research, provided key support during the research process, as did Dean Tennant McWilliams. I appreciate the assistance of Richard Wentworth, Laurie Matheson, and Carol Betts at the University of Illinois Press.

I would also like to express my gratitude to those dockworkers who gave of their time to describe their work experiences along the waterfronts of New York City and London. Thanks to Angelo Pacifico, Pete Bell, Sebastian and Leonard DeFazio, "Eddie," Frank Barbaro, Larry Sullivan, Jose Villa, Arthur McMillon, George Pye, Joe Bloomberg, John Donovan, and Ted Johns. A special thanks to the retired dockers at the Dockers' Club, London. Thanks also to I. Philip Sipser, Vincent Longhi, Harold Mailman, and Audrey West.

During the writing of the book I lost two dear friends: my mother, Audrey, and a younger sister, Brenda. Each of them in her own way solidified my interest in history. Finally, my wife, Susan Swider, and my beautiful daughters, Stella, Ava, and Madeleine, gave me more than I've deserved—a family life of love and challenge.

Waterfront Revolts

INTRODUCTION

During the early 1950s a London dockworker and militant, Joe Bloomberg, paid a fraternal visit to New York City. During his time there, he met with Joe Ryan, the trade union president of the International Longshoremen's Association (ILA). It was no secret that Ryan's union was infested with gangsters. Sitting in Ryan's office, the two men initially engaged in a friendly conversation. According to Bloomberg, Ryan then half-jokingly declared, "You know what we do with a guy like you, don't you? . . . You'd never be sitting there. You'd be buried."[1] This extraordinary statement goes to the core of the relationship between established trade union leader and insurgent rank and filer on the docks. In the parlance of the New York waterfront, the word "buried" could literally mean just that: dead in a lime pit in New Jersey. London's trade union leadership more than likely wished a similar fate for militants like Bloomberg in the Hackney Marshes.

Following World War II, dockworker union leaders on both sides of the Atlantic Ocean battled men like Bloomberg for the hearts and minds of their rank and file. Throughout the early years of the cold war, New York and London dockworkers directly challenged an array of institutions that included their union leaders, employers, and central governments. Unlike earlier confrontations involving recognition of unions, post–World War II struggles centered around issues of rank-and-file estrangement from union leaders, government fears of disruption of national economies by Communist-inspired agitators, and employer frustration with unions' lack of control over their members. Work stoppages and contests for power within labor unions were common during the postindustrial era. Dockworkers stood at the center of these unfolding dramas and faced the wrath of governments determined to maintain cordial relations with trade union allies and ensure free avenues of trade.

The reasons why New York City and London dockworkers directly confronted both their trade union leaders and their erstwhile government allies go to the heart of workplace activism. The respective oppositional movements were charged with pent-up anger, as well as impelled by outside forces that nurtured such resistance. Since the late nineteenth century the climate of work had little changed, but the expectations around it had. Dockworkers demanded better working conditions. The circumstances driving these men to confront their union leaders may have been different in each city, but the workers shared the same weapons of solidarity and a growing sense of menace. The fury of these men was the glue that bound them together. But the hold was temporary. Once initial issues had been resolved, or partially addressed, the men returned to their waterfront jobs.

This study compares New York City and London dockworkers in order to identify the structural and cultural forces that lay behind the emergence of rank-and-file dockworker movements. Its purpose is also to gauge their ability to challenge union hierarchies and to wring concessions from national governments. A comparative examination of dockworker movements and the various responses by central governments builds on important new developments in historical research. Scholars in the historiography of labor and of politics have recently pointed to the importance of the state in shaping working-class protest. Known as the "new institutionalism," this historiography posits a vision of the state as a relatively autonomous force, rather than an instrument dominated by one class or faction.[2] Many of the "new institutionalist" studies are confined, however, to a national approach. Generally, one specific national phenomenon is examined and held up as the mirror of lived experience. Labor historians, it seems, have been lax in utilizing comparative methods and analyses. As George Fredrickson recently asked, "Why haven't historians of American labor and class relations become as cross-cultural and as systematically comparative as those interested in gender, race, and nationality?"[3]

Those few comparative labor histories that do exist end their studies in the early twentieth century, leaving the post–World War II period unexplored.[4] To a large extent, many U.S. and British labor historians have been distracted by the debates over "American exceptionalism" and the "peculiarities of the English." While useful for its intellectual rigor, this discussion has not necessarily led to new approaches that encapsulate the comparative paradigm. Instead, the debate has focused on whether each history is "exceptional" or "peculiar."[5] Historians in other subject areas have not been so focused on such narrow questions. They have produced comparative studies of topics ranging from racial identification and struggle to urban and business history.[6]

This study of dockworkers in New York and London will focus on the connections and differences between the two work forces. This effort will necessarily entail discussion of culture, political economy, and race. But the connective tissue that links these two cases is the world of work, and the quest for dignity on the job and in the union hall. The common characteristic is one of struggle. The comparative approach will reveal the similarities and differences among the struggles of these transatlantic workers.

Comparative history can strengthen U.S. history by situating it in an international context. Moving away from the parochial study of American history will usher in a more complex, exciting, and refined assessment of time and place, as well as of the structural and cultural determinants of human behavior. Grounding the study in the immediate postwar era sheds light on the development of the cold war in the United States and Great Britain. Employing the comparative method reveals how workers, trade unions, and nation-states directly influenced cold war politics, economics, and culture across geographical borders. Shared but distinct experiences emerge in sharp relief.

It is the commonality of the experience that encourages a comparative approach. Studying two similar work forces, contextualized by different national structures and cultures, can broaden one's understanding of political choice during the emerging cold war period. The dockworkers' perception that democracy was absent in their respective unions nurtured their resistance. Their strike actions, on the face of it, undermined calls for loyalty to industrial capitalism during these years. Traversing national boundaries, the comparison of New York and London dockworkers dismantles the themes of exceptionalism and peculiarism. Each group fought simultaneously against not just trade union hierarchies and governments, but also perceptions of consensual or stable industrial relations. By forcefully rejecting their trade unions, these workers took on the mantle of rebels during a period that extolled the virtues of conformism. Thus it is the joined experience that informs the comparative study.

Questions that surround the usefulness of comparative history have a charged pedigree. Recently, the Organization of American Historians (OAH) has taken tentative steps to address the complex topological character of United States history. The OAH LaPietra Report grappled with the questions of the internationalization of American history. Terms such as "internationalization," "cross-national," "transnational," and "comparative" all were given their due in the LaPietra Report. The report was commendably vague in its conclusions, but it finally agreed that U.S. historians should ground their national studies in an embracing paradigm of "larger processes." The point is to "deepen its contextualization and to extend the transnational relations of

American history." Unfortunately, the report stopped there because of the fear that internationalizing U.S. history might result in "subsum[ing]" it "under the umbrella of world or global history."[7] Such tentativeness merely reinforces parochial views. The contradictory impulses to think big but restrain such analysis to the shifting boundaries of what constitutes the national experience surely relegates the others' histories to secondary importance. Using the comparative approach, but with a close eye to the U.S. experience, historians can bridge the chasm of indifference and dismissiveness. The aim therefore is to incorporate the "other" history, while simultaneously spotlighting the American experience.

A study of dockworkers is perfectly situated for such an approach. Port cities were vital points of social and economic connection. Dockworkers literally handled each other's cargoes. The comparative method can allow U.S. labor historians the opportunity to place their work in a larger context while strengthening their appreciation of human agency and structural impulsion. Sharply delineating connections and differences provides a clear sense of both historical congruence and specificity. This is how both comparative and new institutionalist histories can merge. Demonstrating the actions and logic of oppositional culture, and the means by which the respective nation-states acted both as agents shaping workers' lives and as arenas within which class conflict was fought out, will go far in providing explanations of movement design. Such a model embraces a keener understanding of U.S. history framed by the distinctly international human conditions of defiance, conflict, governance, and power.

The emphasis of this book is on conflict, especially that which was largely centered around workplace issues and the ways trade union leaders were regarded. The cultural turn in historical studies of recent years has downplayed the paradigm of union, employer, and state conflict. Studies of institutional conflict have been perceived as unjustly leaning toward a more deterministic impression of human existence.[8] Union-centered histories then are dismissed as merely representative of a small fraction of the working population, ignoring either the totality or specificity of working-class experience. Nonetheless, this study is grounded in the era during which union membership hit its impressive height and trade union leaders enjoyed unprecedented national influence and significance.

But even if one was to choose a segment of the working population that was nonunion, this strategy would not necessarily weaken the case of conflict-ridden workplace experiences. Strikes, for example, do not occur just in union shops. Work is the central experience for most workers. As Paul Thompson has argued, "most people's lives are structured by work."[9] By their daily clocking in, the workers give the employer their most precious object, themselves. Such an action is invariably tension-filled. The labor is not volunteered but merely provided for the basic needs of putting food on the table, and a few extras. For dockworkers, the hazards of the job and frequent collisions with employers and government officials ensured a culture of recalcitrance and suspicion. Such cynicism stretched forth to union officials, whom the workers regarded as not fighting hard enough for their work interests. In turn, these same dockworkers looked elsewhere for leadership.

The contesting of power highlighted a unique form of "dependency" on the part of the rank and file. While the dockworkers in question used their most potent weapon of resistance or rebellion—the strike—to challenge their top union leadership, to a degree they followed a path already laid down for them. In both New York City and London, the initial clashes were framed by workplace issues, but the decision to take the struggle further was generally made by either local union officials or outside agitators. Thus, the conflict became one of competing realms of authority.[10] In essence, multiple groups fought for control of the two cities' docks. The battle between parallel forces at least gave the relatively powerless work forces cause to cheer. Dockworkers in London and New York felt a deep alienation from their respective union leaderships, and they were wooed by groups or individuals purporting to represent their best interests. One of the purposes of this book is to identify and examine these complementary forces, and to examine how at times they coalesced into a unified posture of rebellion.

None of these forces operated in a vacuum, however. On both sides of the ocean, the solidification of a union presence on the docks created distinctive problems. The dockworkers were no longer fighting for institutional survival of their union organizations. Rather, their struggle had moved on to heightened concerns of workplace democracy. The new focus was on both wages and working conditions, and union democracy. These correlative issues had bypassed each group. Consequently, dockworkers looked to local union officials to represent their views. These officials' proximity to workplace struggles naturally enlisted them in the cause to rectify the problem through forceful action against the top leadership.

Central and local governments at times tried to regularize class relations on the waterfront. Governmental trade policies were largely dependent on the efficient and constant labor of dockworkers. Governments at every level—central, state, and city—looked on any threat to trade, whether real or imagined, with keen interest. The lifeblood of the nation could be at stake. Government attention was also influenced by political alliances with trade union leaders. There was an intimate connection between dockworker unions and political administrations. Each had developed a collaborative relationship that necessarily entailed close political links. But governmental interest did vary with each port. While the British Labour government was critically interested in stable work relations on London's docks, this was not necessarily the aim of U.S. federal authorities. In New York City, state and local governmental administrations took a keen interest in labor relations because waterfront strikes had an immediate impact on New York City's metropolitan economy. So in the New York City area, a multitude of governmental agencies were involved in the strife on the docks.

Dockworker rank-and-file movements were inherently unstable but potent cultural forces during the early cold war period. These movements were cultivated either by mid- or lower-level trade union officials, or by outside groups battling for influence. Persistent public displays of rebellion, most notably strike action, galvanized the dockworkers and gave a heightened legitimacy to their existence. The role of the state was to act as both arbitrator and disciplinarian. This Janus-like posture was required to protect trade routes and stanch the rise of Communist influence, as well as to buttress trade union allies. Union leaders, insurgents and their allies, and government officials all had their roles to play. The site of contention shifted constantly from the docks to the union to the corridors of government power.

Both sets of workers, then, shared a common existence. The waterfront was a theater where conflicts over job allocation and discipline were daily played out. The two groups shared deep-seated feelings of alienation from their respective trade union officials and national governments. Separating the two, however, was the method of obtaining work—one casual, the other institutionalized by government authority. Nonetheless, expressions of grievances by each group were the same: work-gang solidarity and wild-cat action. Differences of ethnicity and racial identification also distinguished the two sets of workers. New York longshoremen labored in a racially segmented work force. A strict division of labor existed: Irish Americans stood at the apex followed by Italian, African American, and Hispanic workers. During strike activity, such differences tended to submerge under the strategic need for solidarity. Once strikes were over, however, the rigid racial and ethnic hierarchy encouraged friction once again between longshoremen and within their union.

This book will simultaneously map the New York City and London experiences of dockworkers, outlining their respective work cultures; the sites of conflicts with employers, unions, and states; the creation of alternative rank-and-file movements; and how the response by governments molded such conflicts. Chapter 1 discusses who these workingmen were—that is, their ethnic and racial profiles—and how their respective racial standings determined entry into the work force. Chapter 2 will detail the work of the dockworker. What is clearly evident is the shared sense of skill, danger, and the importance of nicknames as identifying signals. The use of pilferage as a form of rebellion and entitlement was also common. Chapter 3 details the alienation that each work force felt for both employers and top trade union leaders. Although the union cultures were different, the frustrated and angry response by the New York City and London dockworkers held common characteristics.

Chapters 4 and 5 investigate the 1948 strikes in the respective ports. These wildcat, or unofficial, strikes established viable oppositional movements that, while in flux, nurtured rhythms of rebellion. Governmental authorities recognized the shifting power relations and tried to contain them. Differing reactions, one openly hostile, the other more accommodating, were determined by an urgent need to protect trade and reestablish effective communications with trade union allies. Chapters 6 and 7 then detail continuing confrontations on the waterfronts of New York City and London. The confrontation in New York revolved around a trade union that came under intense government scrutiny because of its ties with organized crime figures. Spurring on such attention were continuing rank-and-file revolts. With the union leadership under pressure, rank-and-file leaders were emboldened to increase their attacks. Just as important, the American Federation of Labor (AFL) worked to rid the union of gangsters, even at the extreme of expelling the ILA from the established labor movement. In London, dockworkers were on their own. Throughout 1949–54, they fought unaccompanied against the combined weight of an angry trade union leadership determined to retain control and a hostile central government. Even as leaders of the rank-and-file revolt were punished, the momentum of the movement did not slow as new insurgents emerged to take on the mantle of the opposition.

Chapter 8 takes the study further into the realm of racial conflict on the New York docks. Black and Hispanic longshoremen challenged union and employer discrimination, forming a second social movement on the docks. At times, this action existed concurrently with rank-and-file insurgency between 1948 and 1954. While this latter movement almost disappeared from the scene by 1954, racial contestation continued. The demand for racial justice created its own form of identity and friction. Subsequently, the New York docks witnessed a concerted campaign by both black and Hispanic longshoremen, and their allies, for dignity in hiring and promotion on the job.

Throughout this study the purpose is to situate the dockworkers' lives in the swirling world of work and conflict. The two went together. Whether in New York or London, the daily work pattern was one of relentless toil and danger. Refusing to blindly accept their lot, these workers developed a cantankerous nature that on occasion rejected simultaneously both employer and union prerogatives. When pushed beyond a certain point, both New York and London workers reacted forcefully and created oppositional movements.

This study seeks to capture and enlarge our understanding of two social movements. The focus is as much on the players as on the play. The study is ultimately one of men who worked and died loading and unloading ocean-going ships. Fighting to have a voice in determining their own work conditions gave them hope for recognition both along the waterfront and in their communities. While doing so, they helped create and nurture a crusade for dignity. The battle gave meaning to these men. The intimidating forces aligned against them were strong, but their belief in the righteousness of their cause gave them the necessary courage to carry on.

Notes

1. Joe Bloomberg, interview with author, August 8, 1996. Unless noted otherwise in this book, all interviews by author were audiotaped and the tapes are in his possession.

2. See, for example, Eileen Boris, *Home to Work: Motherhood and the Politics of Industrial Homework in the United States* (New York: Cambridge University Press, 1994); James E. Cronin, *The Politics of State Expansion: War, State and Society in Twentieth-Century Britain* (New York: Routledge, 1991); Alan Dawley, *Struggles for Justice: Social Responsibility and the Liberal State* (Cambridge, Mass.: Belknap Press, 1991); Melvyn Dubofsky, *The State and Labor in Modern America* (Chapel Hill: University of North Carolina Press, 1994); David Montgomery, *The Fall of the House of Labor: The Workplace, the State, and American Labor Activism, 1865–1925* (New York: Cambridge University Press, 1987); Henry Pelling, *The Labor Governments, 1945–1951* (London: St. Martin's, 1984); Justin Davis Smith, *The Attlee and Churchill Administrations and Industrial Unrest, 1945–55* (London: Pinter, 1992); Christopher L. Tomlins, *The State and the Unions: Labor Relations, Law, and the Organized Labor Movement in America, 1880–1960* (New York: Cambridge University Press, 1986); Peter Weiler, *British Labor and the Cold War* (Stanford: Stanford University Press, 1988). It can be argued that many of the aforementioned studies were influenced by Peter Evans, Dietrich Rueschemeyer, and Theda Skocpol, *Bringing the State Back In* (New York: Cambridge University Press, 1985).

3. George Fredrickson, "From Exceptionalism to Variability: Recent Developments in Cross-National Comparative History," *Journal of American History* 82 (September 1995): 604.

4. See, in this regard, George Fredrickson, *The Comparative Imagination: On the History of Racism, Nationalism, and Social Movements* (Berkeley: University of California Press, 1997); Nancy L. Green, *Ready-to-Wear, Ready-to-Work: A Century of Industry and Immigrants in Paris and New York* (Durham, N.C.: Duke University Press, 1997); Jeffrey Haydu, *Making American Industry Safe for Democracy: Comparative Perspectives on the State and Employee Representation in the Era of World War I* (Urbana: University of Illinois Press,

1997); Neville Kirk, *Labour and Society in Britain and the USA* (Aldershot, Hants., Eng.: Scolar Press, 1994); John H. M. Laslett, *Colliers across the Sea: A Comparative Study of Class Formation in Scotland and the American Midwest, 1830–1924* (Urbana: University of Illinois Press, 2000); Craig Littler, *The Development of the Labour Process in Capitalist Societies: A Comparative Study of the Transformation of Work Organization in Britain, Japan, and the U.S.A.* (Exeter, N.H.: Heinemann Press, 1982); Gary Marks, *Unions in Politics: Britain, Germany, and the United States in the Nineteenth and Early Twentieth Centuries* (Princeton: Princeton University Press, 1981). Victor Silverman's *Imagining Internationalism in American and British Labor, 1939–49* (Urbana: University of Illinois Press, 2000) does focus on the post–World War II era.

5. The literature on the subject of "American exceptionalism" and "English peculiarism" is exhaustive. A good introduction to this ongoing discussion is Rick Halpern and Jonathan Morris, eds., *American Exceptionalism? U.S. Working-Class Formation in an International Context* (New York: St. Martin's, 1997). See also James E. Cronin, "Neither Exceptional nor Peculiar: Towards the Comparative Study of Labor in Advanced Society," *International Review of Social History* 38 (1993): 59–75; Sean Wilentz, "Against Exceptionalism: Class Consciousness and the American Labor Movement," *International Labor and Working Class History* 27 (1984): 1–24, and the responses by Nick Salvatore and Michael Hanagan in the same issue, 25–30, 31–36, respectively. Much of the debate regarding the "peculiarism" issue followed Edward Thompson's "The Peculiarities of the English," in *Socialist Register 1965,* ed. Ralph Miliband and John Saville (New York: Monthly Review Press, 1965), 311–62.

6. For studies in other areas, see George Fredrickson, *Black Liberation: A Comparative History of Black Ideologies in the United States and South Africa* (New York: Oxford University Press, 1995); James T. Campbell, *Songs of Zion: The African Methodist Episcopal Church in the United States and South Africa* (Chapel Hill: University of North Carolina Press, 1995); Peter Kolchin, *Unfree Labor: American Slavery and Russian Serfdom* (Cambridge, Mass.: Belknap Press, 1987); Norbert McDonald, *Distant Neighbors: A Comparative History of Seattle and Vancouver* (Lincoln, Neb.: University of Nebraska Press 1987). For a general comparative study, see David Englander, ed., *Britain and America Studies in Comparative History, 1760–1970* (New Haven: Yale University Press, 1997).

7. "The LaPietra Report: A Report to the Profession," <http://www.oah.org/activities/lapietra/final.html>, accessed July 17, 2001.

8. For a discussion of work and union-centered history as having submerged the cultural turn, see Jonathan Prude's critique of David Montgomery's *The Fall of the House of Labor* in "Directions of Labor History," *American Quarterly* 42 (March 1990): 136–44. Of course, discourse analysis was perceived as putting an end to political economy. This is considered in Gareth Stedman Jones, *Languages of Class: Studies in English Working Class History* (New York: Cambridge University Press, 1983). For outstanding rebuttals to discourse theory see Bryan Palmer, *Descent into Discourse: The Reification of Language and the Writing of Social History* (Philadelphia: Temple University Press, 1990); Neville Kirk, "History, Language, Ideas and Post-modernism: A Materialist View," *Social History* 19 (1994): 221–40.

9. Paul Thompson, *The Nature of Work: An Introduction to Debates on the Labor Process* (London: MacMillan, 1983), 4.

10. The strained relationship between the rank and file and labor bureaucracies has

caught the attention of labor historians. See, for example, Jonathan Zeitlin, "'Rank and Filism' in British Labor History: A Critique," *International Review of Social History* 34 (1989): 42–61. See also the responses in the same issue by Richard Price, 62–77, and James E. Cronin, 78–88; Mark Leier, "Which Side Are You On? Some Suggestions for the Labor Bureaucracy Debate," *International Review of Social History* 36 (1991): 412–27; Steven Tolliday and Jonathan Zeitlin, *Shop Floor Bargaining and the State: Historical and Comparative Perspectives* (New York: Cambridge University Press, 1985).

1 The Men

The New York and London dockworkers in the post–World War II period engaged in work that had changed only slightly since the late nineteenth century. Cargoes were still handled by men. Winches and cranes were uniformly used to carry sling-loads of cargo, but it was the dockworkers who placed the cargo in the sling and moved it from the sling to the hold. Working in gangs, dockworkers developed a communal sense of work and responsibility to one another. Decades of conflict and struggle had imbued them with strong feelings of responsibility and reciprocity, both within and between work gangs. What was remarkable about the New York and London dockworkers was that even though they worked in different port cities, they shared characteristics of work, struggle, and hostility to outsiders, whether union officials, employers, governments, or other members of the working class. But in important ways they were inherently different from one another. In New York City the work force was segmented by race and ethnicity. In London the dockers shared a common "English" working-class outlook, although this character was mitigated because large numbers of London dockers boasted an Irish heritage.

The contradictory impulses and shared sense of time and space can best be understood by examining who these dockworkers were and how they obtained their work. Such an approach reveals a picture of enormous complexity. The hard and dangerous work led the dockers to perceive themselves in contradictory ways, with both high and low levels of self-worth. They developed a form of gallows humor and used nicknames and slang to stamp their identity on their working lives. In the decades up until World War II, both

New York City and London dockworkers had strived to control access to jobs. Their strategies included the physical reproduction of the work force, ensuring that family members followed one another onto the docks. They also gained job access by trade union agitation, rank-and-file action, and government design.

In London, familial recruitment was particularly prevalent and by the late 1940s was codified by governmental labor boards. As early as the late nineteenth century, London dockers had created a familial lineage to guarantee work. Since that time, the work force had been split among stevedores, dockers, and lightermen and this multiple work force further ensured familial control. The craft/job division rested on job control and trade union development. While dockers loaded and unloaded cargo, the stevedores exclusively performed the job of loading, while lightermen worked from barges (lighters) docked alongside the ships. Each group adopted a strategy of passing the job down from father to son, uncle to nephew, and cousin to cousin. At least by creating a family hierarchy, they could obtain a form of job control. Ethnicity informed this familial control in the nineteenth and early twentieth centuries.

To a large extent job transference on the River Thames was ethnically based. Irish migrants came to dominate the docks. First used as navvies to dig out the docks, many remained to work along the waterfront. The Irish who emigrated to London were predominately from Munster and the counties of Cork and Kerry. By 1861, 107,000 had moved to London, ensuring an Irish community of 178,000.[1] Of course, this movement was part of the Irish diaspora of the famine years, 1847–48. Although Liverpool and Glasgow were the primary destinations of the Irish who left their home country, London also received a large influx of desperate immigrants. Migrants moving to London either caught ferries or tramped from the north of England. The largest Irish settlement was in the Borough of Tower Hamlets, which encompassed much of London's east-end dock area. The Borough of Southwark, which covered some of the docks south of the River Thames, also saw significant habitation. Cheap lodgings were the main reason why so many Irish migrants settled into communities bordering the River Thames.[2] Because of this riverside settlement and the immigrants' rural backgrounds, men were attracted to the casual labor of dock work. As the reformer Beatrice Webb observed in 1888, "Paddy enjoys more than his proportional share of dock work with [all] its privileges and miseries." Employers also came to prefer Irish laborers because of their tendency to accept hard work and low wages. As one employer remarked, "Without the aid of the Irish . . . the business of the docks would be seriously impeded."[3]

By the end of the nineteenth century, workers with an Irish heritage dominated the dock trades, and family relationships nurtured such authority. Irish workers on the London docks commonly brought their sons into the trade, establishing a continuum wherein the Irish dominated the work and thereby the union. This was particularly true of the stevedores union. Stevedores ranked themselves as the most skilled of the waterfront workers because they loaded cargo, a more practically skilled job. Hoping to dominate such work, the Irish created what John Lovell has termed a "close hereditary corporation."[4] This command of dock work and the union was particularly evident in the 1889 "docker's tanner" strike. The strike leaders, Ben Tillett and James Tooney, traced their ancestry directly to Ireland.[5] In another important example of the overwhelming Irish influence, it was Cardinal Manning who helped settle the strike, while Protestant clergy stood indifferently on the sidelines. According to Gareth Stedman Jones, even following the success of the 1889 strike, "casual workers . . . of Irish extraction" listened more to the "homilies of Cardinal Manning than to the torrent of speeches from the Social Democratic Federation." The dockers thus accepted leaders like Tillett "not because of their socialism but in spite of it."[6]

Placing Catholicism as the primary identifier, however, does not recognize fully the complexity of Irish and British-Irish identity. To emphasize Catholicism over class and ethnicity betrays a simplistic notion of the dockworkers' experience. In his study on the Manchester Irish, Steven Fielding argues that the migrants and the generations that followed were "neither simply Irish, Catholic, or working class, but an amalgam of all three."[7] Although Fielding's appraisal may hold true for the late nineteenth and early twentieth centuries, following World War II, class appears to have taken the upper hand among London dockers. Additionally, in identifying the amalgam, most authors have examined only northern cities where the sectarian divide was more in evidence. As Sam Davies has found in Liverpool, attachment to religion was more prevalent than allegiance to social democratic principles.[8]

But this allegiance to church was being broken down by the end of World War I. In London, many Irish customs were being adapted to suit an anglicized context. The English Roman Catholic Church did much to transform the Irish Catholicism of Celtic magic and religion. The Irish language was also subsumed. But among Irish traditions the funeral wake did transfer to England and was the "one major folk ceremony brought to London." Yet even this ritual underwent change in London's East End by the 1940s. According to Patrick Hanshaw, the son of a docker and also third-generation London Irish, "The deceased still lies at home in state for at least four or five days. . . . However, the body is always segregated in another room, so if there are those who are a little bit squeamish or nervous at looking at a dead body, they don't have to."[9]

The wake was also a site where Irish identity was reaffirmed through song. John Donovan, a stevedore, related how as a child in the early 1920s his father would sing, "Dear homeland, far across the sea, do they wonder if I'm at peace, do they think of me?" According to Donovan, a melancholic atmosphere prevailed following the singing of the song. Only after his mother punched some of the mourners in the arm and began singing, "Let's all be happy again . . . and battle our cares away," did the sad mood pass. Irish Americans also sang songs at wakes that mixed "sorrow and hilarity." Although Irish American wakes included singing, dancing, and drinking, in London during the 1940s such frivolity had fallen out of favor. According to Patrick Hanshaw, when the wake of his grandmother became rather rowdy with singing and the playing of musical instruments, his Aunt Noah yelled, "Shut that f***ing racket down. And if you don't piss off out of this flat in the next few minutes, you will be wearing that f***ing accordion like a dog collar." This exchange, according to Hanshaw, "was a marked division between the old and new," that is, his grandmother's generation as opposed to that of his aunt.[10]

Increasingly during the closing years of the nineteenth century, the Irish identity of dockers was undermined by their allegiance to a trade union, the National Transport Workers' Federation. Although Irish Nationalists tried to maintain a feeling of Irishness among migrants and their descendants, creating such organizations as the Gaelic League, London dockers of Irish descent looked more to their union and the burgeoning Labour Party as their representative economic and political organizations. This was particularly true following World War I. East End dock areas were politicized clusters that adopted the "local road to socialism." Unlike other areas in London, the East End continued to adhere tightly to left-wing political action.[11] Dock work also entailed a cohesiveness that embraced both workplace identification and language. As Lynn Hollen Lees argues, "Occupational loyalties helped to break down ethnic separatism." This was particularly evident in the 1920s, once the partition of Ireland had occurred. Correspondingly, according to David Fitzpatrick, "Irish Nationality would never again be the focus of political activity for Britain's Irish population."[12]

London's dockers of Irish ancestry increasingly identified themselves as workers and trade union members. John Donovan's generation perceived themselves therefore as members of the London working class. As he put it, they were "just Londoners." Unlike in the segregated Liverpool docks, the London work gangs in the 1940s were mixed. Not only were there groups of dockers of English and Irish heritage, but there were "no Catholic or Protestant gangs," according to Donovan.[13] This was attested to by dockers with English ancestry. Joe Bloomberg, who worked in the docks from the early 1940s up until the 1960s, said that "you had the [Irish] names" but the gangs were "all mixed." As he explained, dockers of Irish descent "thought no more about the Irish [than the Irish] thought about them." It was residential and class quality that brought the dockers together. As Bloomberg pointed out, "We were all brought up together. . . . It was Wapping or Stepney . . . and it was what you'd done during that time" that provided character or identity.[14]

By the end of World War II a dramatic transformation had taken place among East London docker communities. Although retaining a Catholic identity, their Irishness was fast disappearing. The generation that had grown up in the 1920s and 1930s, although cognizant of their Irish past, regarded themselves as Londoners. To be more exact, when asked for their identification they invariably described themselves as "East Enders," or even more specifically, as from "Wapping" or the "Island" (Isle of Dogs). Like other Londoners, they defined themselves by the borough or even the neighborhood in which they lived. There continued a sense of being apart but it was not necessarily a separation based upon ethnicity; rather it was based upon class. By the late 1940s it was dock work that separated dockers from people in other working-class neighborhoods. As one stevedore from the Isle of Dogs remarked, "we were different . . . a clannish big family. . . . [We] couldn't talk about anybody at a bus stop" for fear of being overheard. This sense of being apart was reaffirmed on the many occasions when bus conductors refused entry to dockers returning from work because of their dirty and at times foul-smelling clothes.[15]

It would be wrong, however, to suggest that all traces of Irish identity had disappeared. For some in London's East End there remained a sentimental or strong imaginative vision of their Irish past. An idealized image was (and still is) conjured up to describe or validate certain behaviors or outlook. Ted Johns, who worked as a lighterman along the docks, claimed his militancy in the union and community was tied to his "Celtic background," although he was third-generation London Irish. Just like the Irish, according to Johns, London dockers were regarded by employers as "expendable," and when British troops unloaded cargo during postwar strikes the army was perceived as "an occupying power." But although there was evident "a strong sense, not of Irishness, but Irish influence," according to Johns the "class issue overlaid everything else." It was a powerful case of "us" against "them." As Johns explained, it was like the "attitude that all coppers are bastards. . . . [The] same in the dock industry, all employers are bastards."[16]

Patrick Hanshaw echoed Ted Johns in his attachment to Irishness, but at the same time Hanshaw gave an overarching class appraisal of dockers' lives.

In his autobiography, *Nothing Is Forever: Growing Up in Wapping in the Post-War Years,* Hanshaw described his sentimental veneration by explaining, "I am true to my Irish ancestry and tend to be a dreamer, going off at tangents into things that happened in other times and places." After detailing his formative years and the continuing Irish influence of song and religion, Hanshaw, just like Bloomberg, pinpointed the village quality of Wapping. Comparing his area to that of neighboring Shadwell, he relates a common ditty of the time: "Wapping for wit, Shadwell for shit." Wapping is not any more Irish than Shadwell, but Hanshaw is reflecting a common cockney parochial sense of place. As with Ted Johns, the enemy was not English culture or other working-class neighborhoods per se, but employers. Hanshaw explained that the docker was at "constant war against the guvnor. . . . To the guvnor, the docker was just one in a sea of faces. . . . Somebody to be used and discarded when he had outlived his usefulness. Attitudes that had developed over a period of generations would never die. . . . For the docker, the guvnor was the only opponent. He had to be engaged in mortal combat every working day."[17]

By the late 1940s, the differences between stevedores and dockers were also evaporating. Evidence submitted to the 1946 Doughty Inquiry showed that stevedores had the "right to discharge and the right to load" in the Surrey and in the West India and Millwall docks. In the Royal docks, stevedores worked alongside dockers. But it was made plain at the inquiry that dockers were becoming more numerous, while the stevedores were declining in number. The stevedores had been unable to add new members throughout the war because the main register had been closed to them. Robert Barrett, the stevedore representative at the Doughty Inquiry, argued, "I would say that 250 [sons] should be admitted [to the register]. . . . We are entitled to fight to preserve the organization we belong to." Tim Condon, the Transport and General Workers' Union (TGWU) representative, responded by arguing, "I am going to say that they [stevedores] are not a better class of men because there are . . . dockers . . . in the port equally competent to do the loading and discharging and it is altogether wrong to create an impression that the stevedores are a special class. They are special class only because they belong to a different union."[18]

Dockers continued to supplement their numbers with relational recruits. The board of directors of the National Dock Labor Corporation reported on June 19, 1946, that "natural wastage is being counterbalanced by the recruitment of dockers' sons to the main register."[19] Although this type of recruitment was culturally acceptable, the large numbers of sons applying to join the register caused no end of headaches for trade union officials. The sons' demands for dock jobs outstripped supply, leading to friction between officials and fathers insisting their sons get on the register. As Tim Condon explained, "On the question of recruiting members' sons you make more enemies than you make friends, and I can assure you the enemies are legion."[20]

Such organized recruitment of sons was instituted by the Dock Labour Scheme, which was introduced in 1947. By December 28, 1948, 27,435 dockers were on the London Register. During the one-year period of the scheme, 1,209 dockers' sons had been recruited, constituting 5 percent of the work force. This hiring of sons was replicated at the national level. The National Dock Labour Board reported that between 1947 and 1949, "out of the 6,425 recruited . . . 3,369 were dockers' sons."[21]

The Dock Labour Scheme codified the securing of work, discipline, "appearance payments," and dispute resolution. Dockers and stevedores would appear to procure work every day at call stands along the docks in the port. Men would then be dispatched to ships to load or unload. If work was not available, they would be paid "appearance money" for showing up and ordered to return for an afternoon call.

The need to end the casual form of hiring on the nation's docks had been an important issue since the end of World War I. Ernest Bevin, as general secretary of the TGWU, had pushed hard for decasualization. The system produced an overabundance of labor that had always weakened the TGWU. More important, the casual system had engendered an atmosphere of insecurity and fear. Not knowing if a job was available from one day to the next caused widespread anxiety among workers. Bevin correctly identified the weakness that an oversupply of dockworkers created. Throughout the 1920s and the depression years of the 1930s, he was successful in getting a register established for dockworkers. Although there remained a surplus of labor, at least the work was reserved for dockworkers and not for the general unemployed population looking for a few days' work.[22]

The momentum to decasualize the industry increased during World War II. Again, Bevin played a leading role. As minister of labor for the wartime coalition government, Bevin worked hard to guarantee dockworkers payment for turning up to work. This "attendance pay" gave dockworkers an incentive to work where directed. As Bevin pointed out, "They must work as, when and where they are required under the rigorous conditions of modern warfare. In return they will be given some measure of security."[23] The war had provided the needed wedge at last to decasualize the docks. Dock labor was considered strategically important, and to guarantee adequate numbers the prewar casual recruitment patterns were swept away. Instead, dockers were registered and then dispatched to docks where their labor was most needed. In some cases this could mean regulated movement not just from dock to dock, but also from port to port. The National Dock Labor Corporation was formed to create a national register of dockers and to regulate movements between ports. The Ministry of Transport ran a parallel scheme.[24]

Following the end of World War II, some continuation of regularized employment was seen as necessary and justified. Assessing a March 1945 London stevedores' strike, the Ammon Inquiry found that "decasualization during war-time by the establishment of a regular pool of labor and the payment of attendance money to men who attend" was effective. That strike, however, highlighted resentment against corporation officials. The inquiry found that the "Corporation Officers . . . are acting arbitrarily, harshly and unsympathetically." The inquiry recommended that a "Special Advisory Committee" of employer and trade union representatives be established to oversee issues of discipline.[25] The Ammon Inquiry showed that consensus was forming that decasualization should continue, but also that trade union officials should have an equal say in adjudicating disputes. The newly elected Labour government was also convinced that decasualization should be maintained. To provide time to study the issue, the government extended the lives of the corporation and Ministry of Transport schemes, and it created the 1946 Forster Inquiry to investigate the problem and come up with recommendations.[26]

The Forster Inquiry came down heavily on the side of decasualization. Framed by the postwar support of government ownership of industry and the advocacy of business-union cooperation, the inquiry advocated additional regulation. Basing its conclusions on the postwar "labor shortage" and "the need for closer co-operation of employers and workpeople . . . [which] is much in the public mind," the inquiry supported the continuation of a permanent register of dockers, the creation of a national labor board, and the formation of "Local or Area Boards" to "meet the needs" of individual ports. Dockworkers would be guaranteed attendance money for turning up at set calls for work; in return the dockworkers were obliged to accept work that was offered. For disputes or issues of discipline, the dockworker could appeal to the Local or Area Board.[27] The recommendations were accepted and in 1947 the Dock Labour Scheme became law. Although general wage rates would remain in the hands of the National Joint Council of employers and trade union officials, the day-to-day determination of differing rates for hazardous or dirty cargoes was at the discretion of viewing committees.[28]

After 1947, the London dockworkers were registered, ending decades of casual labor. Making themselves available every day at the respective call stands throughout the port, the dockworkers were entitled to attendance money. Dockworkers could not be arbitrarily fired or disciplined without a fair hearing in front of a board of employer and trade union representatives. Although dockworkers were guaranteed either a job or attendance money, the system was not universally accepted. As will be seen, the new employment relations aroused new forms of frustration and anger, leading to a string of work stoppages and portwide strikes.

For New York City longshoremen, obtaining a job was still set by the rhythm of the shape-up, also known as shaping. Unlike their brothers on the West Coast, the New York longshoremen were forced to stand in a semicircle around a hiring boss and wait anxiously to be picked out of the crowd to work. Through strike action in 1945 the men had obtained at least the partial victory of attending just two shape-ups per day—one at 6:55 A.M. and the other at 12:55 P.M.—rather than three.[29] The shape-up system and its corresponding surplus of labor guaranteed subservience and employment insecurity. Louis Waldman, the chief counsel for the International Longshoremen's Association (ILA), the union that represented dockworkers on the Atlantic and Gulf Coasts, concluded that "this is one of the rare exceptions in modern industrial relations to have men come to the employer's establishment [each day] and make themselves ready and willing to work with no obligation on the part of the employer whatever to take them."[30]

The shape-up also encouraged rampant discrimination against African American workers. Blacks for the most part worked in Brooklyn and were segregated in the Jim Crow Local 968. Appearing every day along with white longshoremen for the shape-up, the black longshoremen were exposed to the racism of the hiring boss and the attendant union official. One black longshoreman described the humiliating experience: "Sometimes standing on the pier with my union button and my union book, the hiring boss acts like he hates me. . . . It happens all the time."[31] The "hate," of course, resulted in the worker's not obtaining a job for the shift. Audrey West, a Communist organizer, described a shape-up of black longshoremen in Brooklyn as "a slave market." After not being accepted for work, "most of them would just be turning around and going back home. . . . There might be a little grumbling . . . but never anything that sounded like they were ready to do anything about it."[32]

Cleophas Jacobs, president of Local 968, charged that the "shipping companies . . . in collaboration with various local union officials and the hiring bosses, have an agreement whereby the available work is given to the other nine [white] locals in Brooklyn, to the exclusion of our men." Underscoring the problem was the lack of black representation in the ILA, where not one African American had been appointed organizer even though Local 968 had a membership of a thousand men. Jacobs complained bitterly to Joe Ryan but was met with a chilling silence. Protection of jobs then was informed by racist sentiment. President Morgan of Philadelphia Local 1291 expressed the racist attitude by claiming that blacks could not be trusted as regular workers: "Negroes accept most of the dirty work on the riverfront because of economic necessity due to their own lack of frugality. Many of them work for one or two days, draw their pay, go on a spree and do not return to work until their funds are exhausted." Such a perspective could only reinforce the stereotype of the lazy black longshoreman who should not be given steady work.[33]

Union officials used discrimination and workers' insecurity to line their own pockets with kickbacks. It was standard practice for a worker to pay a bribe to either the foreman or a union official to get picked from the shape-up. The form of the bribe depended upon the system established on each pier. In some cases it was an individual activity, such as directly paying money, buying drinks before or after the shape-up, or purposely losing a card game. One longshoreman known only as "John Doe" testified to the 1952 New York State Crime Commission (NYSCC) that he paid the hiring foreman two dollars per week and "once in a while on Fridays—buy him a pint of whiskey." The kickback and the buying of whiskey was expensive. "[It was] more than I could afford," John Doe explained, "but in order to keep the job and support my family you got to do those things."[34] Kickback clubs were also used. Situated in apartments, saloons, barbershops, or storefronts, the clubs would gather cash from prospective workers before adding their names to the call-up list. Pat Wilson explained to the NYSCC that for years following World War II, men would shape-up in his basement. In an astonishing admission, Wilson explained that his wife would pick up from longshoremen the identification checks or brass discs that showed the men had worked and she would collect the wages from the payroll office. Although he denied that he or his wife received kickbacks, it was obvious that some form of payment was made.[35]

The shape-up was not the principal form of hiring. Regular work gangs operated throughout the port. There are no hard statistics available to document how many dockers were part of such gangs, but a series of sources does provide some information. Depending on the dock or pier, approximately 60 percent to 75 percent of the longshoremen belonged to work gangs and were hired as such. The remaining workers were casuals shaping-up to fill temporary positions within the respective gangs. For the most part the gangs could be divided into two categories, regular and extra. Regular gangs were given priority for either ships or holds, while extra gangs were called upon when larger ships needed to be unloaded. When work was not available on their respective piers, members of the gangs joined the casuals in shaping-up.[36]

Prior to World War II, the employment of regular gangs began to pick up pace. To a large extent the hiring of regular gangs was directly linked to the work because it required experienced longshoremen to load and unload complex cargoes. The needs of the wartime economy further encouraged regularized use of gangs. The armed forces took direct control in regularizing employment. In Brooklyn, for example, the "army base pioneered a system of 'steady gangs' early in the war. . . . Longshoremen were assigned to the same gang every day and dispatched to the same pier."[37] By end of the war and into the late 1940s, then, the majority of longshoremen were hired as gang members and not as individuals. But on any given day the large numbers of casuals shaping-up were joined by roving underemployed regular gang members, ensuring a hectic and at times unfair distribution of work.

Unlike the London groups, the New York work gangs were ethnically and racially segmented. To a large extent the Irish influence in New York City was even greater than in London. A form of Irish identity was evident among the waterfront communities of Manhattan's West Side, where Irish Americans dominated the docks and the union. Many of the migrants who clustered in Manhattan had originated from the Munster counties of Cork and Kerry, although in Brooklyn the migrants were from Donegal and Mayo.[38] As with the London Irish, the New York Irish worked where they lived. Along the West Side, the Irish congregated in specific neighborhoods including Chelsea and Hell's Kitchen. As Calvin Winslow described it, "The Irish lived there, crammed in between streets and warehouses, in neighborhoods known for big families and saloons."[39] Even as late as the 1940s, the Irish continued to dominate the docks or longshore industry in the area. As Larry Sullivan, a onetime longshoreman, explained, "The dock gangs were mostly all Irish."[40] Sheer numbers ensured possession of power. The regular Irish work gangs were the key, and their continued use of ethnic or racial identification helped maintain their position. Ethnic and racial calculations, and the attendant solidarity of work gangs, cemented a commanding authority over the work and union.

Feeding the Irish dominance on Manhattan's waterfront was the unprecedented flood of Irish immigrants. The Irish diaspora to New York dwarfed the influx to the British Isles.[41] Approximately 1.8 million Irish migrants landed at New York City during 1847–51. Most of these migrants moved inland to other states, but many stayed in New York. By 1860, for example, 200,000 Irish-born immigrants lived in New York. By 1870, the Irish born constituted 21 percent of the city's population. No wonder that New York was labeled as the preeminent Irish city in the United States.[42] Such overwhelming numbers gave the Irish a form of political and economic dominance in New York City. Irish migrants were able to comfortably capture the political reins of power, from the Tammany Hall era in the nineteenth century to the immediate post–World War II period. A string of Irish American mayors and bosses dominated New York City. Mayor William O'Dwyer's election in 1945 and again in

1949 was the last hurrah of Irish political control. Irish political supremacy was replicated on New York harbor's docks, where the Irish were the dominant group up until the early 1890s.

Employers first challenged Irish control of the docks by introducing Italian and African American strikebreakers. The Irish longshoremen tried to counter the increasing numbers of Italians and blacks by refusing to work on the same ships where they worked. As Charles Barnes related in his 1912 study, "If a gang of 'Ginnies,' or 'Dagoes,' as they were called was put in the hold with the Irish, the latter would quit." At times Irish American longshoremen engaged in political strikes supportive of Ireland's desire to separate from British authority. Of most concern, however, was the continuing battle by Irish American longshoremen to dominate the work and the International Longshoremen's Association. Such efforts were effectively challenged by Italians who came to control the dirtier jobs of handling coal and gained a foothold on the piers in Brooklyn.[43]

Although unable to stop the rapid influx of Italians and other ethnic groups, the Irish reserved for themselves the better jobs in and around Manhattan's West Side docks. By the turn of the century, Irish Americans controlled the easier dock and deck jobs, leaving the more strenuous and dangerous jobs in ships' holds to new arrivals from Ireland or other countries. The Irish American longshoremen held onto a more ethnicized class identity simply as a response to ethnic succession and the strong ethnic character of New York working-class life.[44] Thus much of the Irish cohesion was predicated on keeping other ethnic and racial groups out of their areas of operation. Such a strategy reaffirmed their Irishness. From as far north as Hell's Kitchen to the southern tip of Manhattan, the piers on the West Side became a series of Irish fiefdoms. Such control continued up through the 1950s. In Brooklyn some Irish activity continued along Third and Fourth Avenues, but as a one-time longshoreman, Paul O'Dwyer, pointed out, "The Irish were dying out really and the Italians were becoming more numerous."[45]

Irish control of Manhattan docks was predicated on the generational transfer of jobs. As in London (and throughout the world), familial relations played a key role in getting and reserving jobs.[46] Larry Sullivan experienced this phenomenon. He began his dock job in 1942 for the U.S. Lines Shipping Company. Although, as he explained, many men got jobs because the hiring boss knew their fathers, he followed two older brothers. As he said, "They got me hired as part of a gang. I was extra. You shaped every day and you went to work or you didn't go to work." Sullivan and the other longshoremen lived near the waterfront. As he described it, "That's what it was, Chelsea was Irish American." The ease of walking to work was the common denominator: "At one time, when I started there was 80 percent walked to work and 20 percent traveled."[47]

But even by the 1940s, the pattern of ethnic and racial exclusion was beginning to break down. On the Grace Line piers, Italian and black gangs labored. Even traditionally Irish gangs were being transformed. Sullivan remembered that "all the members picked were mostly Irish with a mixture of Italian." In these mixed gangs it was the Italian members who invariably worked in the hold. This sort of division existed even within ethnic groups. When native-born Irishmen were hired, Sullivan reported, they too worked in the hold or hatch because "Irish Americans did not want to go down in the hatch." Thus "Irish" identity was a qualified concept. It was one thing to be from the neighborhood, or to be "American," but it was quite another to be an immigrant. Angelo Pacifico, who had been a longshoreman, explained the phenomenon in the Hell's Kitchen area of Manhattan. Hell's Kitchen was a "mixed neighborhood. Strong Italian, Irish was the biggest nationality." A similar ethnic hierarchy was in place where, Pacifico said, "Predominately on the dock [there] was Irish. . . . and hold jobs, they were predominately Italian, Yugoslav, Polish, Czech."[48] So even though the Irish controlled the easier dock jobs, their grip on the waterfront jobs was being gradually broken as the nineteenth century gave way to the twentieth.

Irish dominance on the West Side and on the Brooklyn piers was also being undermined by the appearance of regular gangs of other ethnic groups. This was especially the case for those longshoremen from the ethnically mixed area of Hell's Kitchen. Just like their East End counterparts in London, Hell's Kitchen longshoremen were unified by their class position. Angelo Pacifico related his experience with his best friend, who was a longshoreman with an Irish background: "No matter where we were, wherever we went out, wherever we socialized, wherever we drank, he was never going to leave me, I was never going to leave him. I don't care if we are in an Irish neighborhood, or he was on the East Side in the Italian neighborhood. I don't care. I don't turn my back on him. He was like my brother. We grew up together, we went to school together."[49]

In Manhattan by the late 1940s, ethnicity no longer exclusively defined friendship and job control. Although ethnicity continued to determine success in getting a job and holding union office, the gradual withdrawal of the New York Irish from the waterfront was undermining their power base. Contributing to the Irish retreat was their physical movement from the waterfront areas of the West Side. The Irish moved to other areas of Manhattan and to Queens, as well as to the suburbs in Long Island and New Jersey, and to Nassau, Westchester, Rockland, and Bergen counties in New York. This migration signaled the end of Irish political influence in New York City. Just as important, it drew away many Irish workers from the job market in New York.[50]

Although Irish Americans continued to dominate the port in the early twentieth century, they were eventually forced to share power with Italian Americans. The arrangement was based upon numbers and raw power. Italians came to control the piers and union locals in Brooklyn, Staten Island, and the Lower East Side, as well as on the New Jersey shore. Such an arrangement reflected somewhat the changing political complexion of the city. As the Irish hold on City Hall was loosened, so too was it eased in the city's labor movement.[51] But as power shifted from the established Irish groups to others vying for control, Irishness or Irish identity did not diminish; indeed, it was strengthened.

Elsewhere in Manhattan, especially along the East River, the work force was far more mixed but nonetheless rigidly divided by race. The Standard Fruit and Steamship Company dominated the East River and used Pier 13 to unload bananas. Ten gangs worked Pier 13. While some were "mixed," five were Puerto Rican and one was "colored." The Puerto Rican and black gangs worked the banana shipments exclusively. The Puerto Rican gangs, just like some of the black gangs in Brooklyn, were recent arrivals on the New York waterfront. A sample of one Hispanic gang showed that most of its members had started work on the waterfront between 1945 and 1952. Of the 20-man gang, 16 were born in Puerto Rico, 2 in Cuba, and 1 each in Venezuela and Santo Domingo. The average age of these twenty longshoremen was forty-six. The men in this East River gang had to travel far to work. While the pier was below East Fourteenth Street, the majority of the gang lived in East or West Harlem or further north in the Bronx. Only one member of the gang lived close by on Delancey Street.[52]

The complex interplay of race and ethnicity certainly influenced workers' success in obtaining jobs on the New York waterfront. In Brooklyn, Staten Island, and the Jersey shore, Italian Americans were the predominant group, although large numbers of other racial and ethnic groups were clustered along the piers. "In Brooklyn," one former longshoreman, Sebastian DeFazio, remembered, "we were strictly Italian, a few Irishmen, a few black guys, [but] we made friends." Again, familial relations determined entry onto the docks. DeFazio told how he got his first job: "So being my father was a deckman . . . he knew people there, and I got in." His older brother, Leonard, followed a cousin onto the docks. Standing at the shape-up but not wearing "the proper clothes to work down the waterfront," he attracted the attention of the hiring agent, who pointed to Leonard and asked, "Who's that kid over there?" The cry came back, "That's John's kid." "Well, he better change those clothes and put [on] some working clothes," the agent retorted. Fortunately, within days Leonard could abandon shaping-up after he obtained a slot within a regular gang. "My uncle . . . introduced me right into the gang."[53]

There were relatively large numbers of blacks working on the Brooklyn docks. Without access to union and company records it is difficult to give an accurate count of their numbers in Brooklyn. There were, however, specific "colored" gangs. Large numbers of these black longshoremen were southern-born. Migrating to New York around World War II, they gravitated to the Brooklyn waterfront as casual laborers. The shape-up was a system they could use to get at least a few days' work as extras. Of one 26-member gang, 19 were born in Alabama, Georgia, North Carolina, South Carolina, and Virginia. The remaining members originated from Arizona, Washington, New York, and New Jersey, and one other came from the West Indies.[54] Of those from outside the New York area, 8 had arrived between 1924 and 1941, 9 between 1945 and 1947, and 4 between 1948 and 1950. Although technically a Brooklyn gang, the members traveled far and wide to get to work: 15 were from Brooklyn, but 3 were from Queens, 2 from the Bronx, and 5 from Manhattan.[55]

The influx of southern blacks to New York during World War II was part of a general migratory phenomenon. The incredible expansion of economic activity encouraged geographical change by both blacks and whites. Unlike the negative impetus of earlier migrations, wherein migrants were escaping economic and political oppression, the motivation for the World War II black movement was mostly positive: workers were drawn to high-paying jobs. Between 1940 and 1942, approximately one million blacks moved to urban areas in the North and West Coast. Key states were California, Pennsylvania, Michigan, Illinois, Delaware, and New Jersey. The numbers of migrants to New York City were relatively low compared to those to other cities; nonetheless, movement into the city and its metropolitan area was significant. A 1946 study estimated that twenty-five thousand new arrivals had made New York City their home. Like other migrating African Americans, those in New York City intended to stay once the war was over.[56] Fortifying this worker migration was the influx of ex-servicemen at the end of the war. The wartime military experience of mobility provided an alternative vision for blacks. Moving from farms and breaking away from repressive southern conventions gave black servicemen and women a broader view of the world. Just as vital, it took them away from a community-based safety net. Southern black communities had always provided a tenuous buffer from the harshness of Jim Crow strictures. Military service merely replaced this community and sited it in another place, often outside of the South. During and following World War II, two general migratory movements were in play: one driven by economic opportunism, the other by the military experience of separation. In each case, migrants found common ground by rejecting oppressive southern norms of behavior and seeking opportunity.[57]

Arthur McMillon, a longshoreman, represented both migratory paths. Born in 1923 in Lee County, South Carolina, he was drafted into the army in 1943 but "got out" because he "had flat feet." His limited army experience and that of growing up in South Carolina convinced him to move north. As McMillon explained, "The white folks down there, I don't care how big you was, you had to tell them 'Mr.,' their children too, 'Mr. so and so.' . . . I was always a 'boy' or a 'nigger.'" In the army for nine months, McMillon discovered two important aspects of his new life: there was an alternative to the oppressive southern experience and he could make a commitment not to stay in South Carolina. Although not happy about military discipline, he was determined not to address white men and boys as "Mr." As he declared, "Weren't going to do that no more." "After I found out what living was" in the army, McMillon said he pledged to himself that "when I got out [of the army] I wasn't going to stay there [South Carolina] no more." After a three-day stay in South Carolina to bid farewell to relatives, McMillon headed to New York City in 1944.[58]

Joining a brother and sister in New York, McMillon got a job in the Brooklyn Navy Yard. Occasionally after finishing work he would shape for jobs on the waterfront. While working at the Navy Yard he had a disagreement with a white foreman and walked off the job. McMillon blamed his southern experience for the incident: "I thought he was like people down south but he wasn't . . . but too late, I [had] quit." He then regularly shaped for longshore work on Fulton Street in downtown Brooklyn. The men shaping with him, "all of them from the south, figured they'd do better. . . . [They were] mostly from Alabama, Georgia, South Carolina, got a few from Barbados." There were New York–born blacks who had fairly regular opportunities on the docks. As McMillon explained, "There were some black people who had a good job and even blacks as foremen, but I didn't know these people. I was from down South, I was new."[59]

Unable to obtain steady work, McMillon drove cabs to supplement his meager income. But like other casual workers, McMillon paid a kickback to ensure some form of waterfront work. After collecting his pay "through the window," he handed over his contribution: "I don't know whether you had to do it or not, I figured he would give me a job in a day or so, so I gave him $10. He'd take it and thank me . . . I thought it was what you were supposed to do if you wanted to get hired." The system was a lucrative one for the hiring foreman. McMillon was not alone in giving kick-backs, creating a cycle of obligation and insecurity. As McMillon explained, "Maybe for a day or so he would shape me but he would have other people. . . . He'd work you one day and work the other guy another day, that mean he'd get money from me and the other guy."

McMillon and other recent arrivals from the South were separated from blacks who were more established. Nonetheless, even experienced black longshoremen were forced by entrenched racism to hire on as extras. Italian Americans invariably reserved for themselves the better-paying jobs, whether it be loading cargoes or working in the center holds of the ships. Italian American union locals dominated certain piers, but the Jim Crow Local 968 did not enjoy such a privilege. Thus blacks had to shape-up as extras and worked only rarely as gangs. Working as an extra generally meant that blacks worked on those cargoes that white longshoremen avoided. As I. Philip Sipser, a lawyer who represented Local 968, put it, the black dockers "got the worse piece of shit . . . every lousy job that had to be filled because white workers wouldn't do it." Banana shipments, for example, were generally considered black cargo because of their odious quality. As Sipser explains, in the banana boats there were "rats as big as cats down there. . . . [The] stink was terrible. . . . [It was] dirty work."[60]

In some rare cases some white gang or hatch bosses would hire black longshoremen. Leonard DeFazio, a hatch boss in Brooklyn, brought blacks into his gang after older white members retired. "I had a lot of old guys in my gang, they retired, so I was approached by some black fellas. 'Hey, Lenny, could I come in your gang?' So I said, 'Yeah, sure, come in tomorrow.' . . . I had about four or five." DeFazio was criticized for his action, he said. "That made the other hatch bosses resent what I was doing, why I was [*sic*] hiring the blacks?" But for DeFazio it was the need for reliable workers that was the determining issue: "I wanted a worker. I didn't want him because he's white, black or pink. And that was that." DeFazio also had to endure criticism from the white crew of a South African ship. As DeFazio explained, the ships's mate "was trying to pick on me because he resented I had black working with white." A black gang member witnessing the confrontation from the hold of the ship yelled up to the ship's mate, "Hey, you leave my hatch boss alone. I'll come up there and throw you in the river."[61]

Frank Barbaro, a Brooklyn longshoreman and later a politician, also worked in mixed gangs. "We had three African Americans, three or four Puerto Ricans, two Cubans and a Norwegian, and the rest Italian," he recalled. Such a mixed gang, however, "got the hardest work." As Barbaro explained it, "You got to understand, my gang was reflective of the work." Another white longshoreman, Pete Bell, worked in a black gang in Brooklyn. The gang was the

"8th gang, meaning it was the third extra gang [and] most of the time we did not have work." So when the black hatch boss, Tommy Howard, had a "short" gang he invited Bell to join the gang: "I was the only white guy in the gang. . . . [It] didn't make any difference to me, at least I was getting somewhere on the pier . . . on the foot of Jorelomnon Street." Working together did not always ensure enlightened relations, however. One longshoreman complained of sharing a pail of water with black longshoremen: "The men pass the pail around and they all drink out of the same one. . . . It is particularly bad when there are mixed gangs of Negroes and whites. They [employers] should at least put some paper cups on the draft."[62]

For the most part the integrated gangs of DeFazio, Barbaro, and Bell were exceptional. The Brooklyn waterfront was essentially an Italian fiefdom. Other ethnic and racial groups worked there but only as extras, and sometimes in mixed gangs. As Barbaro pointed out, "The gang that was integrated like ours was an oddity."[63] Black and Puerto Rican longshoremen worked the dirtier cargoes or least desirable hatches, while a lucky few joined an Italian gang. There still remained a smattering of Norwegians who worked in Brooklyn, but just as in Manhattan an ethnic and racial hierarchy was in place, and it was Italian at the top.[64]

Jersey City was also dominated by Italians, but there the ethnic and racial mix was even more diverse. According to "Eddie," an otherwise anonymous longshoreman, a range of groups labored on the city's docks. "When I started [in 1946] we had everybody, blacks, Italian, Pollacks, Irish, Czech. . . . In one gang we had a black deckman, Jew in the hold, Pollack on the dock." Elsewhere on the Jersey shore, ethnic diversity predominated. Eddie said that in "Hoboken [the] Sullivan brothers were running the waterfront. . . . If you didn't have an in you didn't work."[65] Hoboken gangs periodically migrated to Newark. The Hoboken men were then hired as extra gangs. As in Jersey City these extra gangs were mixed, where there could be "four Yugos[lavians], four Cubans, couple of colored guys."[66]

The Newark work force exhibited a similar rigid form of racial and ethnic division. Italians dominated, while Puerto Ricans and African Americans constituted the other principal subgroups. Just as in Brooklyn, blacks had their own "colored" union, Local 1233, and the bulk of the black longshoremen were from the South. According to Arthur McMillon, who began working in Newark in 1960, "all the blacks was . . . from down South," although "two or three were born here in Jersey."[67] Local 1235, on the other hand, was a combination of Italian and Puerto Rican workers. According to one longshoreman, Jose Villa, there were eleven gangs in Local 1235; "four to five were Spanish and the rest Italians. We used to get along good." If regular gang members of Local 1235 were absent, particularly "around the holidays, when people [were] on vacation," blacks came in from Local 1233 "as extra, not steady, [but] on a day-by-day basis."[68]

If a dockworker was unable to get into a gang because he lacked familial or ethnic/racial connections, an alternative was to work consistently hard as an extra in the hope of being noticed. When Eddie first started work, he was assigned clean-up work, in which he "cleaned the hatches of the ship . . . pick[ing] up dunnage after the longshoremen had finished." Only after he proved himself to be a reliable and hard worker would he be brought into a regular gang. As he explained it, "They'd observe ya. . . . One guy tells a foreman, 'He's a good worker, I want to keep him,' . . . [and] maybe in two weeks you get steady." Pete Bell experienced a similar entry into "steady" work as a Brooklyn longshoreman. An Italian gang boss "saw the way I worked . . . knew I didn't know what I was doing half the time, [but] he knew I was big strong guy, I wasn't a stiff."[69]

Bell's race and strength went a long way in his securing a regular job on the Brooklyn waterfront. For black longshoremen like Arthur McMillon, however, strength alone could not guarantee a regular job. Confronting a strict racial and ethnic hierarchy ensured that black newcomers, as well as those who were more established, were forced regularly to shape-up as extras.

For New York and London dockworkers, obtaining and maintaining a job after World War II was based upon two different systems. In London, the recruitment of sons was institutionalized with the establishment of the Dock Labour Scheme. As in the late nineteenth and early twentieth centuries, familial relations provided the cohesion for the reproduction of the work force. To obtain a job, the London dockworker was expected to attend calls in the morning and the afternoon. If no work was available, then the dockworker was entitled to "attendance payments" and he returned for the following call. The work force took on a distinct "cockney character," as family connections were important indicators of worth. Unlike their fathers and grandfathers, however, the postwar London dockworkers defined themselves for the most part as "English." Although for some there remained a sentimental attachment to an Irish past, allegiance based on ethnicity was replaced by one based on class.

New York City longshoremen did not enjoy such regularized employment. The shape-up remained the principal form of job acquisition, just as it had been since the nineteenth century. What had changed, however, was that regular gangs worked throughout the port. But when work was not available they were forced to join the small army of extra gangs and individuals searching for work. The shape-up continued to define the procurement of work.

Unlike their London counterparts, New York dockers were not guaranteed payment simply by turning up for work. Ethnicity and race were just as vital in gaining employment. Entrenched "white" ethnics throughout the port codified control of the work. An elaborate hierarchy was in place, with Irish on top, followed by Italians and then an array of other ethnics. At the bottom were African Americans. Blacks in extra gangs counted themselves fortunate, while others found that the task of obtaining steady work was almost impossible.

It is the work of the longshoremen that is the subject of the next chapter. Just as vital in establishing identity as race and ethnicity, the work regime stamped a clear impression on the dockworkers' world view. The job, with all its trials, helped form a distinct temperament that separated the dockworker from the surrounding society, and also from other members of the American and British working class. The meshing of racial/ethnic identity with that of a unique work experience ensured a working-class character like no other.

Notes

1. Lynn Hollen Lees, *Exiles of Erin: Irish Migrants in Victorian England* (Ithaca, N.Y.: Cornell University Press, 1979), 19, 46.

2. Frank Neal, *Black '47: Britain and the Famine Irish* (New York: St. Martin's, 1998), 52–53, 255, 271; David Fitzpatrick, "Irish Emigration in the Later Nineteenth Century," *Irish Historical Studies* 22 (1986): 126–43; D. M. MacRaild, *Irish Migrants in Modern Britain, 1750–1922* (New York: St. Martin's, 1999). For pre-famine Irish migration to Britain see Ruth-Ann Harris, *The Nearest Place That Wasn't Ireland: Early Nineteenth-Century Labor Migration* (Ames: University of Iowa Press, 1994). For later migration to Britain see Kathleen Paul, "A Case of Mistaken Identity: The Irish in Postwar Britain," *International Labor and Working Class History* 49 (Spring 1996): 116–42. More research is needed about English migration into the dock areas of London. See Derek Matthews, "1889 and All That: New Views on the New Unionism," *International Review of Social History* 36 (1991): 2–58.

3. David Fitzpatrick, "A Curious Middle Place: The Irish in Britain, 1871–1921," in *The Irish in Britain, 1815–1939,* ed. Roger Swift and Sheridan Gilley (Savage, Md.: Barnes and Noble, 1989), 20 (first quote); Harrington W. Benjamin, "The London Irish: A Study in Political Activism, 1870–1910," Ph.D. diss., Princeton University, 1976, 54 (second quote). Similar occupational concentration in low-wage jobs was evident in nineteenth-century Lancashire and Cheshire. See Neville Kirk, "Ethnicity, Class and Popular Toryism, 1850–1870," in *Hosts, Immigrants and Minorities: Historical Responses to Newcomers in British Society, 1870–1914,* ed. Kenneth Lunn (Folkstone: Wm. Dawson, 1980), 64–106.

4. John Lovell, "The Irish and the London Dockers," *Bulletin of the Society for the Study of Labour History* 35 (Autumn 1977) : 17.

5. Fitzpatrick, "A Curious Middle Place," 40.

6. Gareth Stedman Jones, *Outcast London: A Study in the Relationship Between Classes in Victorian Society* (New York: Pantheon, 1984), 348. Catholic schools have also been singled out as vehicles of assimilation into British culture; see Mary J. Hickman, "Alter-

native Historiographies of the Irish in Britain: A Critique of the Segregation/Assimilation Model," in *The Irish in Victorian Britain: The Local Dimension,* ed. Roger Swift and Sheridan Gilley (Dublin: Four Courts Press, 1999), 236–53.

7. Steven Fielding, *Class and Ethnicity: Irish Catholics in England, 1880–1939* (Buckingham, Eng.: Open University Press, 1993), 2.

8. Sam Davies, *Liverpool Labour: Social and Political Influences on the Development of the Labour Party in Liverpool, 1900–1939* (Keele, Eng.: Keele University Press, 1996); see also John Belchem, "The Irish in Britain, United States, and Australia: Some Comparative Reflections on Labour History," in *The Irish in British Labour History,* ed. Patrick Buckland and John Belchem (Liverpool, Eng.: Institute of Irish Studies, 1993), 19–28.

9. Lees, *Exiles of Erin,* 186–88 (first quote); Patrick Hanshaw, *"Nothing Is Forever": Growing Up in Wapping during the Postwar Years* (London: Wapping Neighbourhood, 1992), 18 (second quote). For an excellent study of how religion and education played a part in homogenizing the London Irish, see Mary J. Hickman, *Religion, Class, and Identity: The State, the Catholic Church, and the Education of the Irish in Britain* (Brookfield, Vt.: Ashgate, 1995).

10. John Donovan, interview by author, London, July 9, 1996; Kerby A. Miller, *Emigrants and Exile: Ireland and the Irish Exodus to North America* (New York: Oxford University Press, 1985), 557; Hanshaw, *"Nothing Is Forever,"* 17.

11. James Gillespie, "Popularism and Proletarianism: Unemployment and Labor Politics in London, 1918–34," in *Metropolis-London: Histories and Representations since 1800,* ed. David Feldman and Gareth Stedman Jones (New York: Routledge, 1989), 163–67. Other than in the East End, Londoners were particularly fickle in their allegiance to the Labour Party and trade unions. See Paul Thompson, *Socialists, Liberals and Labor: The Struggle for London, 1885–1914* (London: Routledge, 1967); Gareth Stedman Jones, "Working-Class Culture and Working-Class Politics in London, 1870–1900: Notes on the Remaking of a Working-Class," in *Languages of Class: Studies in English Working Class History, 1832–1982,* ed. Gareth Stedman Jones (New York: Cambridge University Press, 1983), 179–238.

12. Lees, *Exiles of Erin,* 242; Fitzpatrick, "A Curious Middle Place," 44. Roger Swift echoes Lees's claim of ethnic diffusion because of workplace identification, writing that by the late nineteenth century, "economic growth . . . may have helped to reduce ethnic rivalries." Roger Swift, "Heroes or Villains? The Irish, Crime, and Disorder in Victorian England," *Albion 29* 3 (Fall 1997): 420.

13. Donovan interview. For religious segregation of Liverpool gangs, see Eric Taplin, "The History of Dock Labour: Liverpool: Circa 1850–1914," in *Comparative International History of Dock Labour, c. 1790–1970,* ed. Sam Davies, Colin Davis, et al. (Amsterdam: International Institute of Social History, 1997), 14.

14. Joe Bloomberg, interview by author, August 8, 1996.

15. George Pye, interview by author, August 14, 1996.

16. Ted Johns, Interview by author, July 11, 1996.

17. Hanshaw, *"Nothing Is Forever,"* 27 (first quote), 42 (second quote), 144 (third quote).

18. London Labour Force—Doughty Inquiry, 1946, book 29/11, Public Record Office, Kew (hereafter PRO), 3 (first quote), 6 (second quote), 17 (third quote).

19. "Meeting of the Board of Directors," National Dock Labour Corporation, June 19, 1946, National Dock Labour Board (hereafter NDLB), BK 29/8, PRO.

20. London Labour Force—Doughty Inquiry, 44.

21. "Changes in Workers Register, Port of London, as of December 28, 1948," NDLB, BK 27/9, PRO; "Review of the National Dock Labour Board, 1947–1949," NDLB, BK 2-1218, PRO (quote).

22. Alan Bullock, *The Life and Times of Ernest Bevin,* vol. 1, *Trade Union Leader, 1881–1940* (London: Heinemann, 1960), 116–42, 461–75.

23. Peter Weiler, *Ernest Bevin* (New York: St. Martin's, 1993), 132 (quote); Alan Bullock, *The Life and Times of Ernest Bevin: Minister of Labor, 1940–1945, Vol. 2* (London: Heinemann Press, 1967), 30.

24. *Port Transport Industry: (Forster) Report of Inquiry of the Schedule to the Dock Workers (Regulation of Employment) Act, 1946* (HMSO, 1946), 5–8. Ernest Bevin played a large but behind-the-scenes role for the passage of the Dock Labour Scheme. Although he was foreign secretary, Bevin encouraged George Isaacs, minister of labor, to work patiently for the scheme's acceptance by both unions and employers. Alan Bullock, *Ernest Bevin: Foreign Secretary, 1945–1951* (New York: Oxford University Press, 1983), 229.

25. London Dock Dispute, March 1945, Report of the Committee of Inquiry, Ammon Inquiry, LAB 10/580, PRO.

26. The Labour government passed the Dock Workers (Regulation of Employment) Act on February 14, 1946, which in effect prolonged the Ministry of Transport and National Dock Labour Corporation schemes until July 1, 1947. *Port Transport Industry,* 7.

27. Ibid., 11–16.

28. Report, July 1957—Government Attitude to Joint Industrial Councils, Joint Industrial Councils, LAB 10/1499, PRO. The report found that World War II "led the Government to encourage the setting up of GAUCHOS in many industries where they had hitherto been absent, such as the distributive trades. During the war years 46 GAUCHOS were set up."

29. Howard Kimeldorf, *Reds or Rackets? The Making of Radical and Conservative Unions on the Waterfront* (Berkeley: University of California Press, 1992), 154–55.

30. "Excerpt from Testimony of Louis Waldman in Arbitration Proceedings Before William H. Davis, November 21, 1945," International Longshoremen's Association, box 3, folder: Hiring Hall, 1942–54, Tamiment Library, New York University(hereafter ILA-TAM).

31. Malcolm Johnson, *Crime on the Labor Front* (New York: McGraw-Hill, 1950), 116.

32. Audrey West, interview by author, August 5, 1995.

33. "Testimony of Cleophas Jacobs," Senate Committee on Labor and Public Welfare, *To Clarify the Overtime Provisions of the Fair Labor Standards Act of 1938, As Amended,* 81st Cong., 1st sess., 1949, 488–91; James I. (Carfare) Keys, "Notice—To All Members of Local 1291," box 3, ILA-TAM.

34. "Testimony of John Doe," New York State Crime Commission—Public Hearing, No. 5, Port of New York (Waterfront), vol. 3, 1802–3, New York City Municipal Library.

35. Ibid., 1807–12.

36. Vernon H. Jensen, *Hiring of Dock Workers and Employment Practices in the Ports of New York, Liverpool, London, Rotterdam, and Marseilles* (Cambridge, Mass.: Harvard University Press, 1964), 31–33.

37. Kimeldorf, *Reds or Rackets?* 152.

38. John T. Ridge, "Irish Counties Societies in New York, 1880–1914," in *The New York*

Irish, ed. Ronald H. Bayor and Timothy J. Meagher (Baltimore: Johns Hopkins University Press, 1996), 275–300.

39. Calvin Winslow, "On the Waterfront: Black, Italian, and Irish Longshoremen in the New York Habour Strike of 1919," in *Protest and Survival: Essays for E. P. Thompson,* ed. John Rule and Robert Malcolmson (New York: Norton, 1993), 369.

40. Larry Sullivan, interview by author, July 13, 1995.

41. For an excellent discussion of the two migratory flows to the United States and Britain, see Donald M. MacRaild, "Crossing Migrant Frontiers: Comparative Reflections on Irish Migrants in Britain and the United States During the Nineteenth Century," *Immigrants and Minorities* 18, nos. 2–3 (1999): 40–70. For a specific comparative study, see J. Matthew Gallman, *Receiving Erin's Children: Philadelphia, Liverpool, and the Irish Famine Migration, 1845–1855* (Chapel Hill: University of North Carolina Press, 2000).

42. Hasia R. Diner, "'The Most Irish City in the Union': The Era of the Great Migration, 1844–1877," in *The New York Irish,* ed. Ronald H. Bayor and Timothy J. Meagher, 91–92; Kerby A. Miller, "'Revenge for Skibbereen': Irish Emigration and the Meaning of the Great Famine," in *The Great Famine and the Irish Diaspora in America,* ed. Arthur Gribben (Amherst: University of Massachusetts Press, 1999), 180–95.

43. Charles Barnes, *The Longshoremen* (New York: Arno Press, 1977), 8 (quote); Joe Doyle, "Striking for Ireland on the New York Docks," in *The New York Irish,* ed. Ronald H. Bayor and Timothy J. Meagher (Baltimore: John Hopkins University Press, 1996), 357–73.

44. Such a strategy was also used by hard rock miners in Butte, Montana. See David M. Emmons, *The Butte Irish: Class and Ethnicity in an American Mining Town, 1875–1925* (Urbana: University of Illinois Press, 1989).

45. Paul O'Dwyer, Columbia University Oral History Collection, 1962, transcript, 42.

46. Recruitment of sons, daughters, nephews, cousins, and sons-in-law was a common policy used by both employers and dockers around the world during the casual period (generally from the nineteenth century up to World War II) and the later decasualization era. See Colin J. Davis, "Formation and Reproduction of Dockers as an Occupational Group," in *Dock Workers: International Explorations in Comparative Labor History, 1790–1970* ed. Sam Davies, Colin J. Davis, David de Vries, Lex Heerma van Voss, Lidewij Hesselink, and Klaus Wienhauer (Burlington, Vt.: Ashgate, 2000), 542–59.

47. Sullivan interview.

48. Ibid.; Angelo Pacifico, interview by author, July 12, 1995. For experiences of Irish immigrants in New York following World War II, see Linda Dowling Almeida, *Irish Immigrants in New York City, 1945–1995* (Bloomington: Indiana University Press, 2001).

49. Pacifico interview.

50. See the discussion in Marion R. Casey, "'From the East Side to the Seaside': Irish Americans on the Move in New York City," in *The New York Irish* ed. Ronald H. Bayor and Timothy J. Meagher (Baltimore: Johns Hopkins University Press, 1996), 395–415; David M. Reimers, "An End and a Beginning," ibid., 419–38.

51. See the discussion in Stephen P. Erie, *Rainbow's End: Irish-Americans and the Dilemmas of Machine Politics, 1840–1985* (Berkeley: University of California Press, 1988); Roy Peel, *The Political Clubs of New York City* (New York: Praeger, 1975); Theodore J. Lowi, *At the Pleasure of the Mayor: Patronage and Power in New York City, 1898–1958* (London: Free Press of Glencoe, 1964). For the connection between the Irish and the U.S. labor move-

ment, see David Montgomery, "The Irish and the American Labor Movement," in *America and Ireland, 1776–1976: The American Identity and the Irish Connection,* ed. David Noel Doyle and Owen Dudley Edwards (Westport, Conn.: Greenwood Press, 1980).

52. Inter-Office Memorandum, Executive Department, State Commission Against Discrimination, March 2, 1956, series 10409–83, box 13, State Commission Against Discrimination, State of New York, New York State Archives (hereafter SCAD-NYSA).

53. Sebastian DeFazio, interview by author, July 10, 1995; Leonard DeFazio, interview by author, July 12, 1995.

54. Applegate et al. vs. Universal Terminal and Stevedoring Co., Inter-Office Memorandum, Executive Department, State Commission against Discrimination, September 10, 1958, series 10409–83, box 22, SCAD-NYSA.

55. Ibid.; Complaint No. C-5550–58, State Commission against Discrimination on the Complaints of Applegate et al. vs. Universal Terminal and Stevedoring Co., series 10409–83, box 22, SCAD-NYSA.

56. For studies of black migration during the World War II era, see Daniel M. Johnson and Rex R. Campbell, *Black Migration in America: A Social Demographic History* (Durham: Duke University Press, 1981) 102–5; Neil Fligstein, *Going North: Migration of Blacks and Whites from the South, 1900–1950* (New York: Academic Press, 1981), 1–18, 75–92; Oscar Handlin, *The Newcomers: Negroes and Puerto Ricans in a Changing Metropolis* (Cambridge, Mass.: Harvard University Press, 1959), 42–60; Ira De A. Reid, "Special Problems of Negro Migration during the War," in *Postwar Problems of Migration: Papers Presented at the Round Table on Population Problems,* Millbank Memorial Fund Papers (New York: Millbank Memorial Fund, 1947), 153.

57. John Modell, Marc Goulden, and Sigurdur Magnusson, "World War II in the Lives of Black Americans: Some Findings and an Interpretation," *Journal of American History* 76 (December 1989): 838–48.

58. Arthur McMillon, interview by author, March 12, 1999.

59. Ibid.

60. I. Philip Sipser, interview by author, June 29, 1995.

61. Leonard DeFazio interview.

62. Frank Barbaro, interview by author, July 6, 1995; Pete Bell, interview by author, July 7, 1995; "Rudge Report—Survey on Employer and Labor Relations for the New York Shipping Association, December 7, 1956," box 7–4067, Vernon Jensen Papers, Kheel Archives, Cornell University.

63. Barbaro interview.

64. David C. Mauk, "The Colony That Rose from the Sea: The Norwegians in the Red Hook Section of Brooklyn, 1850–1910," Ph.D. diss., New York University, 1991.

65. "Eddie," interview by author, July 9, 1995.

66. Ibid.

67. McMillon interview.

68. Jose Villa, interview by author, December 16, 1996.

69. "Eddie" interview; Pete Bell, interview by author, July 7, 1995.

2 The Work

In his autobiography, *Timebends: A Life,* Arthur Miller described a typical New York City scene in which citizens carried on their daily routines ignorant of the longshoremen's existence: "On the Brooklyn Bridge the waves of traffic moved serenely above the heads of men who were enduring what without exaggeration were *medieval* conditions."[1] Miller's observation of the longshoremen's oppression was essentially correct. The working world of longshoremen long remained a mystery to most New Yorkers. The same could be said of Londoners. Dockworkers in both cities labored in occupations most people regarded, if they thought about it at all, as unskilled work and unworthy of any concerted notice. Not until such men demanded to be recognized through strike action did the general public take heed.[2]

Many employers had their own conceptions of the work and the men who performed it. Generally, employers' attitudes toward their workers were patronizing and at times hostile. One New York City steamship company executive, for example, remarked in 1954, "You make a sad mistake if you try to treat longshoremen like anybody else. You have to understand that they're primitive and they'll just take advantage of you if you treat them kindly." Such a derogatory perception was shared by a London employer: "Dock laborers are a striking instance of brute force and brute appetites. This class of labor is as unskilled as the power of a hurricane. Mere muscle is all that is needed; hence every human locomotion is capable of working there."[3]

The perception that dock work was unskilled was shared even by some of the dockworkers. Both sets of dockworkers had an ambiguous relationship with their job. Some recognized the skills required, while others perceived it as "bull work" with little if any job satisfaction. John Donovan, a London stevedore, represents the ambivalent dockworker. He was engaged in the skilled job of loading, but when asked for his evaluation of the work he responded, "Hard to answer that question, my feelings never went as far as that." When pressed, Donovan used the word "knowledge" to represent "skill." As he expressed it, "The definition of knowledge is experience."[4] Such vagueness suggests that Donovan comprehended the complexities of a hard and dangerous job but viewed the work as having little social value. Such a superficial appraisal lends itself to deprecating the work. But given the opportunity to discuss their work, many dockworkers provided a more nuanced expression of job satisfaction.

The work itself comprised a complex combination of skilled and semiskilled characteristics. Defined entry requirements or apprenticeships were not needed to begin the job, but to do it well required an intricate interplay of abilities that were learned by doing. It took months and even years to acquire the rhythmic motion needed to handle a huge variety of goods efficiently and quickly. Some workers keenly appreciated the nature of moving and handling complex and heavy cargoes. Leonard DeFazio, a New York longshoreman, explained how it wasn't a question of strength but of experience. When loading rails, he said, "You didn't have to be muscular. . . . First you got to marry them . . . so they go right into each other." DeFazio admitted, "It's a real hard job . . . but once you got the knack of it" the job got done. Once a "floor" or cross section of rails was in place, dunnage (wood) was laid down, and the process was repeated.[5]

Skill was the key when it came to handling general cargo. A wide array of goods that could include locomotives, automobiles, rails, drums, and sacks was loaded on one ship. The work had to be organized with heavy loads loaded first, followed by small. As Frank Barbaro explained, "You had to know how to build these floors" and then coordinate with the deckman. "So the hatch boss would say, 'Freddy, I'm on the ground. Give me some heavy stuff.' Freddy would go around and find heavy cargo. And then, 'We're topping off. Give me light stuff.' So this whole organization of a gang was quite difficult. And it took years to be able to develop that group expertise." Such expertise created pride in the work. As Leonard DeFazio explained, "You have to have pride. Otherwise, you're a mess. Believe me, you're in trouble." DeFazio and others did not have a sense that their job was necessarily skilled, but rather that it was a job well done. He said, "Well, I felt that I did the job. And we did it well. We did it the way you're supposed to."[6]

The gang structure gave the workers a collective sense of responsibility and respect. Ted Jones, a London docker, said that the gang was the pivotal unit on the docks: "You got to work together and you've got to have a trust in the bloke you're working with and that's it."[7] Angelo Pacifico, a New York longshoreman, described how the winch operator was key to loading large objects into tight spaces. A worker used hand signals to communicate with the operator, Pacifico said. "You wanted him to pick it up a hair, you know." A specific signal told "when you want him to pull with force and keep a steady pull." The longshoremen on the dock side were part of the cooperative venture: "The people on the dock relied on your expertise that the holdmen secured the commodities properly, so that when it [the sling] came on the dock . . . it would not just fall apart all over the place." Unlike DeFazio, Pacifico felt that the ship rather than the cargo held an intimate attraction. Pacifico wanted to see the ship return, for it literally ensured work. "We knew what each ship meant to us. . . . We didn't want to see any of the ships get lost 'cause we knew as long as that ship came in we worked." The same longshoreman felt connected to the hatch, too: "We knew what the hatch called for and the work it called for. And that work was our work. It didn't belong to anybody else." Such attachment was based on knowledge of hatch design and how best to load and unload in such a confined space. As Pacifico further explained, "We use[d] to be able to walk in on a ship, walk down any hatch and tell you where every rivet was. . . . Everybody [in the gang] knew where to place the snatch block, you know. How to drag different materials in, what the height of the overhead was."[8]

Not all longshoremen were engaged in the skilled loading and unloading of general cargo. Many of them worked on the coffee shipments in Brooklyn. At first glance the unloading of coffee bags appears as unskilled labor. The reality was much different, however, and the workers shared a distinctive view of the job. Pete Bell, who worked with coffee in New York, described a labor process that required skillful partnership and that could give dockers a satisfaction with a job well done. Special hooks were used to grip the forty-pound bags of coffee. It was hard work, but if done properly it was not necessarily exhausting. As Bell explained, the gangs he worked with had "lots of experience with handling this one commodity . . . and they knew how to handle it, how to organize themselves." Bell's initiation into the work was not successful, however: "I started with a friend but the two of us were killing each other." Unable to establish a rhythm, Bell was forced to say to his companion, "'I like you, you're a good friend but you're no fucking good, you're killing me.' . . . Finally we broke up [as partners] because we couldn't coordinate with each other." After changing partners, Bell went on to become a skilled practitioner of the art of loading and unloading coffee.[9]

Completing the job also held meaning for Pete Bell: "You actually see this mountain of bags disappear. It took two days." When loading bags there was the added incentive to get the storage right because failure could mean a shift in the cargo and loss of the ship: "You made sure you loaded the hatch correctly. . . . The wall of cargo . . . had to take the storms or the weather or the movement of the ship and stay up." Loading lumber also held similar satisfaction. Jose Villa worked extensively on lumber ships in Newark, New Jersey. Unloading pine with a "special hook and gloves" was "tough" but Villa "liked lumber 'cause it was clean."[10]

For Bell, the longshoreman's appreciation of the job was based partly on his understanding of the architecture of the ship's hold. As he explained, "Most longshoremen had a good spatial relationship of knowing what would fit in that space."[11] Bell's point of view was not universally shared, and some saw the work as hard and exhausting. For Frank Barbaro, the work did not provide satisfaction; instead it was simply "bull work." As he asked, "How could you be satisfied loading, unloading coffee bags twelve hours a day?" But paradoxically, Barbaro admitted that loading coffee called for a special type of skill. He said, "I mean, it could take a couple of years to be a good coffee worker." In a form of self-criticism Barbaro argued that longshoremen were not always aware of their skilled work: "I think a lot of longshoremen put themselves down and didn't realize what a skilled trade it is." Echoing DeFazio and Pacifico, Barbaro argued that it was a practical skill, one that had to be learned "because you're confronted with problems that there's no textbook." Barbaro gives the example of successfully loading a military tank as evidence of this practical skill: "How do you take a twenty-ton tank . . . and move it into a corner? How do you do that? It requires a sense of engineering, of knowing forces, you know, stresses, strains." When running the cable down from the winch and through a snatch block (a type of pulley used in lifting), Barbaro said, "the force is being changed to ninety degrees. Now, once that tank starts moving, you better have it perfect so it hits the spot you want, because if it doesn't, now you got a problem."[12]

Gaining skill was not always just a matter of acquiring knowledge. Access to the skill could be controlled. In London, the stevedores controlled certain docks and thereby held dominance over loading. In New York, race was the determining factor. One's race controlled entry to the job and also to the skill. This was the case with the job of unloading bananas, a task that was not as simple as it sounds. Over the years a strict demarcation had been drawn between those who unloaded bananas and those who stacked them. On the East River by the 1950s, unloading gangs were predominately Puerto Rican or African American, while those who stacked were Italian. There was a smattering of Puerto Ricans and blacks as stackers, but it had largely become an assignment for Italian workers. When trying to justify such segregation on the piers, union and company officials argued that stacking was skilled work, while unloading was not. Captain Frank Farrar, manager of the John W. McGrath Corporation, a shipper working the banana pier on the East River, argued in 1956 that "carrying bananas from one's shoulder to trucks and stacking them in the trucks in such a manner that they will not be bruised are entirely two different things." Thus stacking was deemed more critical because the bananas had to be loaded on trucks "in a systematic manner" without bruising the fruit. When the issue was investigated by the New York State Commission Against Discrimination, a different finding was reached. It was discovered that the segregation of the work was based more on race than on acquiring skill. More specifically, it was based upon a racial migratory pattern. Because Puerto Ricans were the last immigrant group to arrive on the docks, they were relegated to the least favorable and unskilled jobs, unloading the bananas. As the commission argued, "The pattern of employment in general follows the history of employment of migrant groups—the last arrivals are condemned to the least desirable jobs."[13]

In London, there was a similar appreciation of skill, whereby experience translated into skill; that is, the job had to be learned by doing. George Pye, a stevedore, related that during his first weeks on the job he was forced "to stand there and watch . . . learning." He said that although it was "frustrating, I did watch. . . . You wanted to get involved but you would have been in the way." Ted Jones echoed Pye's viewpoint: "[You] had to be taught the job. And it's a hard job to teach anybody because you had so many things that were custom and practice. You only learn it over the years." As in New York, the dockworker was faced with a variety of different jobs and had to have the flexibility and skill to handle each one. George Pye told how the job of loading was "very skillful." The "ceiling of the ship is forty feet" and the cargoes could range from "cement, sugar, steel rods, cartons solidly packed, others delicate, furniture, cars." When mixed or general cargoes were being loaded, as in New York, dunnage had to be laid to create false flooring, which resulted in a complex, "giant jigsaw." The laying of dunnage was necessary to separate the cargoes and provide structural integrity, although as Pye explained, dockworkers "weren't paid for laying dunnage." There was not necessarily a strict division of labor among workers and foremen. According to John Donovan, in some instances the foreman might work alongside the men or he "just checked out the work."[14]

Experience came with age, and the London work force had an abundance of both. Large numbers of older workers continued laboring on the docks. The London "live register" of December 28, 1948, showed a total of 1,546 men sixty-five and older working on the docks. This constituted approximately 9 percent of the total work force of 17,922. Of the 1,546 older men, at least 50 percent were considered Category "A" workers; that is, they were expected to be "general all round worker[s] able to give a full week's work." The remainder were Category "C" workers, who were generally the "aged" men who engaged in "light work."[15] John Donovan explained how older men or those "set-back" (injured) tended to be consigned to the job of winch operator. The London Dock Labour Board wanted to rid the port of older men but in an October 1947 meeting the board was forced to admit that "nothing could be done in cases where men had good records." The concern was generally over employer liability and how some men were "at risk to themselves and others."[16]

The full employment of the postwar years played a role in the prospects of the aged work force. With plenty of other jobs available, there was difficulty in attracting new men to the physically demanding dock work. The National Dock Labour Board perceived older men and the general aging of the work force as particular problems. Nationwide, in 1947 over 65 percent of the work force in Britain was over the age of 41; and even more glaring, 13.5 percent were between 61 and 70 years of age, while 2.5 percent were over the age of 70. The NDLB was uncomfortable with such large numbers of older men. As the board explained, "This trend must be reversed. . . . An intake of young men of the right type is essential if the industry is to safeguard its future."[17]

Unfortunately, the age breakdown of New York longshoremen is not available. Although New York longshoremen and London dockers were differentiated by race and ethnicity, respectively, they engaged in similar work. One might assume that the universal characteristics of loading and unloading a ship ensured common attitudes toward work and employers.

Another significant common denominator was the dockworkers' attitude toward pilferage. Whether goods were taken for immediate consumption or for use beyond the dock gates, the dockworkers shared an abiding sense of entitlement and opportunism. In Brooklyn, food shipments were particularly valued by the longshoremen, who came prepared to enjoy the fruits of their labor. As one New York docker, Sebastian DeFazio, explained, "When we used to get [pilfer] tuna fish, we used to bring our bread, our onion. Oh, there were so many things you could do down there [in the hatch]. . . . We used to have a picnic with frozen steak, . . . put it on the manifold and have a steak dinner. And then we used to get a lot of ice cream. . . . We were a bunch of crooks and we took everything that wasn't nailed."[18] The availability of food apparently induced longshoremen to perceive it as theirs. This sense of entitlement encouraged pilfering throughout the port. On Manhattan's West Side there was similar on-board consumption of food, accompanied by the drinking of alcohol. According to Angelo Pacifico, "You ate the fruit cakes. You ate the candy. You would drink whatever liquor there was you could get your hands on. There was wine, or whiskey or scotch."[19]

Alcohol could be conceived as both a perk and as an analgesic to help dockers cope with the hard and dangerous work. According to "Eddie," drinking on the ships in Jersey City was very common, often leading to drunkenness. You "opened one case of beer . . . got ice . . . and drank beer while you were working. . . . By the time you go to the tavern you were half-charged and by the time you got back home you were stewed." Such drunkenness was not acceptable in Brooklyn, according Frank Barbaro. Yes, Brooklyn longshoremen would "take a swig. . . . But that's not like drunk."[20] Elaborate methods to steal whiskey were also used in Jersey City. "Eddie" explained how women sewed special pockets in their husbands' long overcoats for just such a purpose. The whiskey "bottles would just fit nice into the pockets in the jacket . . . looked natural."[21]

The New Jersey docks were susceptible to widespread pilferage. Russian fur shipments at the Linden Avenue docks were a prized item. As Charles Strang, a longshoreman, explained, "cloth bags" containing the furs "were easily ripped by a longshoreman's hook." The next step was to get the furs off the ship and dock without being detected. Winter clothing helped the transfer, however: "Swag coats—that is a coat that's twice as large for him—they used to really stuff it." When unloading U.S. Army vehicles, dockers always had the opportunity to steal something of value. Cases of tools were favored items. The theft of army equipment was endemic, according to Strang: "They got a little of everything there. Every longshoreman looked more like an Army man than the Army did itself."[22]

Most items were pilfered for immediate consumption on the ship. The men had a sense of taking what was there or taking advantage of the situation. As "Eddie" explained, "It was there like taking a cigarette—it was a habit." Frank Barbaro had a similar interpretation. If a shipment of beer arrived at the dock, he said, "That's like a gift from heaven." The sense of entitlement was born of low wages and hard work. If an opportunity was provided, the workers took advantage of it. Sebastian DeFazio succinctly expressed the providential initiatives of longshoremen: "We'd send one guy to the kitchen [of the ship] to see what's in the refrigerator. He'd come back with everything from the refrigerator."[23]

Stealing could be dangerous, however. One New York longshoremen toppled overboard while carrying cans of sardines. There was also the danger of being caught. Charles Strang explained to the 1951 New York Crime Commission how one man attempted to steal silk: "The fellow coming out one night got quite a bit of silk wrapped right around his body and he had so much, and he looked so fat that when the customs stopped him and asked him to bend, he couldn't bend at all." His testimony brought a laugh from the commissioners. Although watchmen were present throughout the port, they were physically and verbally intimidated into not enforcing the rules. In one case where a watchman prevented the theft of some cases of meat, the hiring foreman approached him with a dollar note in his hand. The watchmen explained that the foreman told him "he was making a collection for flowers for me and that I was going to be throwed overboard."[24]

Although the value of the pilfered goods is very difficult to measure, the 1952 New York Crime Commission estimated that "possible pilferage" totaled $5,186,485. The North River docks, on the West Side in Manhattan, led the way with an estimated value of goods stolen reaching $2,180,917. Brooklyn followed with $1,986,243; and Jersey City and Hoboken with $501,394; Staten Island, $276,779; the East River, $163,388; and Port Newark, $10,265. These figures show that the more heavily used North River and Brooklyn docks experienced the heaviest losses. Nonetheless, the Jersey City, Hoboken, and Staten Island figures were disproportionately high since those docks were relatively small.[25] But in any of these locations, much of the reported theft could be linked to activity by organized gangsters. The cost of pilferage by longshoremen would not have reached of millions of dollars. As will be shown, gangsters ruled over crime on the waterfront.

In London, goods were generally pilfered for consumption onboard the ship. Unlike in New York, pilferage in London had dire consequences. Highly trained police forces were conspicuous throughout the port and had powers to gather evidence even in the homes of dockers. As the *Sunday Pictorial* reported, "It is significant that London is the only Port Authority which has its own police. Training and conditions are almost identical with those of the Metropolitan Force."[26] Once caught and convicted, the guilty party's career as a dockworker generally came to an end. The uniform policy of the National Dock Labour Board was to remove convicted dockers from the register. This meant that the dockworker could not get a job in London or in the country's ports as a whole. The National Dock Labour Board frowned upon pilfering primarily because it was expensive. In 1949, goods worth £17,301 were stolen, of which £7,416 worth were recovered; but it was a paltry sum compared to that of New York.[27]

London pilferage records for the first six months of 1948 reveal an array of goods stolen. Of the 62 cases that went to court, 23 involved stealing "food and drink"; 14, "liquor"; 14, "clothing"; 5, "toilet goods"; 2, "cigars and cigarettes"; and 3, "miscellaneous." The court sentence for such thefts could be particularly severe. A docker convicted of stealing a "piece of meat weighing 4lbs wrapped in a newspaper," worth three shillings and sixpence, was sentenced to six weeks in prison. A docker who stole three bottles of rum "concealed in pockets and tied to his waist" was also given six weeks. Supposedly, stealing clothing was not considered as serious an offense. A docker who stole a "white shirt worn underneath his own shirt" was given one month's imprisonment.[28]

NDLB officials were convinced that dockers were not deterred from pilfering by losing their "ticket" or enduring heavy fines and imprisonment. As S. C. Parkin, general manager of the National Dock Labour Board, complained, "Despite the knowledge that conviction is almost invariably followed by dismissal, the number of dockworkers affected is not diminishing appreciably and I fear that the eleventh commandment is still 'Thou shall not be caught.'" It's difficult to tell the breadth of pilferage, other than by the numbers of those caught and convicted. During 1948, out of a work force of 27,435, a total of 162 London dockworkers were dismissed for pilferage.[29] For dockworkers generally there was a difference between stealing and pilferage. It was one thing to consume goods on board the ship, but quite another to attempt to get contraband out of the dock. The worksite was therefore the boundary between acceptable and illicit behavior.

According to George Pye, "out of twelve to thirteen in a gang, one or two" would actively steal. The men as a whole would eat bananas, or help themselves "if a case of sweets came open. . . . But only a few walked out of the gates [with pilfered items]. . . . It's not worth it to get caught and lose your [registration] ticket." Thus for the most part, goods were pilfered for immediate consumption onboard the ship or lighter. Just as in New York, though, some dockworkers grabbed an opportunity to steal. George Cosey, a lighterman, testified that some men were "braver than others." Cosey said that if, for example, there was a cargo of "export bikes, I've known them to sort of ride out the dock on one, and all that sort of thing." But unlike New York longshoremen, London dockworkers, "in the main," did not steal when the opportunity arose to do so.[30]

The cause of pilfering is sometimes attributed to a sense of entitlement, to opportunity, or to a culture of theft, but another cause may have been the tenuous work environment on the docks. The number of accidents on the London and New York City docks was exceedingly high, on many occasions equaling or exceeding that of other dangerous occupations. Perhaps dockworkers reasoned that with a high likelihood of injury, it was foolish not to take advantage of "benefits" when the opportunity arose.

The dockworkers' fear of injury was well founded. In both London and New York, dockworkers had similar types of accidents and incurred similar injuries. (See tables 1 and 2.)

The type of injury and the part of the body where London dockworkers were injured indicate much about their work. London dockworkers suffered double the rate of accidents that New York workers suffered due to "handling," and double the number of wrist and hand injuries. Injuries to these appendages constitute the bulk of injuries recorded. Ted Jones remembered handling tins of tea and the attendant danger: "Tin cans like a bleeding razor blade. If you happen to throw that case wrong or get hold of it wrong . . . you look down, [you see] bleeding blood pouring out."[31] To some extent the difference in "handling" injuries in the two ports reflects the greater use of forklifts on the New York docks and inside the holds. There was also greater use of pallets for handling cargo in New York, particularly for cargo sent between New York and the South American trade routes. This resulted in less hand labor and thus there was less "handling" of cargo than in London, resulting in fewer accidents and injuries. However, the use of pallets might also explain the higher number of accidents reported in New York in which workers were "struck by falling bodies." Such accidents were more likely to be reported because falling palletized loads would cause severe injuries. The feet, ankles, and shins of New York dockworkers came in for their fair share of injury. Loads often were dropped or swung against the dockworker as the crane took the sling out of the hold. Eyes, head, and neck injuries suggest the high volume of falling objects.

A 1954 survey of accidents on London docks identified a series of hazards. Surprisingly, there was no evidence of seasonal fluctuation, but the greatest

Table 1. Causes of Accidents in London (1950) and New York (1942)

	London	New York
Handling	60%	28%
Falling	10	14
Struck by falling body	8	25
Stepping on or striking object	11	13
Other causes	11	20
	100	100

Sources: "Analysis of Accidents at Work, Port Medical Services, NDLB, Twelve Months Ended December 31, 1950," BK 5/31, Welfare Committee Agenda Papers, NDLB, PRO; "Injuries and Accident Causes in the Longshore Industry, 1942," *Bulletin No. 764 of the United States Bureau of Labor Statistics* (GPO, 1944), 17–18.

Table 2. Site of Injury

	London	New York
Head and neck	7.5%	7.0%
Upper limb above the wrist	3.0	3.0
Wrist and hand	56.0	22.0
Trunk and back	4.0	21.0
Lower limbs above the ankle	14.0	14.0
Ankle and foot	6.5	31.0
Eyes	9.0	2.0
	100.0	100.0

Sources: "Analysis of Accidents at Work, Port Medical Services, NDLB, Twelve Months Ended December 31, 1950," BK 5/31, Welfare Committee Agenda Papers, NDLB, PRO; "Injuries and Accident Causes in the Longshore Industry, 1942," *Bulletin No. 764 of the United States Bureau of Labor Statistics* (GPO, 1944), 17–18.

number of accidents involved hand trucks. The survey found that "hand hook accidents though numerous" were surpassed by crane accidents, which "were the most severe." There was, however, an "absence of accidents reported" with fork lifts.[32]

New York longshoremen also labored in incredibly unsafe conditions. In the 1942 Department of Labor report it was found that longshoremen endured the "highest injury-frequency rate" of all American workers. As the report stated, "No other industry . . . had a record even approaching this unfavorable figure."[33] Although the 1942 report may have been skewed due to wartime conditions, reports between 1947 and 1950 found little had changed. Longshore work was still found to have the highest "injury severity" rate. The rate was based upon time lost because of injuries. Only the logging business came close to challenging the longshore industry's dubious distinction.[34]

The 1942 report acknowledged the inherent dangers of the dockworking industry, including heavy lifting, moving slings, machinery (winches) without guards, and the hustle and bustle of numerous men working simultaneously in and on the ship and dock. However, it did single out three specific problems. First, there was the casual nature of the work force. "Strangers" working with one another lacked a "mutual understanding and the ability to anticipate each others' actions and reactions." Second, there was "constant pressure for speed" to unload and load a ship quickly, because the time a ship spent in port was a loss in earnings for shipowners.[35]

While these two factors may be considered structural, the report revealed a third, more human factor: the lack of any safety training in New York. On the West Coast, the International Longshoremen's and Warehousemen's

Union (ILWU) had forced employers to create the Accident Prevention Bureau to investigate on-the-job injuries and recommend reforms. Although at times both the ILWU and employers did not forcefully address the problem, the injury-frequency rate was lower on the Pacific Coast than in New York. In New York, on the other hand, although a safety code had been established and published, "comparatively few of the [stevedoring] offices contacted had a copy on hand or knew what the code provisions were." In addition, unlike the West Coast, the New York industry had "no widespread or continuing safety program" in operation.[36] It becomes clear that in New York safety was ignored and injuries on the job were generally regarded as a hazard of the work. When employers did address the problem they invariably blamed the longshoremen's supposed shoddy work habits for the accidents on the job. Appearing before the U.S. Senate Committee on Labor and Public Welfare in 1948, representatives of the New York Shipping Association, the employer organization, shifted the blame for the high accident rate onto the prior physical condition of the longshoremen: "These longshoremen subject themselves and their fellow workers to definite risks not concomitant with their employment, and in doing so subject the employer to extra occupational risk."[37]

The dockworker's job in New York was so dangerous that it ranked first or second when compared to other occupations. According to the 1945 frequency rate, based on the number of accidents, longshore work was rated 87.6. The average for all industry was 18.6, and only logging beat out the stevedoring industry with a rate of 92. These figures might have been distorted by wartime conditions, but in the following years a similar pattern was evident. For 1946 and 1947, longshore work outpaced logging in terms of "severity rate." The severity rate was calculated according to time lost per disabling injury. In 1946 the severity rate for longshoring was 25.9 days lost per injury, while logging was 9.5; the average for manufacturing was 1.6. In 1947 the longshore severity rate dropped to 10.6, but it still outpaced logging's rate of 9.7. This configuration continued in 1948 and 1949, about which the Department of Labor reported, "As in previous years, stevedoring had the highest injury-frequency among the nonmanufacturing industries."[38]

Some jobs on the docks were more hazardous than others. Men working in the ship's hold (holdmen), for example, were twice as likely to be injured as those working on the dock. Although their duties included "making up cargo into sling" as dockmen did, holdmen were exposed to greater dangers because of the lack of space in which they worked. Because of the confined space, dust was an ever-present danger, leading to long-term health problems. Falling cargo presented a more immediate danger. If cargo spilled from a sling there was little room for the holdman to escape.[39]

Angelo Pacifico attested to the hazard of falling cargo as he recounted what happened when a sling carrying cases of knives hit a beam in the ship's hold: "The cases burst open and knives came down by the thousands. . . . There were blades sticking all over the place." George Pye described the frightening experience of being showered by falling steel pipe. Working in a hold eighty feet down in the ship, he heard the warning yell "under" as "ten or twelve fourteen-to-fifteen-foot steel pipes" came tumbling down. Pye explained it was "interesting to say the least" and that he "dived behind the [ship's] ladder." The ladder could afford little protection, as Pye put it. "It was a bit ludicrous, really, but I had less than a second to think." Some of the pipes "pierced the wooden ceiling [floor]," while others "went twenty to thirty feet up in the air. . . . It was lucky that day no one got touched." The opening to the hold was an extensive space. The larger holds, generally the number 3, 4, and 5 holds, could be up to 150 feet in breadth. The middle of the hold was described as the "square" and it was the most hazardous point. With the constant movement of cargo in and out of the hold, the square was the place of vulnerability for the longshoremen toiling below. As Pye attested, "The particular danger was being left in the square, you're left exposed. . . . A lot of people didn't get out of the way."[40]

Men working on the deck faced the hazard of moving cables. One particular incident involved a man stepping over the winch cable. According to Leonard DeFazio, the cable "caught him in between and wrapped him around into the winch and made mince pie out of him. They had to pick him up with a shovel."[41]

Such dangers were easily recognized by the dockworkers, but a sort of gallows humor was born from such dangerous conditions. Even when caught in a potentially perilous situation, both sets of workers often saw the humorous side of it. Joe Bloomberg, a London docker, provided the example of a man caught in a rope, which he described as "funny but dangerous." Another docker, Mack Palmer, was holding a rope that was easing the ship's mast down; unfortunately he was distracted by a conversation about the Millwall Football Club. Meanwhile the other end of the rope "comes free from where it was hitched" and "up he went." His cries of "help, help" were greeted with laughter. Bloomberg explained, "As dangerous as it was we could see the sense of humor out of it." Another amusing incident involved a circus polar bear. According to Bloomberg, the dockers decided to draw their hooks along the bars of the caged polar. The enraged bear in turn went "potty" and "you've never seen such a run for the ladder . . . you couldn't get out of the hatch quick enough."[42]

For Angelo Pacifico, there was humor in an incident where a sling of cocoa drums hit the top of the hatch and released its load down into the hold. Somebody yelled out, "Look out below," and Pacifico made a dash for the side of ship by the sweat boards, wooden boards that kept condensation from the cargo. His friend was transfixed, however, standing "right in the square of the hatch." As the drums hurtled down and hit the bottom they exploded, sending cocoa dust into the air. Once the air began to clear, Pacifico realized his friend had had a lucky escape: a "drum had landed directly in front of him. . . . He was completely covered in cocoa . . . and sputtering and choking. We clear away his face. Even as we were doing this all we could do was laugh, everybody, you know. Because all that was hurt was really his pride, looking like this."[43]

Such a reaction was centered on the fact that accidents had an arbitrary power. The men fatalistically accepted the day-to-day dangers of the job. One day cocoa dust might be the only hazard, but on another it might be acid. Pete Bell describes the awful experience of witnessing a member of a work gang writhing "in the middle of a pool of acid" from a dropped barrel. Another gang member was so badly burned you "couldn't touch his skin" because it "was coming off him."[44]

The work for both New York and London workers was extremely dangerous. Although both groups tried to lessen the dangers by utilizing their skills and experience, the job could never be made fully secure. They worked with the continual movement of cargoes and men, accompanied by the noise and threat of the machinery. Their respective employers and unions appeared uninterested in bettering their work conditions, and the men were left to themselves to endure and hopefully survive serious injury.

Some of the hazards were not immediately recognized, especially when it came to disease. Working with materials that could burn or smother presented long-term health problems. "Eddie" from Jersey City hated working with "talcum powder and cement" because the dust would "cake on you." Less apparent was the damage to lungs that could be caused by the dust. Unfortunately, statistics of the long-term health hazards are not available. The 1942 American study cites seven cases of "industrial disease," but only identifies the area of the body affected ("brain or skull," "eyes," "back," "finger and leg"). In the category of "Chest (lungs)," 5 percent of the injuries were labeled as disabling. One could infer that at least some of the injuries may have been due to lung disease.[45]

New York and London dockworkers specifically complained of lamp black, a substance integral to the production of rubber tires. George Pye remembers working with the substance and its odorous effects: "You could work on it on a Friday night, go home and have a bath, and Saturday night when you went out and you'd had two baths [by then] and you'd go dancing at the Paillasse and would start sweating, . . . it would come out of you, all of your collars would be filthy."[46] Sebastian DeFazio had a similar experience as a longshoreman: "Oh, my god. My wife used to wash me from my head to my toes, and my back and everything."[47]

Other dangerous cargoes included poisons, animal skins, and asbestos. Animal hides were particularly odious. Angelo Pacifico explained how the hides would "stink" and had "maggots jumping all over them. And you had to handle them, you know." It was not uncommon either that "open containers" of hazardous materials with "skulls and cross bones on it" would have to be handled. When longshoremen complained, they'd be informed, "Don't worry about it . . . you can eat it." On the London docks Ted Kirby experienced being covered by maggots an "inch long" when working on African timber shipments. "Many a time" he ran down the street to his home in the hope that no one would notice: "They thought I was stark raving mad, some of the neighbors, but I had to run past the kids, run into a bit of a yard, take me trousers off and bang them up against the wall" to dislodge the maggots.[48]

When medical officers were present on the docks they quickly identified the diseases endured by dockworkers. In 1951 Dr. C. Buchanan, the London port medical officer, listed the diseases that dockworkers confronted, including anthrax, silicosis, jaundice, and Weil's disease. Even though clearly described, some diseases were not readily known. Asbestosis, for example, remained a silent killer until the 1970s. George Pye remembers his father retiring in 1972 with the disease. Although his illness was confirmed by a doctor, compensation was slow in coming. On-site medical facilities for dockworkers were poor. When accidents occurred it was easier to call an ambulance and transport the victim directly to hospital. Although nurses were available in some of the medical facilities, they were rarely dispatched to accident sites. One London nurse, Sister Aynge, was sent to an accident on July 12, 1954. The injured dockworker was bleeding badly due to a fractured skull. The Medical Center administrator, Robert Wilson, testified that her "presence undoubtedly served to preserve calm and must have meant a very great deal to the injured man who remained conscious all the time." Unfortunately, the number of nurses available for the task throughout the port was inadequate.[49]

The hazards of the work and the employers' disregard of the workers were also found in a virtual absence of toilet and eating facilities on the docks. Throughout the 1940s to the 1960s a series of reports were made about the lack of sanitary facilities in the London docks, but most were ignored. Evidence presented to the 1951 Leggett Inquiry highlighted a litany of reports and recommendations, but no action had been taken. Even earlier, a 1948 joint report by stevedores' and dockers' union representatives described conditions as "scandalous and that little or nothing has been done to make any improvement in spite of the [1946] recommendation from the Port Sanitary Officer." The report concluded that "90 percent [of] existing conveniences are obsolete by any standards." Lavatories were found to be "dirty," with an "absence of disinfectant, badly lit, flush system not working, badly ventilated, ventilators bricked up in war still bricked up, absence of drinking water, [and] washing facilities." Doors were missing from toilet cubicles, as were towels and soap. Joe Bloomberg remembered the toilets as "something to be bloody seen. . . . God help you if you fell in."[50]

New York longshoremen also endured inadequate or nonexistent toilet facilities. A "public official" stated to investigators, "The working conditions on the piers are terrible. Take the toilets for example. They are horrible." Employers blamed the longshoremen for such poor facilities. One pier superintendent, when asked why he didn't improve his toilets, replied, "But what good would that do? They'd ruin it anyway."[51] Such a condescending attitude says much about employers' attitudes toward their work force. Perceiving the longshoremen as mere brutes, employers could not appreciate the needs or basic requirements of the work force.

In London, a similar patronizing outlook was evident. In 1950, the National Dock Labour Board found little had been done to rectify the appalling conditions throughout the country as a whole. Some of the inspectors of the facilities became physically sick from the conditions they observed. As the 1950 report pointed out, "Members making the inquiries for the local reports were amazed and nauseated by what they saw and smelt on their own docks—as lavatories. It is not surprising that the men avoid the lavatories whenever possible and have a real fear of infection." Such a statement not only revealed the atrocious conditions but gave clear evidence of a prior lack of understanding of conditions by union and employer officials. The lack of knowledge was supplemented by a patronizing attitude to the "social change" of "dockers." Identifying a "general raising of standards," the dockworkers were demanding better toilet and washing facilities "which but a few years ago would have seemed irrelevant in dock land."[52] But again little was done. George Pye remembers conditions in the late 1960s as "unbelievable . . . toilet facilities were nonexistent, as were washing facilities."[53]

As for eating, although canteens were invariably recommended, the London dockers went off the docks to eat. Joe Bloomberg remembers eating in "coffee shops" or in Italian restaurants. According to Bloomberg, dockers "were all big eaters, they weren't shy in ordering their food." These coffee shops doubled as meeting places for militant dockworkers. During strikes, shop proprietors would provide free coffee and walk "around throwing twenty cigarettes on each table." Such support was rewarded after the strikes ended: "The man [owner] became very popular and he had wonderful business afterwards."[54]

John Donovan described a different activity whereby the "majority of the men went to the nearest pub." He recalled, "I would have a pint and something to eat, a sandwich or something." The danger of eating in pubs lay in the overconsumption of alcohol, which could be dangerous on the job and in the long-term lead to alcoholism. Donovan told with pride that he managed to control his drinking: "One thing I was proud of was that I never gave in to my thirst . . . [but] I wanted a drink because I'd been working bloody hard."[55] Apprehension over drinking during the day was shared by "Eddie" from Jersey City. Tavern owners kept longshoremen in debt or "on the arm. . . . He had you coming back day after day for years." During lunchtime Eddie's gang "went to the tavern, but one thing about me, I always ate because so many of my friends died from sclerosis [*sic*] of the liver. . . . A lot of them only had a liquid lunch and those are the ones who really went down the drain."[56]

The use of distinctive language was also a common denominator between the two groups of workers. The calls "under" and "look out below" warned of danger from above. For London dockworkers, such language was far more elaborate, a mixture of cockney slang and dock-speak. An array of linguistic descriptions was used for everyday job activities. Some slang words expressed humiliating terms for the job or other dockworkers. If, for example, you were the only one not called for work at the call stand, you were described as "left roasting," while a "piper" was a docker who was not pulling his weight in the gang. Dockworkers from the Tilbury Docks were called "turnip bashers" or "carrot crunchers," allusions to their country origins. The docker who stepped beyond the bounds of good behavior was described as "pulling a stroke," and if someone purposely sabotaged the work of others, he had "queer[ed] the pitch." The area or dock where one worked also had its terms. The "lower pool" was the area around Tower Bridge; "the Surrey" stood for the Surrey Commercial Docks; "the Royals" for the Royal Albert Docks; and "over the West" for the West India Docks. Slang could also denote whether work was obtained or not. If a worker was unsuccessful in getting work and had to get his book stamped to get attendance money, it was called "bomping on," which mimicked the sound of the hand-held stamp. When a longshoreman was unloading a ship and was close to reaching the bottom of the ship, the call went out, "Hitting the ceiling"; if the job was close to being finished, the workers yelled, "We're winning." Jobs that paid well or were easy were described as generating "money for old rope"; men doing jobs that were more difficult and paid poorly were "working for love."[57]

Nicknames were also used extensively on the London docks. Nicknames were generally related to a man's actions or appearance while working on the docks. John Donovan described two individuals who always hung around the ship's galley in the hope of scrounging food as the "ship's cat" and "bulging eyes." "Freddie-the-Fly" was one docker who invariably disappeared once work started: "as soon as he got a job he was gone like. . . . Nobody [would] see him until the job was over practically." The docker who often could be found "over The Rainbow," a local pub, became known as "Judy Garland."[58]

Nicknames could also be used to embarrass or humiliate. Joe Bloomberg remembered Johnny Coe, who "was always like a peacock." One day a "special [tall] bus" was being loaded for France and a large crowd had gathered to ensure it was loaded properly. Unfortunately the bus was too high and the hatches could not be lowered. Bloomberg said, "All of a sudden Johnny Coe has got the idea. . . . He said, 'Don't worry, guv. Reflate the tires.'" Coe had got it backwards, he had said, "Reflate 'em, instead of deflate. . . . Well, everybody burst out laughing." From that day on Johnny Coe's nickname was "Reflate." In New York City, nicknames could describe the dress of the person. When one longshoremen always wore a red shirt to work, Angelo Pacifico recalled, he became known as "the bullfighter."[59]

Arthur McMillon's nickname was "Standby," because of his readiness to work whatever hours were needed to finish a job. As he said, "Every time I could get a job, I worked." This propensity to work also extended to overtime. After finishing one job, he would hang around for the chance to work overtime: "I was always the last to go, that's why they called me Standby, because I'm standing by to work some overtime." Other nicknames could be inspired by what the longshoreman brought with him in his lunch pail. Two longshoremen who worked with McMillon, for example, were called, respectively, "Cheese" and "Chicken." Other longshoremen were nicknamed "Wonderbread," "Pineapple," and "Cauliflower." A similar thing occurred in London where one docker acquired the name "Pork Pie."[60] Some nicknames denoted the home or neighborhood of longshoremen. A hiring boss who worked on the East River in Manhattan was known as "Staten Island Joe," while another longshoreman was known as "Hoboken Henry." Other nicknames were racialized in their description. Francisco Garcia, a gang foreman, was tagged with the nickname "Pancho."[61] Although "Pancho" was a name generally reserved for Mexicans, Garcia was born in Puerto Rico. Garcia's white coworkers must have known that there were no Mexicans working the East River.

Swearing was common on the docks, but within relatively strict parameters. When women—usually ships' "officers' wives"—were present on the London Docks, it was reported that "you never heard a bad word said in the presence of a lady. . . . what they [the dockers] do outside the docks is another matter." Such a qualified class perspective on swearing says much about dockworkers' attitudes toward "ladies" and the women in their own lives. When female nurses were in the vicinity, swearing was also kept to a minimum. One trade union official, Arthur Bird, explained the different perceptions that dockers had of female nurses and male doctors: "Now, these fellows will take all kinds of rough treatment from a nurse, whether it means tearing their hair off their body or removing all kinds of plaster—I have seen sweat pouring off them, and I have known they have been taking it, but there was not a bad word. But boy, oh! If a man had been doing that he would be out of the window. But they would not touch the kid, oh no, she could do what she liked with him." This example mixes issues of gender and class. The female nurse was seen as doing her job, albeit a feminized one. This perception of a nurse as a fellow worker was underscored by both Bird and Dr. C. Buchanan, the London port medical officer. Bird succinctly explained the relationship between the worker-nurse and the attending physician: "Let me say this, the nurses, day in day out, are treating the cases, the doctor comes in, looks intelligent, tells the bloke what is wrong, tells the nurse what to do, out goes the doctor and the nurse gets on with the job." Dr. Buchanan confirmed Bird's observation: "I think Mr. Bird has stated the case very fairly."[62]

The New York City dockworkers were just as colorful as their London counterparts in using slang or nicknames. What separated them further from other members of the working class was their dress and posture. The longshoremen's clothes did more than just keep them warm. As "Eddie" pointed out, "We knew how to dress." Even in the winter he wouldn't wear "a heavy coat" because to work efficiently "you had to have room to move." During the colder months, the longshoremen preferred "normal corduroy jackets" that went just "past your cheeks like a car coat, some had hoods, some didn't." As for their posture, Audrey West described how, when the men waited for the shape-up to begin, "they had a distinctive way of carrying their jackets under their arms, and their hooks in their back pockets."[63] Clothes and footwear were important identifiers among the workers themselves. Wearing the wrong boots could also lead to unintended consequences. Pete Bell's attire on his first day on the docks caused longshoremen to shun him. He arrived to work wearing "high-top shoes," he recalled, and there was a "big crap game" of "forty or fifty guys watching and betting on the side." When the group saw Bell, "the game evaporated" and the yell came out, "'You're not going to grab anyone today' . . . because they thought I was a cop." A few days later, after someone who knew Bell explained the situation, he was accepted on the docks.[64] Distinctive clothing as well as unique language and colorful nicknames comprised a form of working-class identity. Such clear markers ensured that dockworkers could recognize one another, both on the job and off it.

The New York City and London dockworkers shared a great deal in common. Clear markers such as slang, nicknames, and clothing ensured that the dockworkers could recognize one another, both on and off the job. Many longshoremen had a keen (but at times ambivalent) understanding of their skills, whether in loading general cargo or unloading bulk cargo. They also had an attachment to the ship and an awareness of the architecture of the hold. It was a work area like no other, and could vary from ship to ship. The work was exceptionally dangerous and held untold numbers of hazards. Besides sharing a perilous job, both New York and London workers engaged in extensive pilferage. They invariably consumed on the ship what they stole and only occasionally walked out of the dock gate with contraband. Their distinctive work created a subculture like no other within working-class populations. Their culture was seen as being apart from that of the surrounding mass society and other working-class communities.

This notion of apartness was replicated in their respective trade unions. As will be seen in the following chapter, the dockers' working lives were fundamentally influenced by a lack of institutional power. The battles for union recognition had long been won, but the contest to gain a voice within their unions, and to effectively change their appalling working conditions, had still to be fought. The postwar period would witness a series of explosions on these issues of union power and work conditions. By challenging their union leadership, the rank and file would also have to confront their nation states. Such contests exemplified postwar industrial relations, and the dockworkers were in the center of the confrontations.

Notes

1. Arthur Miller, *Timebends: A Life* (New York: Penguin, 1987), 147.

2. For discussion of dockworker self-image and proclivity for striking, see Gordon Phillips and Noel Whiteside, *Casual Labor: The Unemployment Question in the Port Transport Industry* (Oxford: Clarendon Press, 1985); Stephen Hill, *The Dockers: Class and Transition in London* (London: Heinemann Press, 1976); Colin J. Davis, "Working with the Hook: A Comparative Study of London and New York City Dockworkers, 1945–1955," *London Journal: A Review of Metropolitan Society Past and Present* 25 (Fall 2000): 79–95.

3. "Rudge Report—Survey on Employee and Labor Relations for the New York Shipping Association, December 7, 1956," Vernon Jensen Papers, box 7-4067, Kheel Archive, Cornell University, 19 (first quote); "Port Worker's News," May, 1950, 8 (second quote).

4. John Donovan, interview by author, July 9, 1996.

5. Leonard DeFazio, interview by author, July 12, 1995.

6. Frank Barbaro, interview by author, July 6, 1995; Leonard DeFazio interview.

7. Interview, Ted Jones, MSS 371/QD7/Docker/23, Modern Records Center, University of Warwick (hereafter MRC).

8. Angelo Pacifico, interview by author, July 12, 1995.

9. Pete Bell, interview by author, July 7, 1995.

10. Ibid.; Jose Villa, interview by author, December 16, 1996.

11. Bell interview.

12. Barbaro interview.

13. Report of Investigation—Investigation of Allegations, Inter-Office Memorandum, April 25, 1956, case file 10409-83, box 13, State Commission against Discrimination, State of New York, New York State Archives (hereafter SCAD-NYSA); "Determination after Investigation and Conference, December 17, 1956," ibid.

14. George Pye, interview by author, August 14, 1996; Jones interview; Donovan interview.

15. Annual Review, National Dock Labour Board (hereafter NDLB), 1948–49, BK 2/1218, Public Record Office, Kew (hereafter PRO).

16. Donovan interview; Minutes of Local Board—London, December 29, 1947, London Dock Labour Board, BK 2-269, PRO.

17. Annual Report, NDLB, 1947–48, BK 27/12, PRO, 13; Annual Review, NDLB, 1948–49, BK 2/1218, PRO, 16.

18. Sebastian DeFazio, interview by author, July 10, 1995.

19. Pacifico interview.

20. "Eddie," interview by author, July 9, 1995.

21. Ibid.

22. "Testimony of Charles Strang," New York State Crime Commission—Public Hearing No. 5, Port of New York (Waterfront) (hereafter NYSCC), vol. 2, 1058–60, New York City Municipal Library.

23. "Eddie" interview; Barbaro interview; Sebastian DeFazio interview.

24. "Testimony of Jones F. Devlin, General Manager, U.S. Shipping Lines," NYSCC, vol. 1, 162; "Testimony of Charles Strang," ibid., vol. 2, 1058 (first quote); "Testimony of Thomas Launders," ibid., vol. 5, 3249 (second quote).

25. "Cargo Losses: Leaving and Entering Port of New York, 1952," NYSCC, vol. 5, 3480.

26. *Sunday Pictorial,* June 4, 1950.

27. Ibid.

28. "Pilferage Cases—1948, London," BK 2/70, NDLB, PRO.

29. Letter to Rt. Hon. H. Graham White from S. C. Parkin, General manager, NDLB, August 18, 1948, BK 2/70, NDLB, PRO (quote); "Changes in the Workers Register—London," BK 27/9, NDLB, PRO.

30. Pye interview; interview, George Cosey, MSS 371/QD7/DOCKS2/8, MRC.

31. Jones interview.

32. "A Survey of Dock Labor Accidents in the Port of London, 1956," by W. J. Shaw, Port Medical Service—Industrial Accidents, London, BK 2/119, PRO.

33. "Injuries and Accident Causes in the Longshore Industry, 1942," *Bulletin No. 764 of the United States Bureau of Labor Statistics* (GPO: 1944), 1.

34. See the rates reported in *Monthly Labor Review* 65 (October 1947): 445–46; ibid.,

67 (October 1948): 363–64; ibid., 69 (October 1949): 386–88; ibid., 71 (October 1950): 481–84.

35. "Injuries and Accident Causes in the Longshore Industry, 1942," 11.

36. Ibid., 14, 15. The report confirmed the role of union/employer efforts to keep the injury rate down: "The lowest regional frequency rate in 1942 was 122 for the Pacific Coast. In comparison with the rates for the regions, this rate reflects the incorporation of the Pacific Coast Marine Safety Code into the working rules of some ports and the continuous accident-prevention activities of the Accident Prevention Bureau of the employers' association" (4).

37. Senate Committee on Labor Public Welfare, *Longshoremen and Harbor Workers Act—Amendments,* 80th Cong., 2d sess., 1948, S. 2237, 55.

38. *Monthly Labor Review* 63 (September 1946): 393; ibid., 65 (October 1947): 45–46; ibid., 67 (October 1948): 363–64; ibid., 69 (October 1949): 385–88; ibid., 71 (October 1950): 480–84 (quote, 481).

39. "Injuries and Accident Causes in the Longshore Industry, 1942," 10 (quote); National Academy of Sciences—National Research Council, *Longshore Safety Survey: A Survey of Occupational Hazards in the Stevedoring Industry—Maritime Cargo Transportation Conference, Publication No. 459* (Washington, D.C.: National Academy of Sciences—National Research Council, 1956), 25, 47.

40. Pacifico interview; Pye interview.

41. Leonard DeFazio interview.

42. Joe Bloomberg, interview by author, August 5, 1996. For other examples of loading and unloading animals, see R. B. Oram, *The Dockers' Tragedy* (London: Hutchinson, 1970), 125.

43. Pacifico interview.

44. Bell interview.

45. "Eddie" interview; "Injuries and Accident Causes in the Longshore Industry, 1942," 29.

46. Pye interview.

47. Ibid.; Sebastian DeFazio interview.

48. Pacifico interview; interview, Ted Kirby, MSS 371/QD7/1/26, MRC.

49. Evidence of Dr. C. Buchanan, *Report of a Committee of Inquiry on Industrial Health Service, 1951—[Edgar T.] Dale Inquiry,* BK 29/16, PRO, 4; Pye interview; Report to Mr. Saunders, NDLB, from Robert Wilson, Administrator, Medical Center, West India Dock, July 26, 1954, BK 2/119, PRO. Wilson stated, "This is only the second time that I know of when a sister has been called out to an accident in London."

50. "T.G.W.U. and Amal. Stevedores, No. Sector Welfare Committee, August 10, 1948," Committee on the London Docks, Leggett Committee on Docks Inquiry, Correspondence with Persons and Bodies Who May Give Evidence, LAB 10/1041, PRO; Bloomberg interview.

51. "Rudge Report," 34.

52. Report of the National Board on Survey of Dock Amenities, January 4, 1950, BK 5/30, PRO, 3.

53. Pye interview.

54. Bloomberg interview (first and second quotes); interview, Harry Browne, MSS 371/QD7/DOCKS2/5, MRC (third and fourth quotes).

55. Donovan interview.

56. "Eddie" interview.

57. Tom Ash, *Childhood Days: The Docks and Dock Slang* (London: Tom Ash, 1985), 51–78.

58. Donovan interview; interview, Jack Dash, MSS 371/QD7/DOCKS2/10, MRC; group interview by author, Dockers' Club, Boutwell Lane, London, July 28, 1996.

59. Bloomberg interview; Pacifico interview.

60. Arthur McMillon, interview by author, March 12, 1999; "Rudge Report" ("Pork Pie").

61. Inter-Office Memorandum, Executive Department, State Commission Against Discrimination, September 16, 1956, series 10409–83, box 13, SCAD-NYSA; "Rudge Report"; Inter-Office Memorandum, Executive Department, State Commission Against Discrimination, June 28, 1956, series 10409–83, box 13, SCAD-NYSA.

62. *Dale Inquiry*, 19–20.

63. "Eddie" interview; Audrey West, interview by author, August 5, 1995.

64. Bell interview.

3 Estrangement

The work of New York City and London dockworkers instilled in them a unique sense of self. They shared or adopted work habits that reinforced familial control and a strong appreciation of skill or work-gang pride. They also shared an increasing anger toward their union hierarchies. Union leaders were judged to be unsympathetic or sometimes irrelevant and therefore out of touch with their members' concerns. Rank-and-file estrangement from union leadership was therefore common. The impulses underlying such perceptions were altogether different in the two groups, however. In the New York case, workers saw the union leadership as corrupt and unworthy of loyalty. In London, the rank and file believed their union leadership had placed itself in the employer camp and understood little about their concern over working conditions and discipline. While the two groups of workers had different motivations, they were linked by their rejection of union leaders' platitudes. What also connected the two memberships was the means used to challenge union leaders, namely, the strike.

New York City

The increasing restlessness of the New York City dockworkers following World War II was grounded in their deteriorating working conditions and trade union indifference. The New York longshoremen were distressed by heavier sling loads, which increased the intensity of work and made a dangerous job that much more hazardous. The sling loads became heavier due to the use of heavier bearing winches. As one longshoreman complained: "Before the war we worked with a one-ton draft—2,240 pounds. Today the sky is the limit." The problem for the longshoremen was that the collapse of such slings made injuries all the more severe. As the same longshoreman commented, "[There are] lots of accidents because there are no safety provisions and often the gear is rotten, the ropes frayed." The increased sling loads also caused hernias, falls, and cuts from unwieldy cargoes, ensuring that the longshoremen's work environment was an extremely hazardous one.[1] The evidence regarding the severity and rate of accidents confirms the longshoremen's concerns; only logging came close to matching the high frequency of injury and attendant work days lost in dockwork.

Beyond the constant danger of accidents and their potentially disabling effects, another prominent threat to the men was the exploitative shape-up system of obtaining work. Unlike their brothers on the West Coast, the New York longshoremen continued to shape-up for work, standing in a horseshoe configuration around the hiring boss and waiting to be picked out of the desperate crowd. The inequity of the ritual was plain for all to see as the hiring boss began to point out who would work that day. There were two shapes per day, one at 6:55 A.M. and the other at 12:55 P.M.[2] Although up to 70 percent of the work force were in regular gangs, the gangs still had to shape-up for work. And when work was not available at the piers, the men had to shape-up at other piers as individuals. The continuation of the practice can be laid at the door of the International Longshoremen's Association (ILA). Under the leadership of Joe Ryan, the ILA accepted the system because it ensured power over the membership. The ILA controlled the system by choosing the hiring boss or by having a union official present at the shape-up. The advantages for the union officials were twofold: they controlled who got work and they benefited from a lucrative kickback scheme. Because the workmen had to appear for work twice a day, they fully realized the need to comply with union demands. Anyone who questioned the union's actions could easily be overlooked for employment. An attorney representing rank-and-file longshoremen testified in 1948 before the Senate Committee on Labor and Public Welfare that a union leader successfully maintained his power "because he is able to discipline any man who dares to raise his voice in a union meeting. . . . That man does not work anymore." The power of hiring ensured that so-called "troublemakers" were kept "off the waterfront simply by not picking them in the shape-up."[3] The shape-up system and its corresponding surplus of labor guaranteed subservience and employment insecurity.

The shape-up was for the most part a sham. As one observer testified, "You will find that 99 out of a hundred times . . . names were submitted to that hiring boss before the men go to the shape-up." One longshoreman said, "You pretend to shape-up . . . and the other fellows waiting there think they have a chance. But they don't." In some cases the "toothpick gimmick" was used; the hiring boss could recognize those to be chosen from the position of the toothpick held in the mouth or placed behind the ear.[4] Union officials also lined their pockets by "inventing" workers known as "phantoms" or "carried," and every week the officials collected the wages. Thomas Maher, a stevedoring superintendent for the Huron Stevedoring Corporation, testified that Timmy O'Mara, a boss loader, regularly collected the wages of a Mr. Ross that totaled $25,000 for the period 1943–51. Payments to O'Mara guaranteed labor peace because he "settled strikes."[5]

It is little wonder that gangsters were attracted to the New York waterfront. Thugs and members of organized crime fought each other for the distinction of becoming hiring bosses. Kickbacks were at stake, as were loan-sharking, bookmaking, payroll padding, and contributions to "charitable" causes or testimonial dinners. Loan-sharking was a common practice, forcing the men to borrow heavily in order to obtain a job. One anonymous longshoreman explained that a loan shark approached him and asked if he needed money but "if I refused, I didn't get the job." Even those workers fortunate enough to pay off the loan discovered once again that they could not obtain work unless they borrowed some more and got into debt again. The system was a lucrative one for the loan shark. After he paid off the hiring boss for the privilege of working his dock, the 10 percent weekly interest charge (520 percent a year) made for a profitable enterprise. The loan shark would collect the brass disc that a working longshoreman was given to show that he had worked. The loan shark would then turn in the disc at the pay window and collect the longshoreman's wages. Generally, the loan shark would take out the money owed and give the remainder to the longshoreman. On occasion the loan shark would take not only the money owed but the entire wages. If the longshoreman would challenge such action he was reminded of the violent consequences. "John Doe" recounted that "I insisted on getting it back, and I was shown a nice blackjack, and I was afraid to try any more." This same longshoreman also stopped paying a kickback to his hiring foreman. For this action he was dropped as a regular of the gang, and as an extra he was intentionally injured: "I sustained a scar on my face. . . . It was identically [*sic*] done, but I wouldn't make any statement, but it was rather funny, what happened."[6]

Instead of dealing with the loan shark as an intermediary, local union leaders used a more direct method for obtaining cash; they demanded cash contributions for "testimonial dinners" or a supposedly sick worker. The longshoremen felt obliged to buy the five-dollar tickets or kick in the odd dollar or two. In some cases up to fifteen thousand tickets would be sold, but the hall for the event would hold only one hundred people. Obviously, the longshoremen were not expected to attend the event. When propositioned for a cash contribution, "the man who refused might find he couldn't get work, or he might get kicked around. A man soon gets the idea; he doesn't refuse more than once."[7]

The criminal exploitation of the longshoremen could not have occurred without a critical alliance between the ILA and gangsters. In many cases the line between the two was blurred. Malcolm Johnson, a crusading journalist for the *New York Sun,* described the port of New York as "an outlaw frontier." Even the structure of the industry played a role in encouraging delay in loading or unloading. An idle ship cost the stevedore money, and he was therefore more likely to pay cash to offset any threat of a work stoppage.[8]

To a large extent the assimilation of gangsters into the union took place during Joe Ryan's presidency of the ILA. Working as a longshoreman for a few years until injury forced him to stop, Ryan maneuvered his way through the ILA hierarchy, becoming president in 1927. Ryan cemented his control in 1943 by getting elected international president for life.[9] Just like his gangster allies throughout the New York City port, Ryan gained financially from his union position. Through a complex web of semiofficial organizations, testimonial dinners, and outright plundering of ILA funds, Ryan accumulated expensive suits, golf club memberships, automobiles, and luxurious vacations around the world. The most explicit gain came from direct payoffs from employers, the stevedoring companies. John William McGrath, president of McGrath Stevedoring Corporation, and Frank Nolan, president of Jarka Stevedoring Corporation, both testified that they paid Ryan cash every year. After intense questioning by the New York State Crime Commission (NYSCC), James C. Kennedy, president of Daniels and Kennedy Corporation, admitted that he too paid Ryan fifteen hundred dollars every year to maintain labor peace. Kennedy explained that once a year he visited Ryan's office and handed over the cash in an envelope. Kennedy reckoned the only word exchanged between them was "Hello."[10]

Ryan also welcomed convicted felons to the union and appointed them as organizers and in some cases as presidents and secretaries of locals throughout the port. His initial justification was that he was giving the men a second chance, but after being pressed during a U.S. Senate inquiry, he admitted hiring convicts to fight Communist influence and maintain his power. As Ryan exclaimed, "Some of those fellows with the bad criminal records were very handy out there when we had to do it the tough way." One ex-convict, Dominick Genova, later testified to the NYSCC that he had made his first contact with the ILA while serving a prison sentence in Sing Sing. After his release he appeared at the docks, introduced himself, and was given a union book with no dues paid. He was not alone: "Oh, after working there I found many men in the same circumstances as myself, who were ex-prisoners, ex-convicts."[11] It appeared that having a police record did not prevent a man from getting a job on the docks. In fact, Arthur Tischon, who had also served time in Sing Sing, explained to the NYSCC, "Well, I guess the worst record [that] you have, I guess the easier to get the job." Tischon testified that he never shaped-up but just walked in after the morning shape and "played cards, and look[ed] to steal something." Contrary to Ryan's insistence that employing ex-convicts gave them a chance to reform, Tischon argued that it achieved the opposite effect: "I don't believe in sending a man to work where his friends are the same friends he had in prison. . . . You're looking for a fast buck [as are the] people you are hanging around with. . . . The temptation is so much greater than if you worked with a legitimate concern."[12] Organized theft was rampant, and cargo and passenger valuables were regularly stolen. In one daring escapade ten tons of steel were stolen. Jones F. Devlin, general manager for the U.S. Lines (a shipping company) testified to the NYSCC, "That was the most remarkable case of pilferage. . . . Yes sir, ten tons disappeared off the pier. It is remarkable how one can get away with it."[13]

A collection of Irish and Italian criminal gangs carved up the waterfront into a series of fiefdoms. In Brooklyn, particularly the Red Hook area, the ILA locals were under control of the Anastasia brothers. Police attempts to rid the docks of gangsters were at best halfhearted. Following the 1939 murder of Pete Panto, an activist-longshoreman, the Brooklyn district attorney, William O'Dwyer (later to become mayor of New York), investigated the Brooklyn union locals. He found that six of the locals were nominally controlled by the Camarda family, and the dues collected from the membership were "turned over . . . to certain known racketeers." One of these racketeers was the infamous Albert Anastasia. Once it became obvious how gangsters controlled the Brooklyn locals, O'Dwyer called in Joe Ryan and Emil Camarda and asked them to clean up the Red Hook locals. A few years later, however, the same group still held power. The 1952 crime commission hearings discovered that the roster of union officers was virtually identical to the one in place when O'Dwyer and Camarda met.[14]

O'Dwyer himself had not been serious in his efforts to investigate either Panto's murder or the role played by the "Camarda locals." Indeed, he had used the investigation to further his own political ambition to become mayor of New York City. In the complex web of New York City politics, O'Dwyer approached the supporters of both Panto and the Camardas. O'Dwyer "had started his campaign for Mayor on the democratic ticket against Mr. LaGuardia" and saw Panto's lawyer, Marcey Protter, as useful to his campaign. Protter was "active in American Labor Party politics"; accordingly O'Dwyer saw him as a potential political ally. As Protter testified to the 1952 crime hearings, O'Dwyer claimed he was about to "break the [Panto] case. . . . I understand the price for this act was that I would attempt to obtain the support of the A.L.P. for him." Protter was not successful in obtaining such support. O'Dwyer then turned to the Camarda-controlled City Democratic Club in Red Hook for its political support. He attended the 1940 "annual ball" at the club, which was frequented by Albert Anastasia and Murder Inc. cohorts Joe Adonis, Louis (Lepke) Buchalter, and Emmanuel (Meny) Weiss.[15]

The link between politicians like O'Dwyer and gangsters was forged in the late 1930s and early 1940s. O'Dwyer had claimed credit for prosecuting members of Murder Inc., but the strange death of an informer, Abe Reles, on his watch would come back to haunt him in the 1950s. The six police officers assigned to protect Reles claimed they had fallen asleep while Reles "fell" to his death from the window of his Coney Island hotel. With Reles dead, the prosecution of organized crime leaders Albert Anastasia and Frank Costello came to an end. Costello, a notorious gangster known also as the "Prime Minister of the Underworld," rewarded O'Dwyer with money and support in his campaign to become mayor in 1945. By the late 1940s organized crime figures like Costello had a solid grip on Democratic politics throughout New York City. The hand of organized crime reached into the city's labor movement as well. ILA officers were tied to various organized crime mobs throughout the city. These connections were replicated in the garment, construction, and teamster unions. By the early 1950s, Carlo Gambino would control the Brooklyn docks after having Albert Anastasia murdered in a Manhattan barber shop. Anthony Anastasia, the dead mobster's brother, preserved his position as union leader of Brooklyn's longshoremen only after he recognized Gambino's power.[16]

The triumvirate of gangster, union official, and politician maintained an atmosphere of terror on New York's waterfront. To challenge union officials could quickly bring mob-related retribution. The police forces who were in the pay of the mobsters would do little to help. The deaths of both Pete Panto and Abe Reles made clear the alliance of union officials, gangsters, and police/political authorities. The murderous image of the mobsters and union officials was based on a violent reality. Between 1930 and 1949, three ILA union officials were murdered, and mobsters who were engaged in the waterfront rackets also fell victim. Thus the world of longshoremen was beset by fear. To survive, most dockworkers adopted a policy of "d and d": acting deaf and dumb.[17]

In Brooklyn, then, a meshing of local politics, gangsterism, and ILA unions formed the backdrop of the longshoremen's world. The *New York Herald Tri-*

bune aptly described the "Camarda locals" as "among the strangest, most feudal and most undemocratic union groups in the city." During the 1952 crime hearings, even small-scale union officials were implicated. When one financial secretary was asked why his local was paying his insurance premiums and notes on his new car, and why he had a large expense account, he replied, "It's the will of the men." And when Salvatore Camarda, the financial secretary of Local 327, was asked where his records were, he replied, "We moved so many times, they must have got lost."[18]

Staten Island was also under the control of gangster-related union officials. Alex DiBrizzi ran the four union locals along the Staten Island shore. Again, union officials had extensive criminal ties. In 1952 the financial secretary of Local 920, Joseph B. Franklin, admitted he had had four criminal convictions for gambling and bookmaking. When pressed by the crime commissioners, Franklin admitted that his receipt and disbursement books had disappeared, the union local did not have a bank account, and that monies had been stored in either a "novelty jar" or a "drawer." Not surprisingly the commissioners stated that Franklin's performance was the "worst exhibition" of "larceny" they had witnessed during the hearings.[19]

Charlie (The Jew) Yanowsky had controlled the locals and thereby the various criminal activities along the New Jersey waterfront until he was assassinated in 1948. Edward Florio took his place as the kingpin along the shore. Florio's ascendancy coincided with the election of Fred M. DeSapio as mayor of Hoboken. To pay off political favors for his electoral victory, DeSapio, with Florio's blessing, obtained jobs for supporters on the Jersey coast.[20] The alliance between politicians and gangsters was a profitable one in Hoboken. Both groups controlled loan-sharking and the use of alien labor. The "aliens," mostly Italians, numbered "a couple of hundred." Also common was "short ganging." That is, instead of the normal twenty-two member gang, only fifteen to seventeen would be put to work and the "phantoms'" wages were collected. The key intermediary between Mayor DeSapio and Edward Florio was the commissioner of public safety, Michael M. Borelli. As one longshoreman explained, "You can't get a job on the piers unless you see Borelli. If he gives you an okay, he sends you to Florio." According to George Fitzpatrick, a Hudson County commissioner, "every Saturday morning" Borelli, Florio, and other known gangsters would meet at the Borelli Democratic Club and "split the profits" from their criminal activities.[21]

On the West Side of Manhattan, the Bowers gang had gained tenuous control by the 1940s. Their inability to dominate the area led to widespread bloodshed as different gangs fought for control, causing one upper West Side local to gain the infamous nickname the "Pistol Local." The Bowers gang spent some of its time away from the docks planning and carrying out bank robberies. The gang members tolerated limited pilferage by others on their docks, but "if anything big came up they were in on it." As on other piers, these gangsters also controlled hiring and loading by managing stevedoring companies, specifically the Allied Stevedoring Company. Below Fourteenth Street, the Chelsea and West Village piers were controlled by Johnny "Cockeye" Dunn until his 1947 murder conviction (he was executed in Sing Sing in 1949).[22] Testifying to the widespread criminal activity on the West Side waterfront, one observer noted that the standard joke on the docks was that when longshoremen read of murderers in the local newspapers they remarked: "If he can beat that rap he has a good job down here."[23]

The presence of tough guys throughout the port deeply affected the longshoremen. Beyond carrying out numerous criminal schemes, the gangsters were also on the docks to maintain order. Criminals and ex-cons were hired by the shipping companies not just to guarantee peace, but to extract the maximum amount of work from the intimidated longshoremen. The employment of gangsters as hiring bosses was affirmed by one company official who revealed that "if I had the choice of hiring a tough ex-convict or a man without a criminal record I am more inclined to take the ex-con. Know why? Because if he is in a boss job he'll keep the men in line and get the maximum work out of them. They'll be afraid of him." After Frank Nolan was pressed to explain why the notorious Anthony Anastasia was hired by his company, the Jarka Stevedoring Corporation, Nolan replied, "He is resourceful and tireless on the job. He preserves discipline and good order on the part of the men."[24] Clearly, longshoremen both obtained employment and worked in an atmosphere of fear and intimidation. Their daily lives were marked by the unending anxiety of job insecurity and unsafe working conditions.

The men were not only controlled by gangsters but were exploited by union officials. Union officials who accepted payments from management were obligated to stall strike action and control disputes over cargo or rates of pay. Nicholas Joseph Palihnich, vice-president of Jarka Stevedoring Corporation, explained how the intimate relationship between union delegate and management worked: "On the waterfront you can always have differences of opinion between labor and management, and if you don't have a [union] delegate around to straighten things out, and, I mean, call to the men's attention that they're wrong and management is right . . . well, you're just at a standstill."[25]

Some stevedore companies were connected with gangster figures. Paul Castellano, for example, was vice-president of the Sottnek Stevedoring Company. He had ties with the East River gangster boss Mike Clementi, business agent of Local 856. Castellano "loaned" Clementi $11,000 to pay for his daughter's wedding, which was attended by a who's who of the underworld. Castellano would later become the head of the Gambino crime family but was assassinated by John Gotti in 1991.[26]

The complex and sordid relationship between union officials, gangsters, and politicians ensured that few longshoremen would challenge the system. Longshoremen viewed the city's political system as problematic because of its corruption. Union leaders were careful to nurture political support, even going to the extreme of creating their own political clubs, but the longshoremen had nowhere to turn. The cynical use of political patronage kept the body politic, including police agencies, away from the waterfront. Only when political capital could be won would politicians tentatively approach longshoremen. Such behavior merely confirmed the longshoremen's distrust of those politicians who purported to represent them. In turn, longshoremen's cynicism toward the surrounding political elites was confirmed.

The system did not, however, go unchallenged. Some brave longshoremen confronted these atrocious conditions but were quickly silenced—their punishments intended as examples of what awaited those who dared challenge the ILA and the gangsters on the waterfront. As noted earlier, prior to World War II, Pete Panto, a Brooklyn longshoreman who organized a vibrant rank-and-file movement, was murdered by Albert Anastasia, the reputed head of Murder Inc., and dumped in a lime pit in New Jersey.[27] By 1945, however, the rank and file rebelled against ILA rule and embarked on an unofficial strike. Following the strike, however, the two principal strike leaders, William E. Warren and Sal Barone, were viciously beaten, thrown out of the ILA, and warned to steer clear of the docks thereafter.[28]

The lack of any democratic institutional structures within the union hampered efforts to challenge the corruption. Union meetings and elections were rarely held and barely advertised. Mitch Berenson, a longtime Brooklyn rank-and-file reformer, testified in 1949 to the House Committee on Education and Labor, "You know, there are elections and [there are] elections." It was common that the corrupt "guys will put a little notice on a store window and they will say, 'Elections tonight.' And they get 15 or 20 guys together in the local, all in favor of Joe Blow, to be delegate. And that is the end of it." To attend such meetings was to place your life in peril: "They will get 15 or 20 gorillas together in a local, and it is your death to get into that local." Furthermore, ILA officials kept no records of the meetings. An illuminating interchange between members of the 1952 New York State Crime Commission and John J. Gannon, secretary-treasurer of Manhattan Locals 824-1 and 901-1, and president of the New York District Council, highlighted the lack of democracy:

Commr. Proskauer: Have you got any minutes of your meetings prior to 1951?
The Witness: I can't locate them.
Q. They have gone too?
A. Yes sir.
Commr. Proskauer: Gone with the wind. . . .
Q. Didn't you testify that the last election in that local [901-1] was maybe ten, twelve, or more years ago?
A. I would say that.
Q. How about 824-1?
A. We had one there in around 1944, '45; I'm not too sure which. . . .
Q. Since then you have never had a meeting?
A. We had a few meetings, but I don't recall the dates.[29]

Longshoremen rarely turned up at meetings, even when notified. If they did attend a meeting they fully realized what was expected of them, namely, a quiet appreciation of the union officials. Sebastian DeFazio testified to the almost farcical nature of the proceedings: "When they had the meetings, they wanted a full house, you know, so they can shoot the baloney to us. Tell us what they're doing for us—which they weren't." But, he said that if "you'd stand up they'd tell you you're out of order, so you know you're going to get your head broke, if you don't keep quiet."[30] Violence was endemic in many of the meetings. The infiltration of some union locals by gangsters made it very risky to challenge officials. For example, men found that attending meetings of the Watchmen's Union, an affiliate of the ILA, was fraught with peril. A reform group in 1948 challenged the leadership of Local 1516, but the meeting was stacked with tough guys. Charles Gulizia, a member of the reform group, explained that at the meeting, "I see some ugly-looking faces that I wouldn't say belong to the same class of watchmen." A fight ensued before the meeting was called to order, and one of the reformers took "several punches right on the eye and cheek, and he was lucky he wasn't sent to the hospital for several months." Gulizia meanwhile had beaten a hasty retreat: "I ducked under the table in the middle, and I rolled down like a hat and ran out."[31] Challenging union officials on the dock was also hazardous. When Mario Frullano berated his business agent, Paul Crissalli, for increasing dues payments while the men were not "getting any benefits from it," he was physically attacked. As Frullano explained, "While I was arguing with him [Crissalli] these two other men were butting in. . . . I don't know who they were, but they were down there with him, and the first thing you know, I got kicked by somebody." As a result of this kick in the groin, Frullano was forced to miss three weeks of work.[32]

Even when union locals practiced democracy, one still had to confront an unsympathetic district and national leadership. This particularly affected black locals. Although the ILA did not officially bar blacks from the union, it ignored their complaints of discrimination. Having black locals helped some, but other blacks throughout the port were forced to accept shorter and dirtier work. To some extent the ILA's relative acceptance of blacks was tactical, to protect against strikebreakers. As one black union official testified, "We are in the union today because the white man had to take us in for his own protection. Outside the organization the Negro could scab on the white man. Inside he can't."[33] In New York there existed a combination of biracial unionism—wherein blacks and whites had their own separate locals—and free-floating black members. Like the Italians and Irish who formed ethnic locals, blacks were either forced to create their own locals or accept what was available. What set black locals apart, however, was the embedded racism they faced and their inability to control a pier to ensure regular employment.[34]

One thing the black longshoremen had in Brooklyn was a strong leadership. The president of Local 968 was Jamaican-born Cleophas Jacobs. I. Philip Sipser, the lawyer who represented Local 968, described Jacobs as "one of the most intelligent men I have met in the trade union movement or anywhere else for that matter." Jacobs was a "short, squat man" and "a follower of Marcus Garvey." Representing well the New York City and Jamaican connections to Garveyism or black nationalism, Jacobs refused to talk with the newly hired Sipser for over six months. Only after a frank meeting where Sipser explained that "as a Jew he understood some of the pain, not all of it, of black people," did Jacobs accept him. More specifically, Sipser detailed how his family had been "wiped out in the Holocaust," and that he "knew about the back-to-Africa movement." Jacobs represented a recast Garveyism, one that saw labor unions as vehicles for black empowerment and economic independence, but one in which whites continued to be regarded with suspicion and, at times, hostility.[35]

Local 968 was located on Atlantic Avenue, while the majority of the membership came from the Bedford-Stuyvesant area of Brooklyn. According to Sipser, the members came from all around, "Jamaicans, native-born blacks, a whole combination . . . you heard Caribbean." Although trying to get work along the Brooklyn (and at times the Staten Island) waterfront, blacks were not necessarily beholden to the Italian bosses. They were discriminated against during the shape-up, but blacks had little fear of the gangsters who controlled the hiring process. As Sipser explained, "Blacks weren't afraid, [they thought] well what the hell, I don't have a job anyhow." Although rejecting intimidation, black longshoremen still had to pay kickbacks to hiring bosses and borrow money from loan sharks. As Sipser pointed out, "The plethora of ills of the longshoremen affected blacks but double."[36] While Local 968 enjoyed a form of autonomy from the more egregious forms of intimidation along the Brooklyn waterfront, it was unable to control a pier and obtain steady employment for its members. It remained a shadow organization with little institutional power.

There were left-wing groups that were working on the New York waterfront, particularly in Brooklyn. In 1948, an amalgam of Communist, trade union, and American Labor Party activists engaged in a campaign to gain back pay for the New York longshoremen. This movement created an oppositional culture on the New York docks and led to direct confrontation with the ILA leadership, and eventually a strike that would threaten Joe Ryan's rule. The issue of money had a good chance of attracting potential recruits and perhaps creating an oppositional culture. Initially, the key organization was Harry Bridges's International Longshoremen and Warehousemen's Union (ILWU), which viewed the situation as an opportunity to expand its influence on the East Coast. The 1945 strike had convinced the ILWU leadership that the time was ripe for challenging ILA control in New York. Consequently Sam Madell, an organizer with the ILWU and Communist Party member, began working with the New York longshoremen. He picked the issue of pay to galvanize them, starting with a movement to obtain back pay owed the longshoremen under the Fair Labor Standards Act. Working with lawyers, Madell first began a petition among the men, and by 1947 the tenuous alliance was cemented when attorneys helped longshoremen file suits for back pay. Madell explained that the men "were very much interested in this thing because it meant millions and millions of dollars in back pay would be due longshoremen."[37] Back Pay Committees were formed in Brooklyn and Hoboken, New Jersey, and also in Baltimore. According to William Glazier, the Washington, D.C., representative of the ILWU, the Brooklyn Back Pay Committee was the "strongest," with meetings drawing over eighteen hundred attendees. Brooklyn blacks formed their own committee, closely associated with all-black Local 968. The "back pay movement," according to Glazier, had become the "first mass anti-Ryan development" since the 1945 strike.[38]

This amalgam of rank-and-file activists and legal collaborators made for a potentially strong bond that would culminate in the 1948 strike. The rumblings over the back pay issue and the influence of "outside" reformers certainly stirred the waters. But there was a strategic weakness in the movement. While men like Madell coaxed some men to act, the majority of longshoremen stood apart, suspicious of Madell because of his ILWU credentials. Many longshoremen were convinced that the ILWU was tainted by Communist control. Indeed, continual postwar government harassment of ILWU officials, including investigations of the supposed ties of Harry Bridges to the Communist Party of America, nurtured suspicions of the union's intentions. While help and support was welcomed by some New York longshoremen, others had misgivings over the "outsiders" objectives. Bridges's dispatching of Sam Madell to New York City was therefore loaded with uncertainty. Adding to the tension was Bridges's ambiguous politics and union ideals. He always denied he was a member of the Communist Party, but some within the party considered him "influential," that is, closely linked to the party but not a member. Because of this tentative relationship, many in the party suspected he was more trade unionist than Communist. One Communist leader, Joseph Starobin, described Bridges as an anarcho-syndicalist rather than a Communist. Bridges, then, picked Madell because of his trade union allegiance rather than his Communist credentials.[39] Thus the prime reason for Madell's presence in New York was principally to expand the ILWU reach in the hopes of capturing the ILA.

For many New York longshoremen the intricacies of Bridges's political and agitational machinations were not considered noteworthy. For them, there was no separation between the two functions of ILWU leader and Communist. A paradoxical situation existed: the strength of men like Madell lay in their having no connection with corrupt ILA officials, but they were divorced from the day-to-day union and work experience of the men. Just as problematic, Madell's Communist and ILWU credentials made him a suspicious character in the eyes of most New York longshoremen. Being an "outsider" was thus a double-edged sword; it gave validity to one's action while severely weakening one's power position.

London

The London dockworkers in the same period were also a mass of restless energy, and they too directed their frustration and anger at a union leadership they considered ineffectual. The conditions surrounding their alienation, however, were altogether different than those of the New York men. The London dockworkers labored within a system of tight governmental control under the auspices of the 1947 Dock Labour Scheme. Quasi-governmental labor boards were in operation that purported to deal with the grievances and discipline problems of dockers. But dockworkers had a different perspective on what the problems were, and how they should be addressed. Unfortunately, union officials sat on the respective boards. Dockworkers were being judged by both union officers and employers.

The National Dock Labour Board (NDLB) had been created to oversee the workings of the Dock Labour Scheme, including: "regulating recruitment"; discharging "from the Scheme dock workers" who failed to adhere to the regularized employment conditions; "determining the size" of the national "register" of dockworkers; and the "training and welfare of dock workers." The chairman and vice chairman were appointed by the minister of labor and food. The eight officers of the board, "four being appointed to represent dock employers and four to represent dock workers," were to be nominated by the National Joint Council.[40]

A London Dock Labour Board (LDLB) was created to oversee "local" conditions and to administer the Dock Labour Scheme in the city. Again, there would be equal numbers of employer and worker representatives. One of the functions of the LDLB was to provide information on local conditions to its national cousin. Critically, it was also to act as a point of appeal for dockworkers and to establish tribunals to hear such appeals. It was this latter function that would cause so much controversy. When issues of discipline came before the LDLB, the trade union members of the board found themselves performing as judge and jury over their members' work habits and conditions.[41]

Most of the disciplinary cases that came before the LDLB and the respective tribunals concerned noncompliance with the scheme's employment clauses. So, if a dockworker failed to "comply with any lawful order given to him," he could be punished in one of three ways: suspended without pay for seven days; given "seven days' notice of termination of employment"; or be "summarily" dismissed. Infractions ran the gamut of noncompliance; not attending the twice-daily calls, for example, was a common infringement, as was refusing to be assigned a certain job or ship.[42]

Absenteeism became the key problem that the LDLB had to address. The regulation that compelled dockers to attend calls every day went against the casual frame of mind they had developed in the prewar years. The dockers therefore did not universally accept the regulation of work. Many dockers and stevedores who had been weaned on the casual system resented the regulated transfer of jobs. They were accustomed to working for days at a stretch and then taking time off to recover. They took time off as a way of replenishing their energy after particularly hard work. The "continuity rule," established by the 1947 Dock Labour Scheme to guarantee that dockworkers finished the job assigned before moving onto the next, exacerbated the situation. Forced to engage in overtime to complete a job, the dockworker was often exhausted. Even before the introduction of the 1947 scheme, dockworkers resisted directed labor. The Ammon Inquiry, an investigation into a March 1945 stevedores' strike, found wholesale resentment over allocation of work. In the London Dock Survey, presented by the National Dock Labour Board to the

Ammon Inquiry, it was explained that the regulation of work had led to increased worker alienation. Thus "the men contend that the Scheme has deprived them of their freedom to work when and where they will." The survey also suggested some of the specific reasons for absenteeism, including the "need to rest after arduous work," and a "tradition of the dockers' 'freedom'" to choose work.[43]

Some dockers were intimately connected with certain employers and felt comfortable in working day-to-day with those firms. Such a link meant that they were familiar with the company, but it also gave them an understanding that prime cargoes, generally those paying a good rate of pay, were reserved for them. Thus on many occasions when dockers knew of such shipments, they refused to answer the morning call, hoping that by the afternoon call the better-paying job would be secured. Many dockers also resisted being dispatched to outlying areas. The dock survey discovered that dockworkers avoided being chosen for certain types of work. Work that was either particularly easy or well paid was seen as "attractive," but difficult work with little incentive in the piece rates was evaded. As the survey pointed out, "If the work offering is attractive, there is a rush for work; if the work is unattractive, the men become inconspicuous."[44] Employers also played a role in reserving jobs for steady gangs. The 1951 Leggett Report found that "every employer wants his own regular gang and generally gets it."[45]

Dockworkers generally resented the disciplinary powers of both the National and London Dock Labour Boards,which only increased their feelings of anger and frustration. The boards had become disciplinary entities in which the union delegates ended up chastising their members for poor work habits. The system was perceived as particularly inflexible, and dockworkers lodged large numbers of complaints about harsh penalties that were meted out even for justified absences. The August 27, 1947, meeting of the LDLB attempted to address the mounting complaints. The port manager reported to the meeting that in the "cases quoted," where dockworkers explained they had provided "satisfactory explanations," the true situation was otherwise. The policy was that "unless a satisfactory explanation had been forthcoming, disciplinary action had been taken," and that such "action" generally occurred once a third incident had occurred.[46]

NDLB and LDLB members and officials became indignant over dockworker complaints. They saw the difficult job of maintaining the register of twenty-five thousand London dockworkers as a gigantic task. To board officials, the benefits of the Dock Labour Scheme far outweighed the restrictions of the accompanying rules. With attendance pay guaranteed and appeal procedures in place, dockworkers who complained were considered ungrateful and their dissatisfaction was regarded as unwarranted. The bureaucratic constraints of the scheme were seen as a small sacrifice compared to the greater benefits that regulation bestowed. The dockworkers were characterized as unappreciative and ignorant of the mechanics of the scheme. The traditional employer's perspective that dockworkers were hot-headed and unreasonable was carried over to the regulated era. Thus complaints by dockworkers were dismissed as mere ramblings of disaffected children.

The dockworkers, however, considered the system unfair. After disciplinary action was taken by the employer/union members of the LDLB, the membership invariably perceived their mid- and upper-level union representatives as being in sympathy with employers and board officials. As one docker asked, "How many suspensions have occurred since the Scheme started? It's becoming more like the Gestapo in pre-war Germany." This comparison bespeaks a deep-seated fear of strangling authority. Just as critical, the docker linked his complaints with wartime regimentation and accused his union leaders of treachery. He believed that the union leadership had lost touch with its membership: the officials, "ex-dockers themselves who have found an easier job, cleaner[,] and better pay, . . . help convict a docker and bring up his past record and the docker is punished by suspension. . . . No sir, do away with Ibex House [headquarters of the London Dock Labour Board] court martials. . . . They must forget their military ideas and remember we are just plain civilians not criminals nor soldiers."[47] In this testimony, war and betrayal were finely meshed. Such a potent mixture made for a dangerous brew.

The accusation that the LDLB was unjust in suspending or dismissing men was also framed by the feeling that employers were given carte blanche to ignore the Labour Dock Scheme. During the 1946 Cameron Inquiry into the proposed scheme, union officials made known their suspicion that discipline would be directed only at dockworkers. John Donovan, a witness for the Transport and General Workers' Union (TGWU), argued that if the National Board "gets the right to punish and discipline the men, then it must have the equal power and right to discipline the employer." In response, the scheme did include the provision that "where a registered employer fails" to abide by the "Scheme, his name may be removed from the employers' register." But the perception persisted that employers continued to ignore requirements of the scheme. On June 14, 1948, a docker named J. Fitzgerald angrily declared, "I would like to know what power has the NDLB over the Employer that consistently keeps breaking his verbal agreement. . . . And they get off Scot Free."[48]

The dockworkers felt constrained by bureaucratic inertia and lack of flexibility. Although incensed that employers escaped censorship, the dockworkers focused their anger on their union officials. Entrenched in a system of institutional adjudication, union officials became increasingly divorced from their members. This particularly affected the Transport and General Workers' Union. Known as the "white union" because of the color of the union card, the TGWU played the dual role of union and judge. By sitting on the NDLB and the LDLB, TGWU officials followed a path of least resistance and became indifferent to their members' concerns. To some extent this was due to the unwieldy structure of the union.

The TGWU was a union that represented more than just dockworkers. Its principal publication, *The Record,* was aimed at the TGWU membership as a whole and did not focus exclusively on the dockworker. Members of the government committee that carried out the 1951 inquiry into "unofficial strikes in the London Docks" were "repeatedly told that *The Record* is read by only a small minority of dock workers."[49]

TGWU officials were present throughout the port, but in most cases they were separated from the membership. This was particularly true of District Officials. In the London docks there were approximately ten full-time District Officials, whose jurisdictions were based loosely on the sectors throughout the port. Of great concern to dockers, these officials were not elected but were appointed by the TGWU. Branch representatives commonly resented these appointed District Officials.[50] The elaborate structure did not fit well the hurly-burly nature of dock work and its attendant grievances. One of the constant complaints of dockers centered on the apathy or indifference of District Officials. Sitting in offices away from the docks, these officials exhibited little interest in their members' grievances. As Joe Bloomberg explained, "You can't sit in the office and know what is right and wrong." The physical distance separating the union official and the rank and file was therefore an important component of the increasing docker alienation. Satisfaction with a union position made the officials less likely to get involved in disputes. Joe Bloomberg described how the officials became comfortable with their new-found status: "They were in a good corner—if it's nice and warm why make it cold, what do we need this hassle for—but [it was] not a hassle for the men."[51]

The division between appointed TGWU officials and the rank and file had a long history. The TGWU was an amalgam of different trades and occupations. Divided into sections, the TGWU included such diverse workers as dockers, busmen, seamen, and truck drivers. The TGWU leadership charged that branch officials could and did create local fiefdoms controlling access to work and overtime. To counter this localism throughout the sections, the District Officials were appointed by the TGWU executive to oversee the running of branches and general working conditions. Dockers resisted such centralized control throughout the early years of the TGWU. During the early twentieth century the London docks were a hotbed of unofficial movements. Anger directed at officials was a common denominator of intra-union relations. In 1923, dockers rallied around an alternative leadership and challenged Ernest Bevin's leadership. London busmen during the 1930s also created the rank-and-file movement, solidifying a tradition of alternative action within the TGWU.[52]

Other than the specific and traditional separation of union officials from the rank and file, the division was also caused by the close political alliance between the TGWU and the Labour government elected in 1945. The TGWU worked closely with the newly elected government in an effort to restore the competitiveness of the British economy. In essence this alliance entailed control over wages and work conditions. The three-union bloc of the TGWU, the National Union of Miners (NUM), and the General and Municipal Workers Union solidified their coalition with the Labour government. On the surface the policies of the Labour Party and the respective unions were the same, aimed toward the nationalization of core industries and the installation of a welfare system. Although the relationship was at times symbiotic, it was also grounded in the intimate connection between union and political party. Of the 120 union-sponsored members of Parliament, 34 were from the TGWU and 17 from the NUM.[53]

Beginning in 1947, the somewhat cozy arrangement between the government and the unions was endangered by a series of crises. The first to hit was a fuel shortage. It was quickly followed by a financial crisis that posed problems for the country's economic recovery. The decline in value of the pound sterling vis-à-vis the American dollar created a problem of confidence. Unable to meet fully its monetary obligations, the government was forced to select devaluation as a solution in 1949. Of more direct importance to the trade unions was the call for wage restraint as the government grappled with the issue of increasing trade to gather much-needed foreign currency. Although such a move was unpopular with their members, the trade unions agreed voluntarily to go along. For the trade union leadership, there was little else they could do. The point was to maintain their political allies in power, even at the expense of their members' incomes and buying power.[54]

While the TGWU had accepted most of the Labour government's wage-restraint policies, the dockworker membership was not so readily convinced. Most work was paid by the piece-work system. In theory each cargo rate had been negotiated by the National Joint Council. In London "there were well over 40,000 scheduled piece-rates." The huge variety of cargoes and their condition on arrival in the port made for a complex and incendiary situation. Each dock had "its own particular work practices, payment schedules, and traditions of militancy."[55] There was constant tension over the correct rate to be paid, when to break from work because of inclement weather, and issues of continuity, that is, of working the ship until the job was completed. The dockworkers were strategically positioned to take advantage of the situation. Any delay in the shipment of cargo could result in the loss of earnings for employers, who were "only too willing to settle disputes as quickly as possible."[56]

Throughout the prewar casual period, work gangs had used the threat of industrial action to gain on-the-spot rewards. This tradition of militancy was carried over into the regulated postwar era. The transferring of dock labor from one dock to the other had the unintended result of making dockworkers more aware of conditions different from their own. As Joe Bloomberg explained, "Sometimes we'd see standards that was operating in the Albert and West India Dock. We thought we could do with those things as well. It just happened. We were quick to see the advantages of the thing." In Bloomberg's words it was just simply a question of "bloody hell, if they can get it why can't we have it?"[57]

But such action conflicted with the clauses of the Dock Labour Scheme. If there was a disagreement over the rate paid, then branch officials were supposed to clarify the issue. "Viewing committees" were also to be established to set the proper rate. This was particularly the case with "dirty cargoes," where the established rate needed to be adjusted. For example, if bags of cement became waterlogged, the rate had to be adjusted accordingly to account for the added weight. The men resented such mechanisms. It took time for the issue to be resolved and in many cases went against the men's wishes. The men therefore began to feel constrained by the Dock Labour Scheme and a strategic loss of their "opportunistic" power. As the 1951 Leggett Inquiry found, the men believed they would more likely win an issue "while they are still doing the job" rather than "after the job is finished."[58]

One other vital ingredient that went into the mix was the changing attitudes of the postwar period, especially those of a younger generation entering the dock work. Harry Browne, who worked at Hays Wharf, was convinced that the men returning from the war had different expectations than those who had remained in the docks during the conflict: "I do believe the chaps coming out of the forces was the biggest shake-up that the industry ever had, to be honest." NDLB officials and employers were equated with military officers. As Browne said, "All of us who came along in '46 we weren't going to be messed about, you know, we didn't expect a 'land of milk and honey' or 'land fit for heroes,' but we'd had enough, we weren't going to be messed about by this sort of people. Little jumped up dictators, we'd just kill one, you know, so."[59] Evidence suggests that such feelings were widespread among men and women who served in the armed forces. The experience of war and the close contact with officers brought out class antagonism. One impact of the war was an erosion of deference; the arbitrary and bullying actions of officers eroded feelings of respect for "your betters." The breakdown of the social compact was no more apparent than in the army mutinies in Egypt and India. They were no longer just "going to take it."[60]

The relative youth of these men also nurtured a rebellious attitude. Albert Andrews, a docker, understood why his docker father felt that postwar dock work "was more or less utopia" because of guaranteed income, and you "stopped work when it rained." But for members of the younger Andrews's generation, expectations were different. They chafed under the Dock Labour Scheme's rules and regulations and were angered by the supposed indifference of union officials. This generational difference also affected clerks working in the docks. Don Perry represented the "younger blood[s]" who entered the industry just after the war. Perry's cohorts "were a different kettle of fish" from his father's generation. Being "more militant" also meant that Perry and others actively supported the 1948–54 unofficial strikes. Perry pointed out to elder clerks that "by supporting the dockers in their struggles," such support would be reciprocated. Just as important, once clerks went out on strike they brought the docks to a standstill. The older generation "gradually realized the power that they had. And that made them more militant." Thus a dynamic combination of war experience and youth unleashed a more radical and confrontational reaction throughout the London docks.[61]

The changing, or heightened, sense of class antagonism was also influenced by the Labour Party victory in 1945. Mass Observation surveys in the immediate postwar period identified an accentuated class identification. One young working-class man stated to a 1948 survey, "I belong to this class because I was born in it, and because I want to be in it. I am proud to be in it because of its forthrightness, honesty, and capacity for hard work, and because I despise the English middle class." The Conservative Party had been discredited by its appeasement and mobilization policies during the 1939–41 period. Attorney General Sir Hartley Shawcross, a Labour cabinet member, spoke for many in the working-class constituencies when he stated, "We are the masters now."[62] One other important factor that played a catalytic role in radicalizing the English working class, and specifically the London dockworkers, was full employment. The Dock Labour Scheme, and the high demand for labor, tipped the balance of power in favor of the dockworkers in particular. No longer fearful of losing their livelihood, dockworkers exchanged their prewar insecurity for an aggressive posture of defiance.

London dockworkers were both invigorated and angered by factors that were directly related to their work and life experiences. A generational shift had taken place. Younger men had strong ideas of challenging established or traditional ways of looking at the job. Nurturing such a combative stance was a union structure that the men considered unwieldy and undemocratic. Greater societal influences of a Labour Party in power and a stabilization of employment emboldened the men's attack on authoritative structures, whether Dock Labour Boards, union officials, or the central government. This volatile and complex mix ensured that the period 1948–54 would be rocky for all concerned.

Dockworkers' dissatisfaction with the Dock Labour Scheme and their trade union officials, mixed with a more militant spirit, fed a series of disputes throughout the port. During the first six months of 1948, strikes broke out concerning issues such as rates of pay, resentment over dismissal, working in bad weather, manning levels, and watchmen in the hold. If one ignores the June 1948 portwide strike, thirty-five strikes occurred that year, and most involved only one ship. (See table 3.)

By far the most common focus of dispute was pay. Over one-third of the disputes entailed a grievance over "extra payments" for "rough goods" and "dirty cargoes." Four disputes occurred over allocation of work in which dockworkers refused to work where assigned. The four disputes concerning dismissals were linked to absences from work or refusal to work overtime. The link with dismissal disputes and work allocation involved the refusal to accept orders. These issues informed eight, or 23 percent, of the disputes. Manning disputes were linked with disputes over working conditions. The latter dis-

Table 3. Strikes in the Port of London, 1948

Issue	Disputes	Average Number of Men	Average Number of Ships	Average Duration (in Days)
Rates of pay	12	117	1	2.5
Dismissal	4	183	1	3.0
Watchmen in the hold	2	40	1	1.5
Discipline	3	120	1	3.0
Working conditions	4	132	1	4.0
Work allocation	4	96	1	2.0
New machinery	2	276	2	2.5
Interunion conflict	1	5,327	63	3.0
Travel time payments	1	20	—	3.0
Manning	2	138	2.5	3.5

Source: "Statement of Disputes Affecting Dock Workers, From 1st January, 1948 to 31st December, 1948," Statistic—Disputes, NDLB, BK 2/71, PRO.

putes included cases of working in "bad weather" and being forced to deal with an "abnormal amount of loose asparto grass on deck." These six issues were the basis of approximately 15 percent of the disputes.[63]

These strikes constituted the more obvious expressions of resentment against the scheme. The number of viewing committees established to oversee disputes is not available, however. Considering the large number of strikes—and, of course, the June strike that would envelop the port and spread to Liverpool—it would be safe to contend that frustration was rampant. As with the New York longshoremen, London dockworkers found their conditions of work and pay inadequate.

The respective work forces were therefore joined by their intense suspicion of trade union leaders. In New York this mistrust was animated by the lawlessness and arbitrariness of union power. Corruption fed such alienation. In London, on the other hand, the incorporation of the TGWU within a government-sanctioned industrial-relations system nurtured the dockworkers' deep-seated dissatisfaction. Paradoxically, what some New York dockworkers yearned for—stable, institutionalized union-employer relations—was resented by their London counterparts. Thus the surrounding conditions of trade union culture may have been different in the two ports, but resentment against union officials was shared. This disaffection would explode in 1948, as both groups of workers would directly confront their union hierarchies and employers. With this action, the respective nation-states would join the battle, making the conflicts more extensive and explosive.

Notes

1. *Daily Worker,* November 19, 1948, 4.

2. Howard Kimeldorf, *Reds or Rackets? The Making of Radical and Conservative Unions on the Waterfront* (Berkeley: University of California Press, 1992), 154–55.

3. "Testimony of Julius E. Bagley," Senate Committee on Labor and Public Welfare, *Fair Labor Standards Act, Amendments, Part 1,* 80th Cong., 2d sess., 994; Charles P. Larrowe, *Shape-Up and Hiring Hall: A Comparison of Hiring Methods on the New York and Seattle Waterfronts* (Berkeley: University of California Press, 1955), 74 (quote).

4. "Testimony of Ross J. DiLorenzo," Senate Committee on Labor and Public Welfare, *To Clarify the Overtime Provisions of the Fair Labor Standards Act of 1938, As Amended,* 81st Cong., 1st sess., 1949, 272 (quotes); Larrowe, *Shape-Up and Hiring Hall,* 55.

5. New York State Crime Commission—Public Hearing No. 5, Port of New York (Waterfront) (hereafter NYSCC), vol. 1, 257–60, New York City Municipal Library.

6. "Testimony of John Doe," NYSCC, vol. 3, 1798, 1804.

7. Malcolm Johnson, *Crime on the Labor Front* (New York: McGraw-Hill, 1950), 115 (quote); "Testimony of Julius E. Bagley," Senate Committee on Labor and Public Welfare, *Fair Labor Standards Act, Amendments, Part 1,* 80th Cong., 2d sess., 995; Larrowe, *Shape-Up and Hiring Hall,* 56–57. In some cases the loan shark had direct access to the

payroll department and would obtain the money owed directly from the payroll clerk. Citizens Waterfront Committee, *The New York Waterfront: A Report to the Public of New York City by the Citizens Waterfront Committee Setting Forth Our Oldest and Most Urgent Civic Problem—The Condition of the Waterfront* (New York, 1946), 28; Johnson, *Crime on the Labor Front,* 113–15.

8. Johnson, *Crime on the Labor Front,* 91.

9. Bruce Nelson, *Workers on the Waterfront: Seamen, Longshoremen, and Unionism in the 1930s* (Urbana: University of Illinois Press, 1990), 142; Larrowe, *Shape-Up and Hiring Hall,* 26.

10. "Testimony of John McGrath, Frank Nolan, and John Kennedy," NYSCC, vol. 1, 43–44, 94–102, 568.

11. "Testimony of Joe Ryan," Senate Committee on Interstate and Foreign Commerce, *Waterfront Investigation, Part 1: New York–New Jersey Waterfront,* 83d Cong., 1st sess., 447; "Testimony of Dominick Genova," NYSCC, vol. 3, 2144–47.

12. "Testimony of Arthur Tischon," NYSCC, vol. 1, 551–53.

13. "Testimony of Jones F. Devlin, General Manager, U.S. Shipping Lines," NYSCC, vol. 1, 162.

14. "Testimony of Edward A. Heffernan, Assistant District Attorney, Kings County, N.Y.," NYSCC, vol. 3, 1549; *New York Times,* December 19, 1952, 1, 26; *New York Herald Tribune,* December 19, 1952, 1, 14. Three years after the meeting between O'Dwyer and Joe Ryan and Emil Camarda, Camarda was murdered. An amalgam of tough guys took nominal control of the Camarda locals led by Constantino Scannavino and Albert and Jerry Anastasia. "Testimony of Constantino Scannavino," NYSCC, vol. 3, 1589.

15. *New York Herald Tribune,* December 19, 1952, 14; *New York Times,* December 19, 1952, 26; Burton B. Turkus and Sid Feder, *Murder Inc.: The Story of the "Syndicate"* (New York: Da Capo Press, 1992), 323 (quotes). Albert Anastasia was a regular member of the club.

16. Alan Block, *East Side–West Side: Organizing Crime in New York, 1930–1950* (New Brunswick, N.J.: Rutgers University Press, 1983), 95–124, 183–95; Mary Heaton Vorse, "The Pirates' Nest of New York," *Harper's Magazine,* April 1952, 28–35; William Howard Moore, *The Kefauver Committee and the Politics of Crime* (Columbia: University of Missouri Press, 1974), 172–205; Chris McNickle, *To Be Mayor of New York: Ethnic Politics in the City* (New York: Columbia University Press, 1993), 49–50.

17. Block, *East Side–West Side,* 209.

18. *New York Herald Tribune,* December 19, 1952, 1 (first quote); *New York Times,* December 19, 1952, 26 (second and third quotes).

19. "Testimony of Joseph Franklin, Financial Secretary, Local 920," NYSCC, vol. 3, 1854–70.

20. "Testimony of George Joseph Fitzpatrick, County Commissioner, Hudson County," NYSCC, vol. 2, 933.

21. "Testimony of Anthony DeVincenzo," NYSCC, vol. 2, 764, 773; "Testimony of George Joseph Fitzpatrick,"925–50; *New York Times,* December 16, 1952, 25.

22. "Testimony of Dominick Genova," 2172; Johnson, *Crime on the Labor Front,* 165–83; Vorse, "The Pirates' Nest of New York," 28–29, 34.

23. "Testimony of Edward A. Heffernan," 1548–59; Larrowe, *Shape-Up and Hiring Hall,* 22–23; Johnson, *Crime on the Labor Front,* 165–82, 210–13; "Testimony of Father John

Corridan," Senate Committee on Interstate and Foreign Commerce, *Waterfront Investigation, Part 1: New York–New Jersey Waterfront,* 83d Cong., 1st sess., 569 (quote).

24. Larrowe, *Shape-Up and Hiring Hall,* 19, 63.

25. "Testimony of Nicholas Joseph Palihnich, vice-president of Jarka Stevedoring Corporation," NYSCC, vol. 1, 80.

26. "Testimony of Michael Castellana, vice-president of Jules S. Sottnek Stevedoring Co.," NYSCC, vol. 1, 206–7; Vorse, "The Pirates' Nest of New York," 27–37.

27. *New York Herald Tribune,* December 19, 1952, 1; *New York Times,* December 19, 1952, 1; Kimeldorf, *Reds or Rackets?* 124–25. It was reported later that Panto, who had been lured to a house in Staten Island, realized he was in danger and attempted to escape. But as the mobster Mendy Weiss explained, "It was a lucky thing I was there, he would have got away. I grabbed him and mugged him, and when I mugged him, he started to fight and he tried to break the mug, and that's when he scratched me, but he didn't get away." "Testimony of Edward A. Heffernan," 1563.

28. Rank and File Committee, "This Is Our Story," box 3, International Longshoremen's Association, Tamiment Library, New York University (hereafter ILA-TAM). Father Benjamin L. Masse recounted that "the day after the strike ended, Warren reported for work—and fell and hurt himself; i.e., he was beaten up. Nice place, the New York waterfront." Quoted in Johnson, *Crime on the Labor Front,* 158. For an outstanding fictional account of the strike and the violent hazards faced by the strikers and Communist organizers alike, see Thomas McGrath, *This Coffin Has No Handles* (New York: Thunder Mouth Press, 1988).

29. "Testimony of Mitch Berenson," House Committee on Education and Labor, *Amendments to the Fair Labor Standards Act of 1938. Volume 1,* 81st Cong., 1st sess., 1949, 611–12; "Testimony of John J. Gannon," NYSCC, vol. 3, 2000–2001.

30. Sebastian DeFazio, interview by author, July 10, 1995.

31. "Testimony of Charles Gulizia," NYSCC, vol. 5, 3167.

32. "Testimony of Mario Frullano," NYSCC, vol. 3, 1826.

33. Sterling Spero and Abrahm L. Harris, *The Black Worker: The Negro and the Labor Movement* (Port Washington, N.Y.: Kennikat Press, 1931), 199.

34. For an excellent discussion of biracialism among longshoremen see Eric Arnesen, *Waterfront Workers of New Orleans: Race, Class, and Politics, 1863–1923* (Urbana: University of Illinois Press, 1994). For the mix of ethnic and racial groups, see Calvin Winslow, "On the Waterfront: Black, Italian, and Irish Longshoremen in the New York Harbour Strike of 1919," in *Protest and Survival: Essays for E. P. Thompson,* ed. John Rule and Robert Malcolmson (New York: Norton, 1993), 355–93.

35. I. Philip Sipser, interview by author, June 29, 1995; Judith Stein, *The World of Marcus Garvey: Race and Class in Modern Society* (Baton Rouge, La.: Louisiana State University Press, 1986), 272, 275–78; Mark D. Naison, "Communism and Black Nationalism in the Depression: The Case of Harlem," in *Black Communities and Urbana Development in America, 1920–1990,* vol. 6, *Depression, War, and the New Migration, 1930–1960,* ed. Kenneth L. Kusmer (New York: Garland, 1991), 57.

36. Sipser interview.

37. Interview with Sam Madell, New Yorkers at Work: Oral History, Robert F. Wagner Labor Archives, Tamiment Library, New York University.

38. Report to Harry Bridges from William Glazier, August 19, 1948, box 1, ILA-TAM.

39. Peter Wellman, *The Union Makes Us Strong: Radical Unionism on the San Francisco Waterfront* (New York: Cambridge University Press, 1995), 9–10, 51–52. Two hundred thirty-seven Pacific Coast longshoremen were official members of the Communist Party. See Kimeldorf, *Reds or Rackets?* 163; Maurice Isserman, *Which Side Are You On? The American Communist Party during the Second World War* (Urbana: University of Illinois Press, 1993), 93–94, 166; Joseph Starobin, *American Communism in Crisis: 1943–1957* (Cambridge, Mass.: Harvard University Press, 1972), 148 n. 51, 258 n. 50, 286.

40. "Schedule: Dock Workers (Regulation of Employment) Scheme 1947—Arrangement of Clauses," 2–3, Dock Labour Scheme, 1947, LAB 8/2162, PRO.

41. Ibid., 3.

42. Ibid., 7–9. The LDLB appeals tribunal was made up of four persons. Minutes of the Local Board—London, October 2, 1947, Minutes of the Local Board—London, BK 2/269, PRO.

43. "London Dock Survey as Presented to the Committee of Inquiry (Ammon), by the National Dock Labour Board, 1945," Stoppages, BK 9/2, PRO.

44. Ibid.

45. Industrial Inquiries—Leggett Report, 1951, BK 2/1215, PRO.

46. "London Dock Labour Board Meeting, August 27, 1947," Minutes of the Local Board—London, BK 2/269, PRO.

47. Anonymous letter to Arthur Deakin, June 23, 1948, MSS 126/TG/3, Sack 30/31, Transport and General Workers' Union, Modern Records Center, University of Warwick (hereafter MRC). Instead of signing his name, the docker wrote, "Sorry I can't give my name in case of victimization by the Gestapo NDLB."

48. Port Transport Industry—Report of Inquiry Held under Paragraph 5 of the Schedule to the Dock Workers (Regulation of Employment) Act, 1946—Cameron Inquiry, BK 29/12, PRO; "Schedule: Dock Labour (Regulation of Employment) Scheme 1947—Arrangement of Clauses," 7, Dock Labour Scheme, 1947, LAB 8/2162, PRO; letter to the National Dock Labour Board from J. Fitzgerald, June 14, 1948, BK 2/1084, PRO.

49. Unofficial Strikes in the London Docks, Report of a Committee of Inquiry, Ministry of Labour and National Service—Confidential—Final Release, BK 2/1215, PRO, 27.

50. Ibid., 25–26.

51. Joe Bloomberg, interview by author, August 5, 1996.

52. Tony Topham, "The Unofficial National Docks Strike of 1923: The Transport and General Workers' Union's First Crisis," *Historical Studies in Industrial Relations* 2 (September 1996): 27–64; Alan Bullock, *The Life and Times of Ernest Bevin,* vol. 1, *Trade Union Leader, 1881–1940* (London: Heinemann, 1960), 214–16, 239–42; Peter Weiler, *Ernest Bevin* (New York: St. Martin's, 1993), 83–86. See also Stephen Hill, *The Dockers: Class and Tradition in London* (London: Heinemann, 1976), 128–30; Ken Coates and Tony Topham, *The History of the Transport and General Workers' Union,* vol. 1, part 2 (Cambridge, Mass.: Blackwell, 1991).

53. Kenneth O. Morgan, *Labor in Power, 1945–1951* (Oxford: Clarendon Press, 1984), 80; V. L. Allen, *Trade Union Leadership: Based on a Study of Arthur Deakin* (New York: Longmans Green, 1957); Roger Eatwell, *The 1945–1951 Labor Governments* (London: Batsford Academic, 1975); Jim Phillips, *The Great Alliance: Economic Recovery and the Problems of Power, 1945–51* (East Haven, Conn.: Pluto Press, 1996).

54. James E. Cronin, *The Politics of State Expansion: War, State and Society in Twentieth-*

Century Britain (New York: Routledge, 1991), 161–80; Henry Pelling, *The Labor Governments, 1945–1951* (New York: St. Martin's, 1984), 165–86.

55. Peter Turnbull, Julia Morris, and David Sapsford, "Persistent Militants and Quiescent Comrades: Intra-Industry Strike Activity on the Docks, 1947–89," *Sociological Review* 44 (November 1996): 707 (first quote), 711 (second quote).

56. Ibid., 698.

57. Bloomberg interview.

58. Unofficial Strikes in the London Docks, Report of a Committee of Inquiry, Ministry of Labour and National Service—Confidential—Final Release, BK 2/1215, PRO, 6.

59. Interview, Harry Browne, MSS 371/QD7/DOCK2/5, MRC.

60. Paul Addison, *Now the War Is Over: A Social History of Britain, 1945–51* (London: British Broadcasting Corp., 1985), 4–5, 18; Kenneth O. Morgan, *The People's Peace: British History, 1945–1990* (New York: Oxford University Press, 1990), 18–19.

61. Interview, Albert Andrews, MSS 371/QD7/DOCKS2/1, MRC; interview, Don Perry, MSS 371/QD7/DOCKS2/26, MRC.

62. James E. Cronin, *Labor and Society in Britain, 1918–1979,* (New York: Schocken, 1984), 141 (first quote), 143 (second quote).

63. "Statement of Disputes Affecting Dock Workers, From 1st January, 1948 to 31st December, 1948," Statistic—Disputes, NDLB, BK 2/71, PRO.

4 The 1948 New York Strike

By 1948 the New York City and London dockworkers were on the verge of revolt. They were alienated from their union leaderships and no longer willing to go along. Pressure was building among the dockworkers to challenge the entrenched union hierarchies. Although the conditions that fueled such behavior were different in each port, the respective rank and file shared a common dislike for union officialdom that left them on the margins of power. The time had arrived when direct action was the only available weapon. It was a weapon that was at once explosive and unstable, but out of the confrontation emerged new leaders who were able to voice the anger of the rank and file and declare that their demands be heard and recognized.

In New York, the spark for the revolt was a 1948 wage agreement signed by their union leadership. The leadership considered it a "fine agreement"; the members thought otherwise. The leadership had endured nearly two years of conflict with rank-and-file agitators and were surprised by the members' venom. The agitators were encouraged by an alliance group of outside reformers who focused their energies on the New York waterfront, particularly in Brooklyn. The group, which included Communist, trade union, and American Labor Party activists, engaged in a campaign to gain back pay for the New York longshoremen. This movement created an oppositional culture on the New York docks and led to direct confrontations with the ILA leadership and eventually strikes that would threaten Joe Ryan's rule.

The New York City movement emerged against a backdrop of growing unemployment during 1947 and 1948, increasingly heavy sling loads and the corresponding speed-up, and favoritism at the shape-up. The interpretation of the 1938 Fair Labor Standards Act by longshoremen and their attorneys was even more important. The matter revolved around overtime payments. The issue of money had a better chance of attracting potential recruits and perhaps creating an oppositional culture than any other issue. Initially, the key organization in the movement was Harry Bridge's International Longshoremen and Warehousemen's Union (ILWU), which viewed the situation as an opportunity to expand its influence on the East Coast. Consequently Sam Madell began working with the New York longshoremen. He picked the issue of pay to galvanize them, starting with a movement to obtain back pay owed the longshoremen under the Fair Labor Standards Act. Working with lawyers, Madell first started a petition among the men and by 1947 the tenuous alliance was cemented when attorneys helped longshoremen file suits for back pay. Madell explained that the men "were very much interested in this thing because it meant millions and millions of dollars in back pay would be due longshoremen."[1] Back Pay Committees were formed in Brooklyn, Hoboken, and Baltimore. William Glazier, the Washington, D.C., representative of the ILWU, said the Brooklyn Back Pay Committee was the "strongest," with meetings drawing over eighteen hundred attendees. Brooklyn blacks formed their own committee, which was closely associated with the all-black Local 968. The "back pay movement," according to Glazier, had become the "first mass anti-Ryan development" since the 1945 strike.[2] This amalgam of rank-and-file action and left-wing legal collaborators made for a potentially strong bond that would culminate in the 1948 strike.

The movement based itself in the campaign headquarters of Vincent Longhi in Brooklyn. Throughout 1947, rank-and-file longshoremen and their attorneys inaugurated suits demanding back pay. Since 1916, contracts negotiated between the ILA and shippers had established the regular work day as extending from 8:00 A.M. to noon, and 1:00 P.M. to 5:00 P.M. Anyone working outside those hours was considered to be working overtime at time and a half. Longshoremen commonly worked outside of the regular hours, in some cases twelve to fourteen hours at a stretch. The back-pay attorneys showed that men who had worked through the night into the daytime hours were not paid overtime. For example, if a longshoreman worked through to 8:00 A.M. he was paid time and a half, but if he continued working after 8:00 A.M. he would be paid the regular rate. Julius Bagley, one of the attorneys filing suit, simplified the issue by comparing the situation to a person having a birthday on Christmas Day. The person, Bagley argued, expected not just one present but two. The same applied to the issue of longshoremen working through the night shift; they should be paid time and a half after working more than an eight-hour day or a forty-hour week. The longshoremen's attorneys therefore argued, using the provisions of the 1938 Fair Labor Standards Act, that work during the evenings was shift work, and the longshoremen should be paid overtime on top of the time-and-a-half payment.[3]

The suits of the Back Pay Committees were contested by the ILA and the shippers, up to the U.S. Supreme Court. The shippers wanted to avoid paying overtime wages due. As for the ILA, Ryan argued that the courts should not rule on contract provisions negotiated by the union. Ryan and the ILA leadership were therefore fearful of the courts' directly challenging their decision-making powers during the contract negotiations. The Supreme Court in October 1947 agreed with the Back Pay Committees that night work was indeed shift work and any longshoremen working in excess of eight hours should be paid time-and-a-half payments. The ILA and shippers responded by attempting to persuade Congress to amend the Fair Labor Standards Act.[4]

As the debate wound its way through the Senate Committee on Labor and Public Welfare, negotiations for a new contract between the ILA and New York Shipping Association (NYSA) began in early June 1948. Many of the rank-and-file dockworkers, emboldened by the back-pay suits and the Supreme Court decision, closely watched the process. Experience had shown them that Ryan and the District Committee did not always represent their best interests. Most longshoremen had learned of the stevedoring operator who described the bargaining routine as follows: "We call Ryan in once a year or so and say, 'Joe, how much of a raise do you need to keep the boys in line?'"[5] Ryan's tentativeness during bargaining time earned him the nickname "nickel and dime Ryan." Although common knowledge during bargaining talks, what gave the 1948 negotiations such potency was the issue of overtime on overtime. The rank and file believed, with justification, that the issue was going to be negotiated away.

Indeed, the subject of overtime on overtime was a major stumbling block in the negotiation process. The employers, represented by the NYSA, insisted on a "drastic modification downward" of the established overtime rates to compensate for the potential costs of the "overtime-on-overtime" decision. For the ILA, a sharp reduction in the overtime rates would create a series of problems. First, the relatively high existing overtime rate had led to work being concentrated during the normal working hours of 8:00 A.M. to 5:00 P.M. Thus when longshoremen had to work beyond those normal hours they were paid relatively high overtime rates. The ILA feared that if the overtime rates were factored downward, then the men would more likely be hired to work beyond normal hours, causing a cut in take-home pay. Thus, the "overtime-on-overtime" question was the issue that had stalled the negotiations, creating a rift between the NYSA and the ILA.[6] Since they were unable to reach a compromise, it appeared that a strike might follow. At this point, the federal government took the dramatic step of involving itself in the controversy.

Sustaining the government's entry into the dispute was the Taft-Hartley Act. Passed in 1947, the act gave the president of the United States the authority to order a sixty-day cooling-off period and create a Board of Inquiry to investigate a dispute or strike. The only stipulation was that the dispute had to be one that threatened the "national health and safety." The Taft-Hartley Act was the culmination of decades of government interest in industrial relations. Starting in 1888 with the Chicago, Burlington, and Quincy Railroad strike, federal legislation was enacted to contain such outbursts of strike activity. The cooling-off provision and boards of inquiry of the Taft-Hartley Act were modeled on the 1926 Railway Labor Act. Passage of the Taft-Hartley Act was stimulated by the enormous strike wave of 1945–46. The Republican Congress was determined to rein in the new-found power of trade unions, or what was regarded by some as a "labor monopoly." U.S. presidents were not shy about using the national emergency strike provision. From 1947 to 1969, twenty-nine cooling-off periods were ordered, with stevedoring leading the pack with involvement in five disputes.[7]

Federal involvement in the New York City dock dispute was specifically motivated by the potential perils of a protracted conflict. The port consisted of seven bays and the mouths of four rivers and four estuaries. *Fortune* magazine calculated that the "entire port of Antwerp could be stuffed into Jersey City." With its three hundred deep-sea piers, the port of New York handled nearly as much cargo as all the other Atlantic and Gulf Coast ports combined. As many as two hundred thousand workers were directly employed in the longshore industry, not counting insurance and financial companies.[8]

John R. Steelman, a Truman administration official, was the key player in determining the federal government's response to the threat of a strike on New York's waterfront. Truman had appointed Steelman in 1946 to be his personal assistant on labor matters. Steelman had been director of the U.S. Conciliation Service between 1937 and 1944 and was special assistant to the president during 1945–46. The Department of Labor deeply resented Steelman's entrenched power in the White House during Truman's presidency. This resentment was accentuated after the Conciliation Service was separated from the Department of Labor with the creation of the Federal Mediation and Conciliation Service (FMCS) in 1947. David Cole, who served on a series of fact-finding boards during Truman's presidency, attested to the increasing tension between Steelman and the Department of Labor. According to Cole, there was tension because Steelman came from the Conciliation Service. More important, however, was Truman's need for a quick response to the postwar strike wave: "The president perceived the urgency, and he didn't have the patience to wait, and observe strict protocol, or bureaucratic courtesy. He would rather have some action. And John Steelman could give him the action, he felt."[9]

Steelman turned to Cyrus Ching, the newly appointed director of the FMCS, for advice and guidance. Unlike the dealings with the Department of Labor, which were marked by tension, Steelman's relationship with Ching was an amicable one. As Cole observed, "Steelman and Ching were good friends and compatible. . . . Ching did not resent Steelman's intrusion into these things [strikes]. In fact, he would work hand in hand with him."[10] On August 17, 1948, Ching wrote to Steelman outlining his view that the ILA and the NYSA were "stalemated" in their negotiations. Ching argued that it was the ILA that had become the major impediment. Only when the "union definitely commits itself" to solving the "'overtime on overtime' issue," Ching argued, would the situation be resolved. Warning that there was "no possibility of settlement" and that a "strike" was imminent, Ching advised Steelman to have the president create a Board of Inquiry under the provisions of the Taft-Hartley Act. Steelman also received counsel from the United States Maritime Commission (USMC). William Smith, chairman of the USMC, notified Steelman that a strike by the longshoremen "will be a blow to the stability of the national economy." Just as vital, it would "impede the progress" of the Marshall Plan and adversely affect U.S. Army supplies abroad. Thus for Smith, the strike "represent[ed] a threat to the national health and safety."[11]

The enormous size of the port and the immense amount of tonnage that flowed through it guaranteed that the federal government would take seriously any threat to its operation. President Truman, heavily influenced by Steelman, decided to invoke the Taft-Hartley Act to stall for time and prohibit the ILA from taking strike action. Using section 206 of the Taft-Hartley Act, Truman created a Board of Inquiry to investigate the dispute and recommend action to avoid labor conflict. Formed on August 17, four days before the expiration of the contract, the board found that the overtime-on-overtime issue was the major point of contention. As the board reported, "Because of the failure to arrive at an agreement, a cessation of work in this industry is imminent as of midnight, August 21, 1948."[12] Again using the provisions of the Taft-Hartley Act (section 208), Truman obtained a federal injunction that barred the ILA from engaging in strike action for a period of eighty days (the order would expire on November 9) and ordered the contending parties to resolve the dispute through collective bargaining. Truman also reconvened the Board of Inquiry to hold hearings and attempt to get the two parties to settle. To support the board members, conciliators from the FMCS were also ordered in.[13]

Throughout September and October a series of separate meetings was held, with FMCS conciliators shuttling back and forth between the two sides. The sticking point continued to be the overtime-on-overtime question. With the injunction expiring on November 9, the parties by late October appeared ready to sign an agreement. The NYSA held fast and put forward its final offer on October 26, agreeing to pay a wage increase of ten cents per hour and improve the vacation plan (with eligibility reduced to 1,250 hours per year from 1,350). The critical segment concerned the overtime issue; the employers demanded that the agreement be placed under terms of Section 7(B)(1) of the Fair Labor Standards Act. The pertinent section would give the employers an exemption from the overtime provisions of the act.[14] The ILA, although unhappy that a welfare fund had been rejected by the NYSA, nonetheless accepted the offer. Complicating the approval, however, was the government's insistence that the National Labor Relations Board (NLRB) supervise the ballot of the membership. Scheduled for November 6–7, the balloting contributed to rank-and-file resistance to the agreement. The NLRB had declared those eligible to vote based upon the names on the vacation list ending June 30, 1948. Only 12,664 New York and 2,500 Philadelphia and Boston longshoremen were on the list; thus approximately 30,000 East Coast longshoremen were excluded. The ILA also used tried-and-tested tactics of distilling the potential vote by advertising the vote late and holding a series of "quickie meetings" to forestall any opposition. To further counter opposition to the contract, Ryan insisted that it was "a very fine agreement" and only "disruptive elements" opposed it.[15]

The rank and file, unhappy with the agreement and incensed that the vote had been fixed, embarked on strike action on November 10, leaving in their wake an embarrassed leadership that had supported the agreement. Within two days, the rank and file followed suit, closing the port.

To some extent the wildcat strike was but a reflection of the longshoremen's lack of power and their corresponding frustration. Sam Madell said that the men "would go along with all of these terrible things for a period of time, and then there would be an explosion, and the docks would be tied up." Father John Carey echoed Madell's observation by stating the "waterfront was very much like Mount Etna. . . . They [the longshoremen] had no real way to get their grievances answered, and as the frustration increased, "building up a head of steam," it would eventually "blow up all over."[16]

The ILA leadership had seriously misjudged the temper of their members and their own power to control an angry rank and file. A dramatic shift in power had occurred; the members no longer fatalistically accepted their exploitative lot. Years of oppressive hiring practices and the concomitant corruption, increasingly heavy sling loads, and unemployment had taken their toll. Another explosive component was the empowerment that came about as the Back Pay Committees made the members less likely to accept blindly their leaders' promises and threats. The inequities of federal power also antagonized the longshoremen. The dockworkers were hampered by taking strike action through injunctive law, while their ILA leaders and the NYSA ignored the Supreme Court decision on overtime payments. As Alfred Corbett, a member of the New Jersey Back Pay Committee, later testified: "It is hard for us to understand why an injunction against labor . . . can be immediately enforced, whereas a United States Supreme Court ruling can be openly flouted by the shipping interests."[17] As the strike progressed, however, the rank and file quickly learned the precariousness of their position. Having little institutional power within the union, the men would quickly fall victim to an entrenched leadership determined to regain its hegemony.

The two storm centers along the New York waterfront were the Chelsea docks on Manhattan's West Side and the docks in Brooklyn. John J. (Gene) Sampson was the powerful leader of Chelsea Local 791, and his men were some of the first to refuse to work on November 9. Sampson had long coveted Ryan's presidency, and the strike gave him the opportunity to challenge openly Ryan's iron rule. Earlier, in the 1945 strike, Sampson had supported the rank-and-file revolt, only to be outmaneuvered by Ryan and other ILA leaders. The *New York Times* described Sampson and Local 791 as the "spearhead insurgent group," and Local 791 would eventually acquire the term "Mother Local" for such leadership qualities.[18] Sampson was a traditional labor boss in the mold of Ryan, a leader who could be said to hold court rather than office. Just like other locals, Local 791 had no record books of expenses or of the membership. When questioned on the issue, Sampson had replied that the membership figures were "under his hat." With the onset of the 1948 conflict, shippers "attributed it [the crisis] to the longstanding feud between Mr. Ryan and the so-called pretender to the Ryan 'throne,' John J. (Gene) Sampson."[19] The conflict between the two leaders reached a fever pitch on the first day of the strike when Sampson and Ryan publicly clashed during a press conference. Ryan called on the assembled journalists and television reporters to investigate the business dealings of Sampson's brother, Frank, who was politically tied to Mayor O'Dwyer. A "white-faced" Gene Sampson demanded that Ryan "retract everything you said about my brother." Ryan shouted back, "You're a partner of Rogers [Borough President Hugo Rogers], who is a partner of Marcantonio [American Labor Party]." Mirroring the complex interplay of union and city politics, Ryan and Sampson represented different political factions. As the television "cameras ground away," Ryan ordered the reporters present to "get out . . . we are going into executive session."[20] The public tirade of the two would be the last open outburst for the remainder of the strike.

Brooklyn, the other stronghold of anti-Ryan forces, had joined the strike on the first day. The *Brooklyn Eagle* reported that "6,000 were on strike in this borough," including all union locals. On the first day of the strike Brooklyn longshoremen turned up at the 7:45 A.M. shape-up and "booed and laughed at boss stevedores when the shape-up whistles were blown." Gathering in "small knots of men outside the piers," the longshoremen eventually "scattered" to their usual haunts when not working, namely, "diners and taverns."[21] Brooklyn insurgents tried to inject a spirit of action in the strike, but not until the waning days of the strike would they make an impact.

Ryan did not just face rank-and-file opposition, however. Ryan was infuriated by a recent spate of articles by a *New York Sun* journalist, Malcolm Johnson. Entitled "Crime on the Waterfront," the series of articles began on November 8, one day before the strike, and continued to be published throughout the conflict. Ryan tried to use the articles to divert attention from his loss of control of the strike. On November 9, he claimed, "This sudden strike was caused by the articles by Malcolm Johnson." Trying to whip up enthusiasm with the membership, he argued that the articles were a "written insult to our members. It is a serious factor in this strike." In a calculated move, he tried to enroll city and federal authorities in his attack on the *New York Sun.* As he pointed out, "It is a direct insult to the Police Commissioner and the FBI. We are ready to be investigated at any time."[22]

Always the master tactician, Ryan also attacked the Taft-Hartley Act to regain the attention of his members. Ryan called the wildcat strike "a protest against" the act, and he described the eighty-day injunction as merely an interlude but with "nothing to suggest" it would settle the conflict. The men "took the attitude that the injunction was off" on November 9 and walked off the job. Such a stance was attacked in the press. An editorial in the November 14 *Brooklyn Eagle* accused Ryan of contradictory and dishonest leadership. The writer pointed out, that "merely criticizing" the Taft-Hartley Act "for failing to settle a dispute which has been in the making for months is hardly a display of labor statesmanship." For years, the *Brooklyn Eagle* charged, there had been "criticism heard, comments expressed and insinuations made" regarding the corrupt relationship between the union and the employers. It was "stretching the meaning" of the word "wildcat" "when over half the members of the unions involved simultaneously and in a rather orderly manner go on strike."[23]

Under attack from all sides, Ryan and his ILA allies scrambled to regain control of the situation. Ryan had been given a black eye by the unofficial walkout and the public lashing from Sampson, and he embarked on a path to master the explosive situation. In an effort to overpower opposition within the striker ranks, Ryan did a complete about-face and declared the strike official on November 11 for all East Coast ports. This declaration meant that the city and nation then witnessed the first official longshore strike since 1919. As Ryan put it, "As long as we're having a strike, let's have a strike."[24] To avoid further embarrassing public outbursts and to nullify internal criticism, Ryan clamped down on press releases. He ordered that the ILA Press Committee could make statements only in the presence of six members of the eleven-man committee. Gene Sampson was barred from the committee, thus officially muzzling him.[25] Ryan hoped to stifle institutional opposition and also to keep the members in the dark concerning negotiations.

One other, and perhaps more important, method for repressing dissent was to avoid any concerted effort to establish picket lines and informational meetings. The *New York Sun* described a "curious aspect" of the strike scene, which "was the complete absence of any picketing. Strikers seemed content to stand silently near pier entrances."[26] On the surface, the last tactic appeared logical because the NYSA had not planned to recruit strikebreakers. In any event, the ILA had a reputation for toughness and ruthlessness and correctly believed that any potential strikebreaker would think twice before trying to obtain work on the waterfront. Without a fighting strike organization, the members would be left isolated and uninformed about strike strategy. The men were left to meet in bars and street corners throughout the port to discuss strike events. They were thus scattered and unable to formulate their own demands and organization.

All was not lost for the rank and file, however. Interviews with journalists could at least bring their grievances to the public's attention. Although some cited the overtime-on-overtime issue as the catalyst for the walkout, others blamed the method of hiring. A longshoreman identified only as "Bill, a giant of a man," spoke of the inequities of the shape-up: "I only got about four hours that week [just before the strike], even though I was up every morning at 6 for the goddam shapeup." Another striker, described as a "grey-haired, rugged docker," blamed the conflict on the shape-up: "It's a dog-eat-dog affair without rhyme or reason except that it pads the pockets of the stevedores with profits." One aged "docker with five grandchildren" compared his existence with that of other workers: "We are ordinary average workingmen with one big difference. We average a hell of a lot less than most workers."[27]

Strategically supplementing the individual grievances were oppositional organizations, namely the Back Pay Committees. An alliance of the committees was formed under the name Rank and File Committee and a meeting was planned for November 16 at Manhattan Center. Correctly sensing the threat that such a meeting could hold for his tenuous control of the strike and union, Ryan declared that no longshoremen would be present, and as for those "communists" attending, "our men will throw them in the river." Determined that the meeting would not go unchallenged, Ryan, with ILA goons and members of the AFL Seafarers Union, attempted to storm the building. Ryan's forces were able to leave leaflets declaring the meeting a Communist plot, but they were outnumbered and had to beat a hasty retreat. Those present at the meeting included rank-and-file members, Back Pay attorneys, and middle-class reformers. The *New York Times* reported that Ryan's "name was booed lustily." A series of strikers described their respective grievances, and James Longhi, an attorney representing the Brooklyn Back Pay Committee, applauded the "rank and file longshoremen in pressing their demands for wages, lighter slingloads and back pay through the years." Those attending the meeting also observed a minute of silence in memory of Pete Panto and then ended with a call to fight to the finish and to send a delegation to Washington, D.C., to press for back pay.[28]

The unofficial leaders appeared to be significant representatives of the rank and file. They gave voice to an oppositional movement that was able to repel Ryan's physical attack. Nonetheless the meeting marked the end of their active involvement in the strike. The rank and file and their allies, excluded from critical involvement in the strike, were forced to stand on the sideline as frustrated observers. Throughout the remainder of the strike, the ILA leaders and the federal government would take center stage in the unfolding drama.

Government involvement in the strike was predicated primarily on the dramatic effect of the stoppage on the greater economy, but it also was based on the exportation of Marshall Plan goods. The Board of Inquiry spelled out this concern in October when it declared that the employers and longshoremen had a "responsibility . . . to the people of the United States and the world, whose welfare would be seriously impaired by a cessation of work in this most vital industry."[29] The initial casualties were passengers who arrived in the port on the first day of the strike. The actress Helen Hayes and others were forced to unload and carry their own luggage.[30] Railroads serving the port placed embargoes on freight and in turn laid off hundreds of workers. The New York Central, for example, laid off "22 tug crews, totally 132 men and 588 pier freight handlers." The New Haven, Erie, and the New Jersey Central Railroads laid off 250, 270, and 250 workers, respectively. By November 16, large numbers of freight handlers, tugboat men, and custom brokers were idled by the stoppage.[31]

The greatest impact of the strike was the curtailment of mail and cargo. The *New York Times* reported on November 19 that "150,000 bags of outbound mail were piled up awaiting settlement of the strike." General cargo, including $130,000 worth of bananas and $500,000 of chestnuts, was languishing in the holds of ships. The federal government was particularly annoyed by the curtailment of Marshall Plan goods. An official of the Economic Cooperation Administration estimated that 20,000 tons per day were backing up on East Coast docks. The standstill of Marshall Plan cargo forced Paul G. Hoffman, economic cooperation administrator, to appeal to Ryan to release the cargo. Ryan responded that only "army supplies to garrison troops overseas" would be handled. The number of strikebound-ships in the port numbered 84, and there was a total of 179 affected vessels on the Atlantic seaboard. The *New York Times* explained that the number of ships trapped in the port of New York was "unusually small" because "an abnormal number of vessels were dispatched on the last day before the strike, in anticipation of trouble."[32]

Giving the strike a further dramatic quality was its expansion to other Atlantic ports. By November 13, the strike had spread to Boston, Philadelphia, Baltimore, and Norfolk, Virginia. Mirroring the New York situation, rank-and-file dissension was present in these ports, fueling the men's determination to strike. After the strike some of these men explained how they had formed Back Pay Committees and voiced their anger toward a union leadership judged to be hopelessly corrupt. Joseph Kane, a Philadelphia longshoreman, explained how the men in his port formed a back pay organization after the Supreme Court decision concerning overtime on overtime. As Kane pointed out, "We realized we had been deprived. . . . Thirty-five hundred men in Philadelphia immediately filed for back pay." Fueling Kane's frustration was the distinct lack of democracy in the Philadelphia ILA. As Kane continued, the Philadelphia men "have no constitution books, we have no bylaw books, we have no agreement books." For Kane the situation smacked of conspiracy: "I believe they keep us in a state of ignorance in order to dominate us."[33] Like their New York brothers, however, the Philadelphia men were forced to witness the strike from the sidelines. The ILA leadership continued throughout the strike to hold a tight rein on policy and tactics.

The ILA, for example, ordered its Gulf Coast locals to continue working at Jacksonville, Florida; Mobile, Alabama; New Orleans; and Galveston, Texas. The reasoning behind the decision was to continue bulk shipments for the

Marshall Plan and thereby avoid a more aggressive government response. Shippers, however, tried to use the ports as an opening to sneak their goods into the country. Ryan responded by threatening "ship companies that any more diversions of ships or cargoes will result in tying up the South Atlantic and Gulf Coast ports."[34] Ryan also had to administer Canadian members of the ILA. Although not party to the agreement, Canadian dockers took part in a sympathy action, which also made for an effective strike. In the early stages of the strike, shipping companies had begun disembarking passengers at Halifax, Nova Scotia, and transferring them to trains bound for New York City. Ryan responded by ordering ILA members in the port to boycott any ships that used Canadian ports to bypass East Coast docks. The order resulted in a disruption within the Canadian ILA leadership. Under pressure from the Canadian government, J. J. Campbell, the president of the Halifax ILA local, argued that to continue the boycott was contrary to Canadian labor law, and he ordered his members to work incoming ships.[35] Although the Canadian situation concerned the ILA leadership, the situation was not unduly threatening. The Atlantic ports remained sealed shut.

The strike forced Ryan to act the role of union leader. To keep the confidence of the men, he had to appear to hold the line against employers trying to sneak cargo in through southern ports, while at the same time trying not to antagonize government authorities. Thus Ryan could present himself as a responsible union leader holding off both hostile employers and the federal government. Such a posture, Ryan hoped, would show the membership he was acting in their interests even though he had initially accepted the rejected wage agreement.

The New York strike was the linchpin in Ryan's strategy. For this reason Mayor O'Dwyer initially tried to procure a peace settlement. O'Dwyer returned from a California vacation on November 14 after consulting with his police commissioner, Arthur W. Wallender, and the head of the city's labor relations division, Theodore Kheel. O'Dwyer met Ryan the following day. Ryan pledged that domestic shipments of food and fuel into New York would not be affected. In fact, the longshoremen handled little of the fuel because it was transported by barge across the Hudson River. Ryan warned O'Dwyer, however, that his "assurance" that interstate or cross-river trade would not be affected did not apply to "perishables in the holds of ships coming in from Latin America or Europe."[36]

Once the strike spread to other ports, however, O'Dwyer's efforts were overshadowed by those of Cyrus Ching and the FMCS. With little power or influence to procure a settlement of a strike that had spread beyond New York,

O'Dwyer conferred with Ching and, according to the *New York Sun,* "agreed that it was advisable for the Federal agency [FMCS], rather than the city, to direct efforts toward a settlement."[37]

With a critical blockade of cargo in place along the eastern seaboard, the federal government had its hands full. Just as problematic for the government was that the strike, unlike the 1946 rail strike, did not directly threaten the national economy. The nation's foodstuffs and fuel were not endangered. Noting the ambiguity of the national emergency provisions of the Taft-Hartley Act, the government broadly considered the effect of the strike on the greater economy. The government stance was therefore one of containment. That is, the strike was recognized as having a negative impact on the regional economies surrounding the strike-bound ports, which taken together were construed as having a national effect. Also, in an especially shrewd move, the ILA had promised to continue loading military cargoes. Indeed, when rumors emerged that some Brooklyn longshoremen were determined to stop this practice, a hundred policemen and a thousand longshoremen turned up at the Brooklyn Army Base on November 16. An ILA sound truck "blared forth with attacks against 'Commies who would sabotage national defense.'" Once it became clear that no attempt was to be made to interfere with army shipments, "500 longshoremen went to work on five army ships." One of the jobs at the army base was the "unloading [of] caskets containing the bodies of Americans killed in World War II."[38]

The government was therefore not faced with an interruption of military supplies. Unlike previous obstructionist union leaders, Ryan tried mightily not to antagonize the Truman administration. After he made the strike official, for example, Ryan publicly called on Truman to settle the conflict: "Well the President will surely have to get into it." Sounding more like an employer demanding government action, Ryan continued, "This is a national calamity. This harbor will clam up tight, even without picket lines. We realize this has to be settled some time."[39]

Thus the ILA leadership had taken away from the government any real grounds for invoking emergency powers. Food and fuel was reaching New York City; military supplies had not been affected; and the union leadership had called on the government for help. For all that, however, the strike had caused a curtailment of Marshall Plan goods, and the economic effects on the eastern seaboard cities was profound. By November 16, six days following the beginning of the strike, the various port cities witnessed a virtual close-down of their waterfronts. In New York, 118 ships were tied up, including passenger liners; foreign mail was stacking up; and thousands of workers had been laid off. In Boston, 8 ships were trapped; in Baltimore, 49; in Philadelphia, 32;

in Hampton Roads, Virginia, 4. In Albany, New York, 2 "loaded grain ships" were "immobilized," and in Halifax, Nova Scotia, longshoremen had refused to handle any more "diverted" shipping.[40]

In New York City, processing plants were also under threat. Two sugar refining plants in Brooklyn and Long Island City, Queens, were endangered. A similar situation confronted coffee companies. Speaking for the coffee wholesalers, Albert Ehlers, Inc., reported that only ten days of supply were left, and "after that, we will have nothing to work with." Other Brooklyn coffee firms were in a similar predicament, as were sugar refiners in Philadelphia. Perishable fruit was under a particular risk. The *Brooklyn Eagle* reported that "$30,000 worth of fruit was rotting at piers," and that other shipments totaling $140,000 were "due soon."[41]

The Truman administration was informed of the deleterious effects of the strike on the local economies of the port cities. Telegrams began flooding into the White House from shippers and merchants alike calling for government action. The strike at the bulk cargo ports of Philadelphia, Baltimore, and Norfolk was interfering with the export of grain shipments. The Southern States Cooperative Inc. Grain Marketing Service complained to John Steelman that the strike was "severely penalizing farmers in the eastern grain growing states of Maryland, Delaware, Virginia and North Carolina." The specific problem was that grain elevators were full because of the lack of movement from grain elevators to ships. This in turn meant that recently harvested grains and soybeans could not find elevators to be dried. According to the marketing service this handicapped "eastern farmers" from participating in the Marshall Plan. A shipper from New York also complained that a perishable cargo of "fifty-two thousand bags of potatoes valued at $156,000" was rotting in Norfolk harbor. The shipper, Canada Packers, Inc., urged Truman that "prompt and decisive personal action be taken to settle longshoremen's strike."[42]

Shippers of perishable cargoes trapped in New York harbor were particularly vociferous in asking for federal action. One shipper telegrammed the vacationing Truman in Key West, Florida. The shipper asked Truman to influence the "Longshoremen's Union" to unload "5,000 stems of bananas" from the trapped steamer *Cristobal.* The Eastern Banana Corporation also asked Truman to "intercede" and encourage the strikers to "discharge" the trapped perishable cargoes. One toy manufacturer called on Truman to arrange a "truce" so that his Christmas season would not be ruined. A more forceful demand was made by Floyd W. Jefferson, president of the New York Board of Trade. Jefferson urged Truman "to use full power of high office . . . to the end that United States mail be not obstructed, impeded or delayed by pier strike along seaboard. That early tradition 'the mail must go through' be maintained and not be made subordinate to temporary decisions by labor or management."[43]

The strike's serious effect on maritime commerce along the eastern seaboard and on Marshall Plan shipments, and the pressure exerted by shippers and merchants alike, forced the federal government to act. Since July, federal mediators from the FMCS had been in the center of the negotiations. What gave the situation much more urgency was not just the increasingly serious economic effects of the strike, but the growing rift between the ILA and the employers. The employer group, dominated by the NYSA, responded to the official strike call by stating, "We have no more concessions to make." The ILA, on the other hand, had returned to its original demands of a straight fifty-cent increase (the employers had offered ten cents), a company-sponsored welfare plan, and better vacation payments.[44]

Initially the FMCS held off before acting. The two regional FMCS conciliators were Thomas R. Steutel and Howard E. Dunham. When the ILA announced that a newly constituted negotiating committee would meet on November 15, Steutel sat in as an observer, while Dunham conferred with the employer group. The employers were still smarting from the strike so the conciliators decided that a cooling-off period was needed before calling for a joint meeting of the two sides. Employer frustration with the ILA had grown appreciably. Long used to getting their own way, with the connivance of Ryan, the employers were somewhat stunned by the events. They felt badly let down by Ryan and the ILA. An agreement had been in place, one that Ryan had described as "fine," but the strike had disrupted the consummation of that agreement. The employers were annoyed also because it appeared that Ryan had lost control of the situation. The employers had not experienced an official strike for nearly thirty years, but in 1945 and now in 1948, wildcat action had closed down the eastern seaboard.[45]

With no movement from either side, on November 16, Cyrus Ching dispatched his top man, William N. Margolis, assistant director of the FMCS, to New York City to try to bring about an agreement. Described by one journalist as "one of the nation's crack labor peacemakers," Margolis had earlier settled a threatened strike by Western Union workers.[46] Margolis, however, confronted an entrenched employer group, the New York Shipping Association. Although the NYSA had agreed with the ILA to table the problem of overtime on overtime, it became increasingly disturbed by ILA recalcitrance. The ILA had formed a 125-member Wage Negotiating Committee to represent all East Coast longshoremen. This committee took a much stronger line than before. It demanded an increase of fifty cents per hour, called for one shape a day, a reduction in sling loads, and pension and welfare plans.

Margolis arranged for a meeting of the two contending parties on November 19, their first meeting since November 12. The ILA put forth a proposal to cut its wage increase demand to twenty-five cents. The ILA had hoped that its concession would steer the NYSA to accept the agreement. Just as important, pressure on both parties was increasing. On the day of the talks, Paul G. Hoffman, the economic cooperation administrator of the Marshall Plan, publicly appealed to the union and the shippers to allow relief cargo to be loaded. Hoffman argued that if delays continued, they would "not only endanger the recovery of Europe but tend to defeat the will of the America people."[47]

The NYSA held tough on its original offer of ten cents. The NYSA did offer to establish a welfare fund but only after the strike was called off and the men were back at work. While the ILA discussed the offer, Margolis took the opportunity to fly back to Washington, D.C., to meet Cyrus Ching. Following the meeting, Ching was very cautious in his comments. With the deliberateness of a mediator, he stated to the press, "I think this thing is moving in the right direction, but it is impossible to forecast when we will get a settlement." Reflecting well one of principal goals of a federal mediator, Ching further argued, "So long as you can keep the two parties meeting there is hope."[48]

Hope appeared to be dashed when the ILA rejected the NYSA proposal on November 22. The wage committee declared that the welfare scheme needed to be more "specific," and that the committee's wage demand of a twenty-five-cent increase had been ignored by the shippers.[49] With this rejection the NYSA expressed its dissatisfaction over dealing with the 125-member wage committee. The employers "complained privately that union representatives strolled in and out of all the meetings." Just as annoying, the wage committee members didn't hesitate to "interpolate local and sectional issues in the discussions." Confronted for the first time with serious discussions, the shippers were confused and felt betrayed—confused because the ILA had initially accepted the agreement, and betrayed due to the raising of wage demands and other issues. Thus many shippers felt a sense of "futility" with the talks. Additionally, they were frustrated because there was no guarantee that the ILA membership would go along with any agreement negotiated by the two sides. The NYSA was then faced with the unknown; it had endured a thirteen-day strike and a union that had adopted a confrontational posture. In response, the NYSA issued a statement that it would "make no further proposals to the union."[50] By their withdrawal from the negotiating process, the shippers had signaled their determination to wait out the striking longshoremen.

At this juncture, on November 24, Cyrus Ching flew to New York City from Washington to confront the issue. Forcing Ching's hand was the lack of any movement by the shippers and the continued piling up of Marshall Plan cargoes. As the *New York Times* reported, "The strike had virtually wiped out transatlantic cargo and passenger movements." Just as important in Ching's decision to fly to New York was his meeting with President Truman the previous day. When asked if he was in New York by "direct orders from the President," Ching reluctantly acknowledged that the "President did know of his" trip to New York.[51] Ching was obviously trying to protect President Truman's reputation during the conflict but was hampered in his efforts by the lack of power to force an agreement. Other than threatening to take control of the docks, as Truman had done in the 1946 railroad strike, Ching declared to reporters, "We have no authority to make them get together but we want to give them a nudge."[52]

Although lacking tangible power, Ching was the official representative of Truman's administration and intended to use every tactic at his disposal, including bluff. By November 26, and after a series of hectic back-and-forth meetings with the ILA and the NYSA, an agreement seemed in sight. The ILA and the NYSA refused to settle. At this point Ching played a new card, threatening Joe Ryan and John V. Lyon, chairman of the NYSA, with government action. When Ryan and Lyon both asked, "What is the Government going to do?" Ching replied, "I'll tell you at four o'clock." Ching was bluffing because, as he explained later to Truman, "they didn't know what further weapons the Government had, and they didn't realize that the Government didn't have any."[53] Unsure of the minimal threat posed by Ching, Lyon and Ryan agreed to consider making an agreement. The NYSA subsequently agreed to give the longshoremen an increase of 13 cents per hour, one week of paid vacation after working 800 hours per year and two weeks' paid vacation after working 1,350 hours per year, and, crucially, a welfare fund. Ching and Margolis presented this offer to the wage committee on November 25. The committee accepted the offer. Gene Sampson then called on his fellow members of the committee, with Ching, Margolis, Steutel, and Durham present, to pass a resolution of thanks for the mediators' efforts. The resolution was "unanimously adopted" and the mediators "received a rising vote of thanks together with an enthusiastic round of applause."[54] The agreement was turned over to the membership to vote on its acceptance. Sustaining the fears of some shippers, however, the rank and file had yet to voice its approval.

While it appeared that a majority of locals would accept the agreement, in Brooklyn rank-and-file resistance still remained strong. Sparking this revolt was Mitch Berenson, the leader of the Brooklyn Back Pay Committee. Berenson had organized meetings throughout the strike. To help him in his efforts he called on well-known city figures for support. Arthur Miller, for one, was invited to attend meetings. Berenson and Miller had struck up a friendship after Miller had begun writing a play on the subject of New York's longshoremen. But the two key men were Vincent Longhi and Paul O'Dwyer, the brother of New York City mayor, William O'Dwyer. Vincent Longhi was connected to the American Labor Party and had run for Congress from his campaign headquarters at 564 Henry Street, Brooklyn. Berenson and his group used Longhi's headquarters as a base to organize the Back Pay Committee and galvanize the men during the strike. Longhi was intimately attached to the waterfront. His Italian-born father had played a role in creating the ILA and because of his socialist ideals the ILA hierarchy resented him. Just like his father, Vincent Longhi was "always pulled towards the docks." He had met Berenson when working on *L'Unità del Popolo* (Unity of the People), and they shared a "dream," as Longhi put it, "to carry out my father's ideal of cleaning up the waterfront, get rid of Joe Ryan, the Mafia, and the unholy trinity of Tammany Hall."[55]

Longhi in turn invited Paul O'Dwyer to join the fight. According to O'Dwyer, Longhi said, "Give us a hand with this strike in Brooklyn. This is a new group of people, new and young Italians, who are entitled to live right and shouldn't be bound by what went on before." O'Dwyer reported, "So, I said, 'Oh leave me alone. . . . I want to get back to my [law] practice.' And anyway, he said, 'It would be great thing if you came here.'"[56]

Paul O'Dwyer was a good choice to help in the struggle. He was born in County Mayo, Ireland, in 1907 and migrated to the United States in 1925. Thanks to his elder brother, Jack, he got a job as a checker on the Brooklyn waterfront in 1926. Unfortunately, O'Dwyer took the ILA union rule book seriously and, as he recalled, "made a complaint of what I thought was a violation of the union agreement." O'Dwyer had of course "violated" the unspoken agreement between ILA officials and shippers not to make complaints: "And so, I didn't last too long in that job, and, of course, I worked wherever [on the waterfront] I could get employment after that."[57] By 1940, O'Dwyer had obtained his law degree and joined the American Labor Party (ALP). The ALP was closely tied with the Communist Party of America (CPUSA) but was nominally independent. The influence of the CPUSA on the ALP was significant. As O'Dwyer stated, "The great mass [of the ALP] were non-Communist. The Communists were very aggressive, and they found themselves very often in leadership [positions], although numerically they were few. But because of the fact that they had the capacity for working day and night in whatever cause they felt was important, they were also in a position of leadership."[58]

Through his work on the Brooklyn waterfront he witnessed first-hand the daily exploitation of both Italian and "Negro" longshoremen. Short ganging was common in Brooklyn. Under the union contract a normal gang should have been nineteen men, but it was common to have only twelve or fifteen. Thus the stevedore was saved money in wages and the union official received a kickback in return. The men in turn "came there literally with hat in hand as they passed by" the hiring agent, who on many occasions was merely a local gangster. O'Dwyer also understood the reticence of the longshoremen to confront openly the union officials. The tradition of being "completely opposed to the informer" ensured that "both Italians and Irishmen" would hesitate before taking political action. Besides his personal experience and his left-wing politics, familial relations also played a role in O'Dwyer's decision to work with Longhi. O'Dwyer's relationship with his brother Bill was strained. Mayor O'Dwyer was tied with the Brooklyn Democratic party machine, the very forces that Paul O'Dwyer was fighting. As Longhi explained, "Paul was a maverick" in his family; "Bill was not a bad guy . . . but he was not a saint. Paul is a saint, he fought for the honor of his family."[59]

There was another strategy in the decision to bring in O'Dwyer: he could theoretically provide some form of protection from the local Mafia groups that dominated the waterfront. If the brother of the New York City mayor was in one's camp, it might make the local goons think twice before engaging in reprisals. As Longhi explained, "When things got hot, lives were at stake, we were afraid, we thought that Paul through his brother would get us some protection, and there were times when we got it, protection from the cops." Such protection was necessary considering that Longhi and his cohorts would "see them [gangsters] all the time." Each side knew of the other and they commonly rubbed shoulders with one another. Longhi testified to this almost daily contact: "when you walk past their club, their men are outside, 4 or 5 outside, you make eye contact, you say heh, or ho, that's all. They knew who we were, we knew them." Longhi thought that the local hoods were thinking, "Maybe I'll kill them tomorrow, maybe." So the presence of the mayor's brother and police protection certainly tipped the scales in the rank and file's favor.[60]

Paul O'Dwyer's initiation into the rank and file was not without drama. At his first meeting he was asked to speak to the assembled longshoremen. O'Dwyer exclaimed, "This is a new day. The day of the gangster telling you you can't speak is finished. This is emancipation day for the Italian longshoremen of Brooklyn, and you are not bound by the thugs anymore." He said that the "new" era also provided an environment "where a man may speak without fear." O'Dwyer later recalled that a voice from the back of the hall asked, "'Mister, why, you mean anybody can go up there [the podium] and speak?' I said, 'That's what I said.' He said, 'You mean, I can go up there and speak?' And I said, 'That's what I mean. Come on up.' And to my amazement there was a sort of silence and the man got up and took the microphone and said, 'My name is Anthony Anastasia.'" The strained silence was understandable. Anthony (Tough Tony) Anastasia was the brother of Albert Anastasia, the reputed head of Murder Inc. O'Dwyer later said, "I'm afraid my efforts to bring freedom of speech to the workmen backfired somewhat" as the meeting abruptly ended.[61]

Mitch Berenson and his political allies had done much to keep Brooklyn's Italian longshoremen informed of events. While most were not interested in usurping the power of their local union/gangster leaders, Berenson's organization did provide an outlet for the rank and file's anger and concerns. It was more than just mere rhetoric that was absorbed, however. The men could now decide for themselves whether they would accept or reject the agreement negotiated by their leadership.

When news of the agreement was delivered to the Brooklyn membership on November 25, O'Dwyer called a meeting for the following day to enable the longshoremen to air their views. Held at the Livingston Hall on Schermerhorn Street, the meeting was attended by two thousand longshoremen. Indeed, the numbers were so large that many men "had to remain outside, listening to the speeches carried over a public address system." Speaker after speaker called on the men to hold out and ask for more concessions, including one daily shape-up. Ryan responded to the meeting with his usual barrage of anti-Communist rhetoric: "Some of the speakers and the men agitating at the meeting were ex-members of the ILA, and some were known Communists who have tried to keep the waterfront disturbed." Although Ryan's jibe about "ex-members" was aimed at O'Dwyer, journalists at the meeting reported that he had "stressed he was impartial, and would not make any recommendations for or against the strike settlement."[62]

The vote was held on November 27. The majority of the New York locals voted for acceptance, as did the locals in Boston, Philadelphia, Baltimore, and Newport News. The so-called "Mother Local" 791 led by Gene Sampson had voted for the pact, as had the black Local 968. But four Brooklyn Locals and one in Jersey City rejected the pact. They were, respectively, Local 327, Local 327-1, Local 338-1, Local 1199-1, and Local 1247. Mitch Berenson's Local 327 was the first to reject the agreement. He stated to the press, "We have no faith in Joe Ryan and we don't trust him."[63]

Following meetings throughout the day on November 28, O'Dwyer and Berenson were forced to accept the agreement. It made little sense to stand pat when the bulk of the membership was returning to work, and the majority of members of the rogue locals also were planning on returning to work. A final meeting was held at St. Stephens Hall, Hicks Street, Brooklyn, with O'Dwyer presiding. O'Dwyer began by criticizing the agreement as not taking into account the demand for one daily shape-up and a reduction in sling loads: "But the majority of the membership . . . agreed to accept the agreement. . . . We must go along with the majority decision, no matter how much we dislike it; that's democracy." O'Dwyer finished by outlining future demands to be met, including a union hiring hall, sling load reductions, a welfare plan paid by employers, "two extra men in the hold of each ship, with no split gangs," and "overtime pay after forty hours."[64]

The outcome of the strike confirmed the rank and file's power to effect change in the contract and working conditions. The pay increase, improved vacation time, and a welfare fund spoke for the potency of a work force once perceived as crushed and of no consequence. Government action had also played an important role by forcing Ryan to negotiate a contract that the membership could vote on. Once federal mediators and NLRB officials entered the scene, Ryan was confronted with forces he could not control. It was one thing to vigorously contain rank-and-file anger; it was quite another to curb federal officials.

As the strike had progressed, however, it had affirmed the weakness of the oppositional movement in the face of union and state action that critically divorced members from decision making. Only in Brooklyn did a rank-and-file presence continue. Brilliantly using "outside" support in the form of O'Dwyer and Longhi, Mitch Berenson was able to keep the men involved in the strike, even bringing newspaper attention to their demands. The Back Pay Committees would remain in existence and continue to press their claims. It would take another wildcat strike in 1951, and a barrage of crime commission hearings, for the longshoremen to rid themselves of the humiliating shape-up system. The 1948 strike, then, set the scene for a move toward democratic control of the ILA and a more secure and safe work environment.

Notes

1. Interview with Sam Madell, New Yorkers at Work: Oral History, Robert F. Wagner Labor Archives, Tamiment Library, New York University (hereafter NYAW).

2. Report to Harry Bridges from William Glazier, August 19, 1948, box 1, International Longshoremen's Association, Tamiment Library, New York University (hereafter ILA-TAM).

3. "Testimony of Julius Bagley," House Committee on Education and Labor, *Amendments to the Fair Labor Standards Act of 1938, Vol. 1,* 81st Cong., 1st sess., 1949, 621; Vernon H. Jensen, *Strife on the Waterfront: The Port of New York since 1945* (Ithaca, N.Y.: Cornell University Press, 1974), 54–59.

4. For the shippers' and Ryan's opposition to the overtime-on-overtime issue, see "Testimony of Frank Nolan, Chairman, Stevedoring Committee, NYC," Senate Com-

mittee on Labor and Public Welfare, *Fair Labor Standards Act Amendments, Part 1*, 80th Cong., 1st sess., 1948, 381–421; "Statement of Joseph Ryan," ibid., 1063–79. For the original suit and the following decisions through to the Supreme Court, see "Statement of Louis Waldman, General Counsel, ILA," Senate Committee on Labor and Public Welfare, *To Clarify the Overtime Provisions of the Fair Labor Standards Act of 1938, As Amended*, 81st Cong., 1st sess., 1949, 4–35.

5. Quoted in Citizens Waterfront Committee, *The New York Waterfront: A Report to the Public of New York City by the Citizens Waterfront Committee Setting Forth Our Oldest and Most Urgent Civic Problem—The Condition of the Waterfront* (New York, 1946), 13.

6. Report to the President on the Labor Dispute Involving Longshoremen and Associated Occupations in the Maritime Industry on the Atlantic Coast, August 19, 1948, Papers of Harry Truman, Official File, 407-B, Maritime Relations, Harry Truman Presidential Library, West Branch, Iowa.

7. Charles M. Rehmus, "Emergency Strikes Revisited," *Industrial and Labor Relations Review* 43 (January 1990): 176–77; Ruth O'Brien, "Taking the Conservative State Seriously: Statebuilding and Restrictive Labor Practices in Postwar America," *Labor Studies Journal* 21 (Winter 1997): 32–63. Many of the members of the presidential fact-finding boards were dissatisfied with the process; see Arthur A. Sloane, "Presidential Boards of Inquiry in National Emergency Disputes: An Assessment after Twenty Years of Performance," *Labor Law Journal* 18 (November 1967): 665–75; Irving Bernstein, Harold L. Enarson, and R. W. Fleming, *Emergency Disputes and National Policy* (New York: Harper, 1955).

8. "On the Beach," *Fortune Magazine*, February 1937, 75; New York State Crime Commission, *Study of the Port of New York* (New York: New York City Municipal Library, 1953), 27; Benjamin Chinitz, *Freight and the Metropolis: The Impact of America's Transportation Revolution on the New York Region* (Cambridge, Mass.: Harvard University Press, 1960), 2; R. Alton Lee, *Truman and Taft-Hartley: A Question of Mandate* (Lexington, Ky.: University of Kentucky Press, 1966), 76.

9. Interview with David L. Cole, September 20, 1972, Oral History Collection, Harry S. Truman Library, Independence, Missouri.

10. Ibid.

11. Letter to John R. Steelman from Cyrus Ching, director of Federal Mediation and Conciliation Service, August 17, 1948, Papers of Harry S. Truman, box 1183, file 3, Official File 407-B, Harry Truman Presidential Library, West Branch, Iowa; letter to Steelman from William W. Smith, chairman, U.S. Maritime Commission, August 17, 1948, ibid.

12. *Report of Board of Inquiry—Maritime Industry (East Coast Longshoremen)* (Washington D.C.: GPO, 1948), 7 (quote); *Final Report of Board of Inquiry, October 21, 1948* (Washington, D.C.: GPO, 1948), 1–2.

13. Letter to Tom C. Clark, U.S. Attorney General, from Harry Truman, August 20, 1948, Official File 407-B, Harry Truman Presidential Library.

14. "Status Report of Thomas R. Steutel," October 26, 1948, Federal Conciliation and Mediation Service, Dispute Case Files, 1913–1948, box 2357, RG 280. National Archives; "Last Offer of Settlement by the New York Shipping Association and the International Longshoremen's Association, Submitted to the Presidential Board of Inquiry, Thursday, October 21, 1948," Federal Conciliation and Mediation Service, Regional Dispute Files (Nationally Significant), 1948–1950, Category One, box 2522, RG 280, National Archives; *Final Report of the Board of Inquiry*, 3–6.

15. *Daily Worker,* November 14, 1948, 1; *New York Times,* November 10, 1948, 59 (quote); Charles P. Larrowe, *Shape-Up and Hiring Hall: A Comparison of Hiring Methods on the New York and Seattle Waterfronts* (Berkeley: University of California Press, 1955), 32.

16. Interview with Sam Madell and Father Philip Carey, NYAW.

17. "Statement of Alfred Corbett, Chairman, New Jersey Back Pay Committee," Senate Committee on Labor and Public Welfare, *To Clarify the Overtime Provisions of the Fair Labor Standards Act of 1938, As Amended,* 81st Cong., 1st sess., 1949, 341.

18. *New York Times,* November 11, 1948, 1.

19. Ibid.

20. Sampson's hold on Local 791 is discussed in Larrowe, *Shape-Up and Hiring Hall,* 34. For the public clash between Ryan and Sampson, see *New York Times,* November 11, 1, 31; *New York Telegram,* November 10, 1948, 5.

21. *Brooklyn Eagle,* November 10, 1948, 1, 2.

22. *New York Sun,* November 10, 1948, 1 (quotes). For Malcolm Johnson's articles "Crime on the Waterfront," see the *New York Sun,* November 8, 1948, 1, 6; November 9, 1948, 1, 10; November 10, 1948, 1, 10; November 11, 1948, 1, 2; November 12, 1948, 1, 10; November 15, 1948, 1, 5; November 16, 1948, 1, 6; November 17, 1948, 1, 10; November 18, 1948, 1, 6; November 19, 1948, 1, 9; November 22, 1948, 1, 11; November 23, 1948, 1, 4; November 24, 1948, 1, 6; November 26, 1948, 1, 16; November 29, 1948, 1, 7; November 30, 1948, 1, 4.

23. *New York Sun,* November 12, 1948, 10 (first quote); *Brooklyn Eagle,* November 14, 1948, 24 (second quote).

24. *New York Sun,* November 13, 1948, 2.

25. *New York Times,* November 13, 1948, 1; *New York Sun,* November 12, 1, 10; *New York Times,* November 17, 1948, 3; *New York Sun,* November 13, 1948, 2.

26. *New York Sun,* November 11, 1948, 6.

27. "Shapeup, Unemployment Main Issues in Longshore Strike," Fred Zeserson, Federated Press, Eastern Bureau, November 18, 1948, Folder: Agreements, Negotiations and Strikes, box 1, ILA-TAM.

28. *New York Telegram,* November 10, 1948, 1 (first quote); *New York Times,* November 16, 1948, 35 (second quote); *Daily Worker,* November 16, 1948, 6; ibid., November 17, 1948, 2, 11 (third quote); *New York Sun,* November 16, 1–2.

29. *Final Report of Board of Inquiry,* 15.

30. *New York Sun,* November 11, 1948, 1; *New York Telegram,* November 10, 1948, 5.

31. *Brooklyn Eagle,* November 16, 1948, 9; *New York Times,* November 16, 1948, 35; ibid., November 17, 1948, 1, 49 (quote).

32. *New York Times,* November 11, 1948, 31; November 16, 1948, 1 (second quote); November 17, 1948, 1, 49 (third quote); November 18, 1948, 19; November 19, 1948, 23 (first quote).

33. "Testimony of Joseph Kane, Member of the International Longshoremen's Association," Senate Committee on Labor and Public Welfare, *To Clarify the Overtime Provisions of the Fair Labor Standards Act of 1938, As Amended,* 81st Cong., 1st sess., 1949, 255–63.

34. *New York Times,* November 14, 1948, 48 (quote); *San Francisco Chronicle,* November 18, 1948, 1.

35. "Canadian ILA Leader Knuckles Under to Pressure," by Tom Carlson, box 1, ILA-TAM; *New York Times,* November 19, 1948, 1. *New York Sun,* November 17, 1–2.

36. *New York Times,* November 16, 1948, 1. It was reported that "Mr. Ryan indicated yesterday he believed the strike effect on the city would be negligible as far as food and fuel transport was concerned. . . . much of the local coal and food transport is handled by other than ILA men." *New York Times,* November 14, 1948.

37. *New York Sun,* November 16, 1948, 2.

38. *Brooklyn Eagle,* November 17, 1948, 1, 3 (first quote); *New York Sun,* November 18, 1948, 37 (second quote).

39. *New York Times,* November 13, 1948, 3.

40. *New York Sun,* November 16, 1948, 2.

41. *Brooklyn Eagle,* November 18, 1948, 1, 3 (quote); *Wall Street Journal,* November 24, 1948, 4.

42. Telegram to President Truman from George L. Leitze, Southern States Cooperative Inc. Grain Marketing Service, November 19, 1948, and telegram to President Truman from Harry S. Thompson, vice-president, Canada Packers Inc., November 23, 1948, both in Papers of Harry S. Truman, Official Files, 407-B, Maritime Strikes.

43. Telegram to President Truman from Pablo Calvert and Co. Inc., November 16, 1948; telegram to President Truman from Eastern Banana Corporation, November 15, 1948; telegram to President Truman from Samuel Steele, president, Arista Toy Corporation, November 19, 1948; telegram to President Truman from Floyd W. Jefferson, president, New York Board of Trade, November 19, 1948; all in Papers of Harry S. Truman, Official Files, 407-B, Maritime Strikes.

44. *New York Times,* November 13, 1948, 1.

45. Ibid., November 15, 1948, 1; ibid., November 16, 1948, 1. Prior to the meeting, Steutel had "conferred with Theodore Kheel" and "representatives of the New York Shipping Association." *New York Sun,* November 15, 1948, 3.

46. *New York Sun,* November 17, 1948, 1.

47. *New York Times,* November 20, 1948, 1. Hoffman's request was ignored by the ILA and the NYSA. *New York Times,* November 21, 1948, 48.

48. *New York Times,* November 22, 1948, 1–12. Ching was a forceful advocate of the mediated settlement, writing, "Repression in the name of emergency tends to compound itself. . . . Mediators have learned long ago that to date, there is no substitute for the seemingly endless drudgery of prolonged discussion, persistent persuasion, and reasonable argument." Cyrus Ching, "Collective Bargaining and the Emergency Dispute," *Temple Law Quarterly* 26 (Spring 1953): 366–67.

49. *New York Times,* November 23, 1948, 1.

50. Ibid., November 24, 1948, 1 (first quote); *New York Sun,* November 24, 1948, 1–2 (second quote).

51. *New York Times,* November 25, 1948, 1; *New York Sun,* November 24, 1948, 2.

52. Report, William N. Margolis, December 8, 1948, Records of the FMCS, Regional Dispute Files (Nationally Significant), 1948–1950, Category 1, box 2522, RG 280, National Archives; *New York Times,* November 25, 1948, 1 (Ching quote).

53. "Cyrus Stewart Ching," part 2, no. 35, microfiche card 7 of 9, 575, 577, Columbia University Oral History Collection (quote); Report, William N. Margolis.

54. Report, William N. Margolis.

55. Vincent Longhi, interview by author, August 29, 1995. For the influence of the American Labor Party on New York City politics, see Kenneth Alan Waltzer, "The American Labor Party: Third Party Politics in New Deal/Cold War New York, 1936–1954," Ph.D. diss., Harvard University, 1977.

56. "Paul O'Dwyer," Columbia University Oral History Collection, 1962, transcript, 71.

57. Ibid., 1, 34–37.

58. Ibid., 178.

59. Ibid., 39–40, 44; Longhi interview.

60. Longhi interview.

61. "Paul O'Dwyer," Columbia University Oral History Project, 1962, 71–72.

62. *Brooklyn Eagle,* November 27, 1948, 1; *New York Times,* November 27, 1948, 1 (first and second quotes); *New York Sun,* November 26, 1948, 1; ibid., November 27, 1948, 1 (third quote).

63. *New York Times,* November 28, 1948, 66; *Brooklyn Eagle,* November 28, 1948, 1, 48 (quote).

64. *New York Sun,* November 29, 1948, 1 (quotes); *New York Times,* November 29, 1948, 1.

5 The 1948 London Strike

The 1948 New York strike had firmly implanted the notion of insurrection on the docks. Taking on both their union and the national state had energized many of the rank and file and created a new coterie of leaders. In London, conditions were also ripe for an explosion of dockworker anger. Out of this anger came an oppositional movement that raised new leaders who directly challenged established trade union leaders. As in New York, the rank-and-filers directed their frustration at a union leadership they considered ineffectual. However, the conditions surrounding the dispute and the structural components were altogether different from those in New York. The London dockworkers worked under a system of tight governmental control under the auspices of the 1947 Dock Labour Scheme. The dockers felt constrained by bureaucratic inertia and a corresponding lack of flexibility. Grievances covering types of work, special payments, and discipline had to be appealed to the London Dock Labour Board and then, if need be, to the National Dock Labour Board. It could take up to two years before a decision was made concerning individual and group grievances, ensuring that feelings of resentment continued to fester. The suffocating arrangement led directly to the strike of 1948. The dispute became known as the "zinc oxide" strike.

Unlike the New York strike, the London conflict had all the hallmarks of a titanic struggle between the rank and file on the one hand and the trade union leadership and its government allies on the other. The Transport and General Workers' Union (TGWU) was working closely with the newly elected Labour government to restore the competitiveness of the British economy. In 1948, the Labour government was beset with problems, however. On the one hand, the government had pledged to create the welfare state of free medical coverage and to initiate a dramatic nationalization program of core industries. On the other, there was a continuing drain of foreign reserves to pay off the government's debts to the United States, and a low productivity rate. Faced with a hemorrhaging of valuable reserves, the government embarked on a policy of austerity, or as some have put it, "retreat." Thus, rationing of foodstuffs and clothing would continue. Once again women would face long lines outside bakeries and butcher shops; the only alternative was the thriving black market. Just as vital, the trade union movement was convinced to adopt a policy of voluntary wage restraint. Adding to the siege feeling were volatile foreign relations that arose because of the Berlin blockade that had just been instituted by the Soviet Union.[1]

London's dockworkers, although sympathetic to the plight of the Labour government, were concerned over the disciplinary measures of the Dock Labour Scheme. It was one thing to have stability of employment, but quite another to accept the structural constraints of the scheme's administration. The resulting frustration would lead to a portwide strike. Once the strike broke out, the dockworkers would be confronted by the combined might of higher trade union and government officials. The strike would also directly threaten the nation's food supply. Against such a backdrop, the Labour government was determined to lessen the effects of the strike, even using troops to win their cause.

The numbers of dockworkers disciplined under the Dock Labour Scheme reflected the growing tension. Clauses 15 and 16 of the scheme empowered the respective local Dock Labour Boards to discipline any worker "who fails to comply with any lawful order given to him" either by "the National Board" or "by his employer." To encourage other workers to stop work was also deemed an offense. Thus the worker who "behaves in such manner as to impede other workers" was found to be in violation of the scheme. The local board would then hold a hearing and if it found the offending worker guilty, he could be suspended from work, disentitled to attendance pay, or dismissed from employment. The dockworker was entitled to appeal his case to an appeal tribunal.[2]

The number of cases coming before the London Dock Labour Board (LDLB) was indeed high. In the twelve-month period between June 1947 and June 1948, a total of 3,685 men were reported. The number represents 15 percent of the entire work force of 25,546. True, 1,630 of the cases were "not proceeded with," but a sizable section was disciplined in one fashion or another. One thousand fifty-seven men were "warned," while the remainder were suspended from the scheme. The majority were suspended for either three days

(392) or seven days (393). There was of course recourse to the appeal tribunal. Of the 585 men who did appeal, only 150 won or were "allowed," while 256 were rejected or "disallowed" and a further 179 "disallowed but penalty reduced."[3]

The London dockworkers resented the disciplinary sections of the Dock Labour Scheme and the aggressive action taken by the LDLB. The extremely large numbers of dockworkers brought before the LDLB signaled a breakdown of the scheme. The LDLB was increasingly at odds with the work force. Just as crucial, the union members of the board found themselves battling and disciplining large numbers of their membership. In an effort to follow the strict policies of their national leadership, the dockworker leaders punished those who threatened the industry by refusing work allocation or who were involved in work stoppages. The result was simmering discontent by the rank and file. A spark was all that was needed to inflame the situation, and in June 1948 the worst fears of both employers and union leaders were realized.

On May 27, 1948, eleven dockers in the Regent Canal Dock were assigned the job of loading into the S.S. *Theems* 3,022 bags (100 tons) of zinc oxide. Known as the "Coe's gang," the dockworkers became suspicious of the cargo. One of the gang members was Joe Bloomberg, who announced to one of his gang mates, "You're all blue, you're bloody blue. . . . It can't be right." The dockers' clothing and skin was colored by the substance. The men believed that the cargo was dangerous and that extra payment was therefore due. During their lunch hour they marched to Stepney Public Library and looked in a "book of poisonous substances." Discovering that zinc oxide "doesn't do you any good," the gang agreed among themselves not to unload the cargo until paid a "dirty cargo rate."[4]

Returning to the ship, the men refused to continue loading the zinc oxide until the rate of 5 shillings per ton was paid (the rate had been established at 3 shillings and 4 pence). Under the rules of the Dock Labour Scheme, a viewing committee had to judge the men's demand. The following afternoon, on May 28, such a committee found that the initial rate was correct and that men should begin again to load the ship. The men refused and the S.S. *Theems* sailed with only 25 of the 100 tons loaded. The men were then reported to the LDLB as being in breach of the scheme. On Saturday, June 5, the S.S. *Theems* returned and the men were ordered once again to load the remaining zinc oxide; they again refused to do so. Another gang was "engaged" to complete the loading but it also refused to do the job. A further report was made to the LDLB regarding the gang's refusal. Fearing a spread of the dispute, the Port Labour Executive Committee agreed that another viewing committee should be formed and that it should "view the job whilst it was in progress." The committee was made up of two employers and two TGWU officials, Tim O'Leary and Steven Platt. On Tuesday, June 8, the "augmented view committee" watched the men at work and found that the original rate was the proper one. The gang refused once again to accept the rate. During dinner the men were persuaded by other workmates to finish the job, but their earlier refusal had been reported to the LDLB. So the gang had been reported three times for breaching the rules of the Dock Labour Scheme.[5]

The incident highlighted the differing perspectives on the correct rate for the job. Coe's gang plainly saw the issue as one of a dirty cargo and the need for a corresponding increased pay rate. For the union officials and the employers, however, the cargo was not problematic. Adding to the volatile situation was the continuing refusal of Coe's gang to accept the numerous viewing committees' findings. Coe's gang had the right to demand a viewing, but once done it was obligated to accept the decision. After repeatedly refusing to accept the decision, the gang was clearly in violation of the Dock Labour Scheme.

After a complaint was filed by the shipper, the Grand Union Company, Ltd., the issue was placed before the London Dock Labour Board for disciplinary action. The LDLB took up the case the following day. The LDLB agreed that the men were being paid the proper rate and that their subsequent actions were in violation of the scheme. Employer and public members pushed for "instant dismissal," while the union members argued for suspension. In a supposed compromise, the LDLB suspended the men for seven days and ordered that they would not be entitled to any attendance money for a period of three months.[6] This was a particularly severe punishment because the men were still expected to attend calls every day without any compensation if work was not available. This was the first time that the full penalty had been used.

While Coe's gang appealed the decision, a special meeting of shop stewards was held on Saturday, June 12, to discuss the situation. Although angry with the decision, the shop stewards agreed that the membership as a whole should continue to work while the appeal was heard. On the following Monday morning, however, Harold Van Loo, a member of the Docks Group Committee who had attended the Saturday meeting, held an impromptu discussion with dockworkers at the Ratcliff Cross Gate entrance of the Regent's Canal Dock. He put forward a motion to "cease work," to which the men agreed. Thereby seven hundred Regent's Canal dockers refused to work. Van Loo visited other docks on that morning. The regional industrial relations officer, J. H. Withal, reported that Van Loo, accompanied by an unnamed "Strike Committee" member, was "going around the docks this morning, still making inflammatory speeches."[7] By the afternoon the Regent's Canal strikers were joined by segments from the neighboring London and St. Katherines Docks, totaling 1,733 men.[8]

That evening a "Special Meeting" of the TGWU Docks Group Committee (DGC) convened at the union's Tooley Street headquarters. The purpose of the meeting was to try to gauge the mood of the strikers and ascertain what steps could be taken to get the men back to work. In a pointed reference to Van Loo, it was reported that "notwithstanding the decision of the stewards [not to strike], at the Ratcliff Cross Gate a responsible member who had been party to the stewards' decision moved a motion to the effect 'we carry out our previous decision and cease work,' with the result that the men at . . . Regents Canal Dock did not start work." Unfortunately the "long discussion" that followed was not recorded in the minutes. More than likely Van Loo was criticized for his actions because the DGC resolved that, "having heard all the facts concerning the dispute, [it] endorses the action of all the Officers" to get the men back to work.[9]

The attempts by the officers to regain control of the situation were not successful, however. The following morning, a further 1,127 London and St. Katherines men came out, accompanied by 700 from the India and Millwall Docks. On the same day the appeals tribunal met to hear the men's complaint, but "failed to agree" on a decision.[10]

By Thursday, June 17, a reconstituted appeals tribunal met, headed by an independent chairman, Sir Robert Aske. The two "workpeople's" representatives were G. S. Richards, divisional officer of the TGWU-Surrey Docks, and E. C. Harvey, of TGWU Ships' Clerks. Representing the employers were Major K. W. Evetts and A. Wright. Three NDLB officials were also present. The tribunal unanimously agreed that the seven days' suspension without pay should stand. The thirteen-week disentitlement to attendance pay was, however, reduced to two weeks.[11]

Although the period of disentitlement had been reduced to two weeks, NDLB officials appeared happy with the decision. John Saunders, assistant port manager and an official of the LDLB, explained to the NDLB chairman, Lord Ammon, that the loss of a week's pay was important because the gang members were "preference men, whom [*sic*] on average earn over £15 a week." As for disentitlement to attendance money, Saunders explained, "It is the first time that the London Board has implemented this section of the Scheme." Reflecting the attitude of board officials, Saunders smugly remarked that he "hope[d]" that the "disentitlement to the financial benefits is more frequently used in London and other ports in the future."[12]

Saunders made his glib remarks while a total of 12,918 dockers were on strike, idling ninety-three ships.[13] He had seriously miscalculated the temper of the dockers. Once the appeal tribunal's decision was made public on Thursday, June 17, it only inflamed the situation. The men perceived the punishment as arbitrary and therefore unfair. The shop stewards, who had called the earlier Saturday meeting, met immediately after the tribunal decision was made public.

The small group of shop stewards played a key role in calling and expanding the strike. The group's earlier meetings, on June 12 and June 14, had helped create a common purpose and cohesion. By June 17, the group had transformed itself into a strike committee. Responding to the tribunal's decision, the strike committee passed a resolution declaring that the punishment was a "direct attack on all militant workers in the docks. Further we cannot recommend the acceptance of the Tribunals findings." The "no name organization" "demand[ed] a mass meeting of all delegates" with Arthur Deakin, head of the TGWU, and Arthur Bird, head of Docks Group Committee, "in attendance so that we submit to them our grievances against the Scheme."[14] Eventually naming itself the "Unofficial Committee," it was made up of seventeen members, ten of whom were either shop stewards or branch secretaries. Although hoping to brand the committee as Communist inspired, a regional industrial relations officer of the Ministry of Labour was forced to admit that while some members were either "Communist" or "Trotskyite," the "organization is a very mixed bag indeed and includes, I am told, people who are not extremists."[15] While the majority of the committee were not aligned with Marxist parties, some of its officials were. The chairman of the committee was Pat Coleman, a known Communist. Coleman was sixty years old and considered by many an "old man at the time." Because of his age he worked in a warehouse. His Communist politics were well known by the men. Joe Bloomberg remembered Coleman as a "good Communist" in that he "sincerely believed in" his Marxist politics. Coleman was known to bend, but he "would not deviate from it unless you could prove it." Coleman did not proselytize among the men. According to Bloomberg, he "did not try and convince me to become a Communist." Others in the inner group did not share the same left-wing ideology as Coleman. Arthur Upton, for example, was treasurer but he was a socialist. Bloomberg said of Upton: "He knew his business. . . . Our views were the same. . . . He was very sharp . . . a good guy."[16]

Stevedores and Lightermen were also represented on the Unofficial Committee. Two NASD officials, Bert Aylward and John Donovan, acted as press officer and speaker, respectively. Aylward worked in the Surrey Docks and had gained a reputation as a rebel within the NASD. He represented the NASD on the LDLB. It was in this capacity that he infuriated the public and employer members. Aylward publicized LDLB proceedings in a pamphlet entitled *The*

Struggle. His actions resulted in at least one stevedores' strike, and he was subsequently reprimanded by the NASD's London Sectional Committee, Dockers Section.[17]

The Unofficial Committee was indeed a "mixed bag" but unified by resentment against the disciplinary measures of the Dock Labour Scheme. These men were all working dockers and stevedores, not paid union officials. The rank-and-filers then perceived them as representing their best interests in the dispute. Higher union officials were regarded with distrust and were perceived as having played the role of employer lackey. As the strike progressed, the rank and file would witness another vital role played by its union officials, that of government agents.

With the strike spreading, district union leaders scrambled to regain control of the situation. They scheduled a meeting at Victoria Park on June 18. The officials called on the assembled dockers to go back to work. The meeting collapsed, however, after members of the crowd yelled out that it was a "phoney meeting." It was alleged that the "meeting had been faked by the presence of a number of men who were not on strike but whose employer had given them leave to attend the meeting."[18] The meeting had seriously misfired, embarrassing the leadership. Additionally, the debacle encouraged those London dockers still working to walk out the following day.

The night of June 18, Arthur W. Harvey, TGWU district official of the London docks, attended a meeting of what he described as the "no name organization." It was made abundantly clear to him that the "organization" was determined to stand firm until the tribunal decision was nullified. In an extraordinary move, Harvey, with his fellow official Steven Platt, visited the offices of the London Dock Labour Board the following Saturday morning. Meeting with John Saunders, Harvey "gave details of officers and committee of the [no name] organization." Harvey pleaded with Saunders that something "drastic" be done "to placate" the men and to "save the faces of us all." Harvey suggested that the tribunal decision should be suspended "pending a discussion" of the "Scheme." When Saunders asked that Harvey's entreaty be put in writing, "Harvey replied, that he 'expected to be criticized by his headquarters for putting the suggestion forward.'" Shortly after the meeting, Harvey phoned Saunders and pleaded "to forget their visit to the London Dock Labour Board and to treat their interview in the strictest confidence." Harvey's entreaty was to no avail. The list of members of the "no name organization" had already been furnished to the National Dock Labour Board and "forwarded to Mr. Stillwell" at the Ministry of Labour. So Harvey's remarkable visit to board officials merely resulted in the provision of invaluable information to the LDLB and eventually the Ministry of Labour.[19]

Such machinations could not stall the momentum of the strike. By Friday night, June 18, the TGWU clerks had joined the strike, bringing "all ship work to a standstill." Likewise, stevedores "threw in their lot with the strikers" and walked off the job. On Sunday morning an official meeting of the stevedores was held in Surrey Docks. The 1,200 men present at the meeting pledged to remain out on strike "unless the other Unions go back." General Secretary Dickie Barrett spoke but, mindful of the damage of pressing the men too far, was "luke-warm in urging the men to resume [work]." By Saturday, June 19, the port of London had virtually come to a standstill. As the stevedores joined the dockers on strike, the number of men out totaled 19,052.[20]

On the same day, a special meeting of the Docks Group Committee was held to go over the quickly deteriorating situation. Van Loo avoided the meeting, apologizing for his absence. Tom Birkett, a TGWU national officer, attended the meeting as Arthur Deakin's representative. Arthur Harvey again gave his report of the meeting of the Unofficial Committee. Those at the meeting subsequently agreed that the members of Coe's gang "were in breach" of the Dock Labour Scheme by their repeated refusal to work for the proper rate. Justifying such a stance, the attendees of the special meeting found that the proper procedures had been followed with the viewing committees and appeal tribunals. Heavily influenced by the bureaucratic structure of the respective findings and appeals, those attending the special meeting could only conclude that the "majority of the men on strike were not aware of the true facts." "The unofficial leaders of the strike" were blamed for this ignorance. A remedy for the situation was to inform the membership via a "pamphlet" that "should set out the full facts of the case."[21]

The newspapers and radio were also to be utilized to get the message across. If all failed to achieve a "resumption of work," a mass meeting would be called for Tuesday, June 22. Attempts to get the BBC to broadcast the officials' position regarding the strike or appeals to return to work fizzled, however. Lord Simon of Wythenshawe, director general of the BBC, explained that if the BBC allowed the officials to broadcast an appeal, then the Unofficial Committee would have to be given the same privilege. As he stated: "The BBC has a paramount duty to be impartial in all controversial matters, and however much the Governors may sympathize with one side of the case, they are compelled if a broadcast is made on behalf of one side to allow the other side to reply."[22]

Although rebuffed by the BBC, the higher union officials were determined to regain control. Nonetheless, they were reacting to an explosive situation by expending their time and energy trying to get the men back to work. It was the Unofficial Committee that held the upper hand because the men were following its guidance. The Unofficial Committee had had a profound impact on the strike. The initial group of shop stewards had taken on the case of Coe's gang. Their meetings and subsequent calls for action were catalysts in the conflict. Higher union officials were out-maneuvered by such action. These same officials ignored the gang's demand for fair play and tried to forestall action by the stewards and the men in general. Just as important, London and National Dock Labour Board officials also shared the blame for allowing the situation to deteriorate so fast and so far. The same officials enjoyed meting out punishment but were ignorant of the effects of such posturing. Trapped in a bureaucratic straitjacket, the board officials' demeanor was regarded by the men as both patronizing and hostile.

One other vital participant in this evolving national crisis was the Labour government. The government considered the strike as a threat to the economy and to its relationship with the trade union movement as a whole. It was plainly evident to the government that the strike could undermine its efforts to restore the competitiveness of the British economy because exports were the key in garnering badly needed foreign currency. In the immediate sense it was the threat to food rations that took initial priority. The food ration was by far the most important symbol of the country's financial stress. To offset shortages of meat, the government had taken the drastic step of introducing whalemeat, horsemeat, and snoek, a South African fish, into the ration.[23]

The strike then jeopardized the nation's meat supply. John Strachy, minister of food, took the lead in explaining to a nervous press that the situation was under control. At a June 16 press conference he stated, "The only facts I have ascertained at present are that no food is under any immediate danger of deterioration as a result of it [the strike], but we are watching the situation, of course."[24] Behind the scenes, though, apprehension was growing. It was expected that perishable cargoes would be under direct threat by June 21. The cabinet had established a special committee to oversee the government's response and actions. With George Issacs, the minister of labor, on a foreign trip attending an International Labor Organization conference, Ness Edwards, the parliamentary secretary for the Ministry of Labour, became a key player on the committee. On June 18, Edwards informed Prime Minister Clement Attlee of the threat to food supplies and the need to use troops to unload perishables: "The Ministry of Food have made clear that unless work is resumed not later than Monday morning [June 21] alternative labor will be necessary to move certain perishable food stuffs at present held up in the docks." To offset the danger, he said, "Arrangements have accordingly been made for alternative military labor to be made available on Monday morning."[25]

Events abroad gave the dock strike an added sense of urgency. The crisis over Germany that had been brewing throughout May and early June had deteriorated into the Berlin blockade by June 23. Cabinet meetings were then lively and troubled affairs during which both issues were simultaneously debated and decided upon. The Soviet blockade of Berlin added to fears that Communist expansionism was not confined to the European continent. Foreign Secretary Ernest Bevin was convinced that the Soviet Union was a "predatory expansionist power," and the dock strike merely confirmed his longstanding antipathy toward insurgent groups within the union movement, particularly in his beloved TGWU. The two events were seen as connected by sinister forces operating to disrupt Britain's economic strength and thereby its military preparedness.[26]

Just as problematic was the balance of payments crisis. The chancellor of the exchequer, Sir Stafford Cripps, explained to the June 17 cabinet meeting that Britain was facing the prospect of draining its monetary reserves. As Cripps pointed out, "the net drain for the first half 1948 would be over 250 million pounds. . . . This is far more than we could afford." In a nod in the direction of devaluing the pound, Cripps "warned that they would shortly have to consider what adjustments should be made to meet this situation."[27] The strike therefore threatened the loss of badly needed export earnings. So with both food shipments and export earnings endangered, the government was determined to end the strike, even if it meant using troops to unload cargoes.

To rationalize and focus the government's response to the strike, the cabinet formed a Cabinet Emergencies Committee. The committee was made up of Chuter Ede, home secretary; A. V. Alexander, minister of defense; John Strachey, minister of food; A. Woodburn, secretary of state for Scotland; and Sir Hartley Shawcross, attorney general. An assortment of parliamentary secretaries was also in attendance. The emergencies committee's first meeting was held at noon on June 21. The first order of business was the plan to move troops into the docks to unload perishable cargo. Three hundred servicemen and 150 trucks were standing by to unload "20,000 cases of eggs and some 350 tons of tomatoes." A further "200 tons of meat and fruit pulp" needed to be moved, "but the urgency was not quite so great" with this cargo because it was stowed in cold storage. John Strachey expressed his pessimism regarding the use of troops to unload all the cargo trapped in the port. He estimated that at least 15,000 men would be needed. Sir Frank Newsam, parliamentary secretary of the home office, reported that the three armed services "had not been able to offer more than 5,000 troops, together with 2,000 lorries [trucks] and drivers, and that seven days would be required to mobilize this force." A. V.

Alexander, the minister of defense, promised to look into it and work out "a program for the maximum utilization of Service labor."[28]

The issue of Communist involvement in the conflict was also discussed. Police investigation had found no evidence of direct Communist control, however. It was reported that "Scotland Yard was of the opinion that the strike was not being fomented by Communists, but there was some indication that the Communist Party was beginning to take an interest in it for political purposes."

The emergencies committee then discussed Arthur Deakin's intention to hold a meeting at the Albert Hall and convince the men to return to work. Although the committee "felt doubtful whether this meeting would be successful," it wanted at least to give the "Union . . . an opportunity to seek a settlement . . . and preserve their authority." So the dispatching of troops would be delayed "until it was quite clear that the Union could do nothing more." The final point of discussion was over the "legal aspects" of the strike. The conversation was "whether the ringleaders of the strike should be prosecuted." In a glaring admission, members of the emergencies committee had been waiting since the 1947 Glasgow dock strike to "take legal action . . . against the leaders of illegal strikes and the present case might be a suitable one on which to take action." Ness Edwards argued that there might be "some doubt" over prosecuting the "ringleaders" because the strike was not against an employer. That is, the strike was not "entirely . . . a trade dispute"; rather it was a strike "against the enforcement of dock labor regulations." Attorney General Shawcross agreed that he would "examine the legal points" of the conflict.

The discussion within the emergencies committee made clear the intention to battle the strike with every weapon available. Troops were already standing by and others would be recruited for the work of loading and unloading of cargo. The strategy included forming an alliance with the trade union officials, particularly Arthur Deakin. Support was to be given to Deakin, but if he was unsuccessful in his efforts to get the men back to work, then the government was prepared to go it alone. The decision to try to prosecute the "ringleaders" revealed government frustration with unofficial strikes that threatened a weakened economy.

The emergencies committee's report was presented to the full cabinet the following day, Tuesday, June 22. Other than considering the use of troops to unload perishable cargo, the topic of conversation centered around the precarious position of Arthur Deakin and his Albert Hall meeting, to be held that morning. Deakin had earlier refused an offer by the Unofficial Committee for an open-air meeting in Victoria Park. The Albert Hall meeting was therefore an attempt to bypass the power that the Unofficial Committee had in the open-air meetings. Deakin realized the meeting was potentially dangerous and wanted to provide something to the strikers so that they could "return to work . . . without loss of face." Ness Edwards argued in the meeting that Deakin should be given some assurance to forestall any "formation of a breakaway union." During the private notice question time later that day, Edwards suggested that if the "Union asked for a review of the operation of the disciplinary machinery, the Government would be prepared to assist in the matter."

The full cabinet was not as ready as Edwards to placate the strikers. Instead, cabinet members generally agreed that the government position continued to be that the strike was "unjustified." Further, the government "should hold out no hope of an enquiry into the operation of the disciplinary machinery." The cabinet did agree that once the strike had ended "it might be appropriate to examine the matter," but the strikers needed to be convinced that their actions would have little influence on the government. The cabinet found that the TGWU had a role to play in convincing its members that "unjustifiable strike action" would only "undermine the scheme," thus threatening the "benefits" of decasualization. The cabinet finished its meeting by resolving that the unloading of perishable cargo should begin on June 23, and that the three hundred servicemen already assigned should be supplemented with men and equipment "in order to enable the movement" of other cargo. The ministers of labor and transport were also "invited" to compile a report on any "improvements" required of the scheme and to suggest "what propaganda in favor of the scheme could be undertaken among the dockers with a view to reducing the risk of further dockers' strikes."[29]

The Albert Hall meeting was then key to gauging the feelings of the men and the ability of Deakin to control his restless docker membership. The situation was indeed volatile because the Unofficial Committee was just as determined to win the complete backing of the London dockers. Therefore it organized a meeting in Victoria Park, at the same time as the one in Albert Hall. The dockworkers would then have to decide who best represented their interests by publicly attending the meeting of their choice.

Before the Albert Hall meeting Deakin publicly spelled out his concerns that the dockers were being deceived. "I cannot allow the dockers to be misled and sacrificed," he said. Deakin explained that the strike was damaging an influential ally, namely, the Labour government: "A longer stoppage will put the Labour Government on a spot and this is what our political opponents want." Deakin also rejected a meeting proposed by the Unofficial Committee:

"I will not meet any unofficial body. I am going on with my properly-convened meeting."[30]

Deakin's stance struck a responsive chord with a sympathetic labor press. Editorials expressed impatience with the strikers and said there was a potential need for forceful government action to end the strike and "maintain" discipline. On the eve of the Albert Hall and Victoria Park meetings the *Daily Mirror* editorialized, "Today the country has a legitimate grievance against the dockers. . . . It is clear that, if necessary, the Government will have to move in and use all the country's resources to restore discipline at the docks and maintain it." On June 21, the *Daily Herald* proclaimed, "The urgent need this morning is for good sense and loyalty to be shown by all dockers as family men, as trade unionists, and as citizens of a nation fighting for its economic life."[31] Other popular newspapers were more outspoken. The *Hackney Gazette and North London Advertizer* goaded the strikers, shop stewards, and the government. In its June 23 editorial it argued it made little "sense" that a "small but determined body of shop stewards can have a greater influence over the rank and file workers than their own trade organization and official leaders." The dockers "must be compounded of very flabby material when they permit themselves to be molded like clay in the hands of the few, and do so without any hope of receiving strike pay." Finally, the paper accused the Labour government of "allow[ing] events to take their course, instead of mitigating the situation by the employment of troops."[32]

Despite Deakin's public posturing, he did agree to a secret meeting with a "small committee" from the Unofficial Committee. The "small committee" included Ted Dickens (treasurer), Charles Riddell (speaker's panel), John Cowley (press officer), and C. H. Saunders (sector representative). The committee argued that the NDLB officials were "too quick to fly to penalties and suspensions" and that the "union officials should stand up . . . on behalf of the men when confronted with such cases." Deakin responded by repeating his public pronouncements that the strike was hurting food shipments and that "opposition" forces were using the strike as "propaganda . . . to bring the government down." Deakin "hoped that the Victoria Park meeting would be canceled and that the committee would see the Albert Hall meeting was a full meeting." The committee agreed to discuss Deakin's proposals "with their colleagues" on the Unofficial Committee.[33]

The committee did not take seriously Deakin's fear of a government collapse because of the strike. Additionally, the committee was not impressed with Deakin's plea to return to work because he had offered no concrete suggestions as to what could be done with the penalties assessed Coe's gang or with any of the Dock Labour Scheme's disciplinary clauses. The strike leaders therefore continued with their plans to hold the Victoria Park meeting. They were determined to maintain control and the momentum of the strike. They were clearly confident that the men would follow their lead.

Much was riding on Deakin's Albert Hall meeting. For Deakin, it was his own standing within his union and the labor movement as a whole. Attlee's government was delaying sending in troops in the hope that Deakin could persuade the striking dockers to return to work. The meeting was, however, a personal disaster for Deakin. Only two thousand dockers attended, while a greater number were at the Victoria Park meeting organized by the Unofficial Committee. Journalists reported that the Victoria Park meeting was "much larger." The strike leaders promised to expand the strike to other ports, and the meeting supported such action. While Deakin obtained a vote of confidence from those attending the Albert Hall meeting, the damage to his credibility was profound.[34] A Ministry of Labour official described Deakin as having "taken a nasty knock over the business and we cannot exclude a breakaway union from the possible consequences of the strike."[35]

The suggestion that the TGWU was facing the prospect of a "breakaway union" perhaps was made in the heat of the moment, but the Unofficial Committee had certainly made its presence felt. Why the men had willingly joined the committee in rejecting the TGWU's official leaders can be explained by a number of factors. Many strikers resented Deakin's decision to hold his meeting at the Albert Hall. The venue was an alien location because Victoria Park was the traditional setting for open-air meetings. Some dockers suspected that the Albert Hall was a site where the officials would fix the meeting.[36]

Just as damaging to the TGWU was the decision by the port's eighteen hundred lightermen to join the strike. Eighty lightermen had refused to work prior to the Albert Hall meeting, but following Deakin's fiasco, the remaining lightermen joined the strike. Lightermen officials had endorsed the sympathetic strike action in an attempt to maintain control over their members. They also sought a meeting with Prime Minister Attlee to discuss the strikers' cause but Attlee rejected their overture.[37]

Now all of London's dockworkers were out on strike. What had begun as a local dispute had been transformed into a battle between an angry rank and file and union officials. Making the situation even more volatile, the government was mired in the conflict. Hoping to maintain trade relations and reinforce its union allies, the government was headed for a direct confrontation with a shadowy organization and an angry strike force of over nineteen thousand men. The close alliance of the TGWU and the Labour government had made the union leaders' motives suspect. More important was the relationship of the union with the Dock Labour Scheme. The National and London

Dock Labour Boards had become disciplinary entities wherein the union delegates ended up chastising their members for poor work habits. It was no wonder that the membership perceived their mid- and upper-level union representatives as sympathetic to employers and board officials.

The catalyst for the strike was resentment aimed at the Dock Labour Scheme, and more particularly, at the respective Dock Labour Boards' disciplinary powers. But nurturing this resentment was the tactical decision by London dockworkers to confront such power. Entrenched in dockworker subculture was the dockers' need to stand together against a common foe. Such an attitude was formed during the years when dockwork was predominately casual. Being hired from day to day created in the dockers a collective sense of responsibility to one another. Dependency created in turn solidarity. If conditions threatened one gang or on one specific dock, the entire work force recognized that it was an issue for all. Thus the call "one out, all out" became the watchword for the dockers as a whole. This condition was acknowledged by the 1951 government inquiry into the "unofficial stoppages in the London docks." As was pointed out, "the strong tradition of solidarity" was "an important part of the explanation of unrest in the docks in recent years." If dockers refused the call to walk out they faced "ostracism from their mates" and "their wives and families will be made to suffer in their social contacts if they take a stand against unofficial strike action."[38]

For Joe Bloomberg, the "strong tradition of solidarity" was a pragmatic response: "on our own we'll get beat. . . . [Once we've] joined forces we're strong." But there was another factor that made the 1948 struggle unique: the war years had transformed the opinions of many dockers. As Bloomberg explained, the "generation after the war [were a] new breed, they had their own thoughts [of] what was right or wrong." Dockers were no longer just going to take it. As Bloomberg pointed out, "People were changing, views were changing." This sentiment was shared by George Pye, a stevedore. According to Pye, "A lot of the older stevedores and dockers were set in their ways. . . . The younger ones [who] had been shot at, shit on . . . would say 'hang on, we're not accepting this' because expectations were different."[39]

Such an outlook, mixed with resentment toward union officials and the Dock Labour Boards, fueled the dockers' anger and made it more likely that conflict would occur. Thus while union officials were distancing themselves from the day-to-day concerns of their members, the "unofficial guys were putting forth the members' views."[40]

The Unofficial Committee continued to be the recognized voice of the striking dockers. The committee demanded that the labor board punishment be rescinded and called for a union inquiry of the Dock Labour Scheme. It held daily open-air meetings to keep the members abreast of recent events. The committee also dispatched a group of shop stewards to the House of Commons where they demanded to meet their East End members of Parliament. Walter Edwards, the Labour M.P. for Whitechapel, after first refusing to meet the delegation, informed them to "go back to work and use the constitutional machinery [of the union]."[41] The dockers also attempted to gain a meeting with the minister of labor and Prime Minister Attlee, but they were rejected outright.

The hard line of the government to ignore entreaties by the Unofficial Committee was solidified when troops entered the London docks on June 23. The *Daily Herald* reported on June 24: "About 300 Guardsmen wearing denim overalls arrived in lorries and were escorted into the docks by police on motor-cycles."[42] Helping the government's (and the TGWU's) cause was the desertion of two members from the Unofficial Committee, Frank Palmer and John Duhigg. Palmer insisted that the committee was dominated by Communists. The desertion and accompanying red-scare accusations placed the committee on the defensive. The committee issued a statement that "we are entirely non-political," but Pat Coleman, a known Communist, was forced to step down as chairman.[43]

Such a dramatic gesture was an effort to temper increasing charges of left-wing manipulation within the committee. Both Deakin and the cabinet had done much to foster the idea of Communist involvement with and direction of the strike. Indeed, national TGWU officials had encouraged Frank Palmer to bolt from the committee. Deakin had "arranged" for a meeting between Thomas W. Condon, docks group secretary, and Frank Palmer and John Duhigg to "take a statement from them" regarding "communist influence on [the] Strike Committee." The statement was then released to the press. The accusations of Communist involvement built upon a continuing campaign to smear the strike leaders. Encouraged by both Deakin and cabinet members, the *Daily Mirror* had earlier eagerly charged that the strike leaders were politically motivated. A June 23 report argued that sinister forces lay behind the Unofficial Committee's actions: "Cabinet Ministers and members of the T.U.C. General Council believe that the London dock strike has become part of a political campaign intended to destroy solid trade union support for the Government."[44]

Deakin's strategy of smearing the committee was an attempt to divert criticism that he had lost control of his members. By fostering the idea that the membership was being duped by outside forces, he hoped to avoid blame for his loss of control. Additionally, his anti-Communist posturing cleared the path to ask for government support. When troops were dispatched to the docks, they would be seen not as strikebreaking forces but rather as liberators for the national interest. For the government, raising the Communist issue could also better assuage criticism of its earlier decision to hold off using troops until Deakin could convince the dockers to return to work. Once Deakin raised the issue of Communist involvement, the government could go ahead with its plans to use the armed services.

The suggestion of Communist control or influence was moot. The government had learned early in the strike that its effect was minimal. The accusation that Communist agents were fomenting trouble on the docks came first from Anthony Nutting, a Tory M.P. Nutting informed Anthony Eden that he had received a phone call from an unidentified "Mr. X" within the Communist Party hierarchy. "Mr. X" claimed that the Communist Party was determined to "spearhead . . . the fight against the Marshall Plan" by agitating along the London waterfront. The informant declared further that at a June 22 meeting of "Communist Trade Union functionaries who included representatives of the Transport and General Workers' Union, . . . it was agreed that every step should be taken to prolong the Dock strike." "Mr. X" charged that "at the same time" the meeting was ordered "to create the utmost disaffection amongst . . . the Transport and General Workers' Union." Eden handed over the information to Attlee on June 24. After prodding by Tories, the Home Office in turn engaged in an investigation. Subsequently, the Home Office discovered no evidence of a conspiracy to disrupt Marshall Plan shipments or the TGWU. In a report to Attlee, the Home Office explained, "Extensive enquiries have been made by the police but nothing has been found to support the . . . theory that the strike was part of a Cominform inspired campaign against the European recovery program" and the TGWU.[45]

Official Communist Party policy would suggest that the Home Office report was correct. Under the leadership of Harry Pollitt, the Communist Party of Great Britain (CPGB) had actively supported the government's nationalization policy. Following the 1945 electoral triumph of the Labour Party and the growth of Britain's debt to the United States, the CPGB aligned itself with government's attempts to increase productivity and thereby exports. For the CPGB, the new policy of efficiency and productivity was to wean the British economy away from the grip of American financial institutions. In sum, the CPGB wanted to help create a more vibrant British economy that could steer Britain toward its ultimate conversion to Communism. In 1947, however, the establishment of the Cominform entailed a change of policy whereby the Labour government was no longer seen as an ally. But as the police report makes clear, the CPGB had not aggressively supported the strike. Rank-and-file Communists had no such restraints. Their allegiance was to the membership; not for the first time did they follow their own path. The CPGB leadership was therefore torn by the strike. It had traditionally supported rank-and-file movements in the trade union movement, but it did not vigorously encourage strikes that posed a threat to the greater economy. As one historian has argued, the policy was to "operate as enthusiastic union loyalists eager to support the new government."[46]

Like the police force, cabinet members were also unconvinced of a Communist threat posed by the strike. Nonetheless, they were determined not to give way to the strikers' demands. Foreign Secretary Ernest Bevin held a particularly hard line. Bevin had been the dockers' leader throughout the confrontations in the 1920s, but his policy in 1948 was not to budge an inch. In a June 24 cabinet meeting he argued "that there must be no sign of weakness on the part of the Government." For Bevin, "whether the strike continued for one week or five, no concessions should be made by the Government." To show the government's determination Bevin even suggested "to move in further troops by degrees over the week-end." The point for Bevin was to stop forcefully the phenomenon of wildcat strikes; failure would mean the "Government would be at the mercy of unofficial strikes for many years to come."[47]

For all the behind-the-scenes maneuvering by the cabinet and Deakin, it was the Unofficial Committee that had regained the initiative. Although stung by Palmer's desertion and by continuing accusations of Communist agitation within the strike leadership, the Unofficial Committee attempted to maintain the momentum of its fight. It decided to raise the stakes of the conflict by spreading it to other ports in the country. The Unofficial Committee hoped that expanding the struggle to the nation's ports would force the hand of the TGWU and the government. With a complete breakdown in shipments, the government would be compelled to promise to reexamine the Dock Labour Scheme and overturn the appeal tribunal's punishment of Coe's gang.

The strike leadership's plan to extend the strike to other ports did not come as a surprise to the NDLB, the TGWU, or the government. As early as June 18 (the day the strike spread throughout London), the NDLB issued a circular to local boards throughout the country warning of the possible spread of the strike to their ports. The circular insisted that "efforts are being made by the Strike Leaders to secure support of dock workers in other ports." Local managers were ordered to "report any local activity in this direction." The TGWU also warned its dock officials of impending trouble: "All ports were 'phoned and put on guard, and asked to keep a strict watch on position and report any developments."[48]

The three principal ports that concerned the TGWU and the government were Liverpool, Southampton, and Glasgow. These ports were the largest after London. The government was optimistic that Glasgow would not be embroiled in the conflict, however. This was largely because of the split of Scottish dockers from the TGWU. The subsequent formation of the Scottish Transport and General Workers' Union (STGWU) had solidified the separation. The Ministry of Labour had learned that "a representative for the Unofficial Committee . . . was proceeding to Glasgow" on June 24, but government officials were not unduly worried. Michael Byrne, general secretary of the STGWU, had reported that he regarded the "London representative with disfavor and intends to exercise strong influence among his members" to steer clear "from active participation in the dispute."[49]

At Southampton, known officially as Area 2, the situation was not so calm. An area meeting had taken place earlier to discuss the London dispute. The meeting was split between those who wanted to take sympathetic strike action and those who wanted to remain clear from the conflict. Those attending the meeting did agree that the Area 2 men would refuse to handle any shipments diverted to Southampton but would show support for the London strikers with "contributions." Although the meeting ended on a cautious note, the Area 2 officers were obviously split on how to proceed. The arrival of Ted Cowley and Ted Dickens, members of the speakers panel for the Unofficial Committee, added to the volatility of the situation. Cowley was invited to address members on June 25, in an open-air meeting on "The Mead." Trevor Stallard, an Area 2 officer, chaired the meeting. Cowley began his speech by giving a brief history of the dispute. To dispel any notion that the London committee was connected to the Communist Party, Cowley clearly stated, "We are not connected with any political body." His main point was that the London strikers were in the vanguard in fighting the disciplinary sections of the Dock Labour Scheme. Cowley charged that the disciplining of Coe's gang was just a "first step" in harnessing dockers throughout the country, and "if they [NDLB] get away with it in London no other port has got a chance." Cowley was careful not to ask directly for supportive strike action. As he pointed out, "I am not here to ask you men what you are going to do about it, I am here to tell you what the London dockers think about it." Cowley finished his address by stating that the London battle was for all dockers: "I say in conclusion that if the London men never took up this challenge our conditions would be in danger." Stallard then took over the meeting by asking the dockers "if they were prepared" to take strike action. The men wanted to have another meeting to discuss the issue. John Bonnin, a local branch member, put forward a resolution for a meeting to be held on the following Monday, June 28. The resolution was passed.[50]

The Southampton men had decided to hold off from a strike decision. The presence of Trevor Stallard as chair of the meeting did not bode well for the TGWU officials. Even R. Chicks, the Area 2 secretary, was initially reluctant to attack the meeting and Stallard's role. Not until three weeks after the end of the strike did Chicks provide Deakin with a report of the meeting. Trying to divert attention from his inaction, Chicks did report that Peter Bonnin was "an active member of the C.P." Although Stallard had stated in the meeting that the only "fair" reporting of the strike came from the *Daily Worker,* Chicks did not identify him as a Communist. The decision by the attendees at the meeting to delay taking action had merely postponed their participation in the strike. Deakin ordered Arthur Bird, national dock group secretary of the TGWU, to Southampton "to cover" the situation.[51]

Although Glasgow and Southampton had been given a breathing space, Liverpool remained an area of acute concern to TGWU and government officials. Liverpool was Britain's second largest port and therefore of strategic importance in terms of effects on the economy. For that reason the London strikers recognized its critical significance. The Unofficial Committee dispatched Harry Constable (a member of the speakers panel) and Bert Saunders to Liverpool on June 26. Constable addressed a meeting the next day. He outlined the desperate financial condition of the strikers and called on the Liverpool dockers, saying, "We want help and we want it bad. We are on the floor. This week it's the pawnshop for us, and the pawnshop next week and the week after."[52]

The battle for the wholehearted support of the Liverpool men was joined by high TGWU officials. Ted Birkett, national secretary of the Waterways Group, traveled to Merseyside and met with the Liverpool and Birkenhead District Committee on June 27. Birkett outlined the course of events and explained that Deakin had called a meeting at Victoria Park that same day. Birkett announced that Deakin was confident that he could convince the men to return to work by agreeing to investigate the Dock Labour Scheme. With such an assurance, the Liverpool and Birkenhead District Committee passed a resolution calling on their members to remain on the job.[53]

Deakin's address to three thousand strikers at Victoria Park was not successful, however. It was his last-gasp attempt to get the men back to work. Deakin stated, "I say the time has come to call it a day and to get back to work tomorrow." Once Deakin had finished, A. E. Tiffin, assistant general secretary of the TGWU, called for a vote to return to work. According to a *Daily Mirror* reporter, while a large number of men voted yes, when those who opposed raised their union books "it seemed apparent that the majority voted against the resolution." Tiffin, however, believed otherwise and stated that the resolution had passed. "Instantly, there was a great roar of 'No' from the crowd." Elements from the crowd charged the platform yelling, "Carve up," and "The ruddy thing's rigged." As a ruffled Deakin prepared to leave by car, an angry docker called on the crowd to overturn the vehicle. The meeting collapsed in disarray, leaving once again a humiliated Deakin and an angry rank and file. A *Times* (London) reporter made clear Deakin's predicament: "the union leaders, however unwittingly, have done themselves much harm by allowing ill-feeling on the voting to persist. . . . As it was the meeting achieved little, except probably to strengthen the hands of the unofficial committee, which was refused a hearing."[54]

Further bad news followed. Once again, officials had misjudged the temper of their men because starting on Monday morning, June 28, the majority of Liverpool and Birkenhead dockers refused to work. By the end of the day the Liverpool docks were virtually silent.[55]

Deakin and his cohorts had lost a series of vital battles with the Unofficial Committee. Each time Deakin personally tried to convince the men to return, he publicly failed. The Albert Hall and Victoria Park meetings left Deakin lost in acrimony. The Unofficial Committee had become the clear leader of London dockworkers. Its leadership of dockers, stevedores, and lightermen made it a potent body. By capturing the loyalty, however tenuous, of the rank and file, the Unofficial Committee had become a force to be reckoned with. Because of the committee's newfound power, the Labour government looked for a way to at least neutralize it.

Once the strike had spread to Liverpool, the Attlee government decided on draconian action. Propelling the government were direct threats to food shipments and therefore the nation's ration. A Ministry of Food circular declared on June 24, nine days after the strike became citywide, that a "substantial temporary reduction in the issue of carcass meat is unavoidable." By June 28, sixty "food ships" were affected in London, "carrying 86,000 tons of cereals and flour, 10,000 tons of meat and bacon, 1,000 tons of butter and cheese, and 78,000 tons of other foods, mainly sugar." With the Liverpool men joining the strike, further food shipments were affected, including twenty ships carrying "85,000 tons of food, mainly cereals and sugar." The Ministry of Food estimated that "some failure of sugar distribution" would occur by July 11. Flour distribution was also reported to be jeopardized. In addition to meat supplies, the Ministry of Food reported that by July 18 it might "not be possible to meet the sugar and bread ration."[56]

The troops working on the London docks had therefore made little impact in unloading the trapped foodstuffs. Since June 21, a small detachment of Coldstream Guards had been dispatched to the Popular Docks to unload perishable goods. By June 28, approximately nine hundred troops were working along the London waterfront, and by June 29 the number would increase to nineteen hundred. Such action was merely a short-term solution. The cabinet was informed on June 28 that "there would be difficulty in maintaining the sugar ration after about a week and in about fourteen days there would be serious shortages of bread, bacon, cheese and butter."[57] Consequently, the Attlee government decided to proclaim a state of emergency. Not since the 1926 general strike had a state of emergency been declared.[58]

Ness Edwards, the parliamentary secretary for the minister of labor, had drawn up the plan to proclaim the state of emergency. Deakin's debacle at Victoria Park and the spread of the strike to Liverpool had spurred the call for action under the Emergency Powers Act. Edwards's plan was contained in a memorandum that outlined why the state of emergency was necessary. First, there could never be enough troops to ensure the loading and unloading of cargo. Second, the NDLB argued that for it to request extra labor would alienate labor members of the board and "would only serve to embitter the situation." The only practical alternative was for the government to call on volunteers to work the trapped cargoes. An order to do that would necessitate suspending the Dock Labour Scheme. Edwards argued that this would "forcibly" inform the strikers of "losing its [the scheme's] advantages." Additionally, the proclamation would place the government "on the offensive against the unofficial strikers." As for recruiting "volunteer labor," the government could postpone such a call, but in the "meantime the employers will automatically be free to take any steps they like." Edwards met with Attlee on the morning of June 28 to discuss the plan.[59]

The full cabinet met the same day to discuss the spreading strike and Edwards's plan. The idea of suspending the scheme was not accepted. It was argued that such an action would not address the strike in Liverpool (it was reported that trouble was also brewing in Glasgow and Southampton). Also, there was "no evidence" that employers could recruit the required number of workers to work the trapped ships. Additionally, such a suspension might give a "victory for those who were exploiting the strike." The cabinet did support the idea of proclaiming a state of emergency, however. Such a proclamation could be assigned to other ports such as Liverpool. It would enable the armed services to requisition buildings along the docks to accommodate troops. The proclamation would also allow a call for volunteers and provide necessary protection and would make possible the banning of sympathetic strike action by other workers. The proclamation would also provide flexibility in cases of violent resistance by strikers or sabotage. As for the calling of volunteers, "there was general agreement that this should not be done for the present."

It was also agreed that "the Government's intentions" should be announced in the House of Commons later in the day, and that Attlee should make a radio appeal that night to the strikers to return to work.[60]

At 9:00 p.m. Attlee made his dramatic BBC radio address. He stated, "The government cannot in any way recognize or deal with those who are leading the unofficial strike. . . . This is not a strike against capitalists or employers. It is a strike against your mates; a strike against the housewife; a strike against the ordinary common people." Attlee charged that the disciplinary action against Coe's gang was "a little thing" that still could be addressed by the National Dock Labour Board. Using the common theme of Communist subversion, Attlee rhetorically asked, "Who advised you to do this [strike] . . . but just a small nucleus who have been instructed for political reasons to take advantage of every little disturbance that takes place, to cause the disruption of the British economy, British trade, to undermine the Government, and to destroy Britain's position." He called on the dockers to use the "constitutional machinery" of their union to challenge or reform the Dock Labour Scheme. Attlee then highlighted the beneficial aspects of the scheme, arguing that nowhere else in the world were men guaranteed money just to turn up for work. Dockers should therefore be grateful. He told them, "Your clear duty to yourselves, to your fellow citizens, and to your country is to return to work."[61]

Following the address and the emergency proclamation, the Unofficial Committee realized the strike could not continue. Taking on the combined weight of the government was seen as pointless. In addition, Deakin's June 27 Victoria Park meeting had been a close call, and the Southampton men had voted not to strike. Realizing that the strike could not continue, the Unofficial Committee called a meeting for June 29 at Victoria Park. It had been arranged that after a few speeches a resolution for a return to work would be made. One of the speakers, Stephen Smith, "dodged his brief" and attacked Attlee and his proclamation. The crowd grew increasingly restless but Smith continued only to be "howled down . . . none too gracefully, from the platform." The resolution was then read: "In view of the complete line up of reactionary forces against us and considering the complacent attitude of the responsible parties—that is, the employers, the higher trade union officials and the government—we, the strike committee, are recommending all men back to work tomorrow." The resolution was overwhelmingly passed by a show of hands, and the London and Liverpool men went back to work en masse the next day.[62]

A mountain of cargo awaited the returning London strikers. The men were confident they would soon move the accumulated goods. One docker exclaimed, "We'll eat this lot. We'll shift it in a couple of days." Fueling such confidence was the prospect of plenty of overtime to grease the way. As one dock manager explained, "They're working like beavers." Another employer was not so sanguine. Angry that the men were working abundant overtime, one employer caustically remarked, "The London docker can expect that the result of his strike will be a special bonus of from 10 pounds to 20 pounds, and the gratitude of the Press for his patriotism in working at week-ends to repair the national damage he has caused."[63] For some London dockworkers the strike had ended on their terms, or they pointed to a more aggressive assertion of newfound power. As one dockworker said, "We were just ready to go back to work, mate." Others regarded the strike as having an activating effect: "They'll be more men at the branch meetings in future. We learned we'd got to use Deakin's precious 'constitutional machinery.' Well, now we'll use it, and from now on some of the local officials had better watch out."[64]

The stevedores and lightermen also voted to return to work. But the men displayed no hostility toward their officials. Edward Thomas, secretary of the Lightermen's Union, had maintained close links with the Unofficial Committee throughout the strike. John Brooks had been the lightermen's representative on the committee. On two occasions during the strike, Thomas had been "congratulated and thanked for postponing official Union meetings to suit the convenience of the Strike Committee." Thomas also attended the meeting where it was voted to return to work. Immediately following the vote, Thomas "took over the microphone" and addressed the meeting. He declared, "The unofficial meeting is now over and the Strike Committee will take a short holiday." Thomas's remark concerning the "short holiday" was reported by a conciliation officer for the Industrial Relations Department, Ministry of Labour, to be "an ominous note if taken seriously." Thomas then informed the men to return to work the following morning. Dickie Barrett, general secretary of the Stevedores Union, had also supported the dockers in their fight. Unlike Thomas, Barrett played the role of reluctant strike supporter. He had used the decision to strike made by the TGWU clerks to bring his men out also. Although directing the men not to work, he avoided any public pronouncements during the conflict. For this he got the grudging respect by the same conciliation officer: "[Barrett] astutely played for safety and managed to avoid public appreciation of his tight-rope display."[65]

The strike had been an enormous black eye for the TGWU leadership and the Labour government. The government's decision to invoke the Emergency Powers Act was a desperate move. It revealed its lack of control over erstwhile allies. To bolster Deakin's standing the government had delayed using troops to unload ships. Just as critical, once the food ration became directly threatened only dramatic action could ensure an end to the crisis. Although it appeared that most of the trade union movement supported the government's action, it nonetheless left a sour taste. The Labour government had used a weapon that the labor movement had associated with the reactionary Conservative forces of the 1920s. William Gallagher, a Communist M.P., tried to draw out the irony of the situation in the House of Commons on June 29. He reminded Foreign Secretary Ernest Bevin he had been the dockers' leader when the Conservative government used the Emergency Powers Act in 1924 to break a dock strike.[66]

The government was pressured to investigate the unofficial action but remained aloof from the idea. The cabinet felt "it would be inexpedient to hold any formal inquiry into the causes of the strike," but it did agree to look into the workings of the Dock Labour Scheme. Ernest Bevin was given the responsibility to undertake the investigation. Another tack taken by the government was to inquire whether specific working conditions had contributed to the dockworker's "discontent." The government asked the NDLB to investigate dockland canteens and bathroom facilities. George Alfred Isaacs, the minister of labor, asked the NDLB chair, Lord Ammon, to undertake personally such an investigation. Isaacs argued that there was a direct connection between the "lack of amenities" and the "discontent resulting in unofficial strikes." Thus if the NDLB was seen as actively addressing the matter it might "tend to allay discontent."[67]

For the TGWU, the strike highlighted its loss of control over the rank and file. Its adoption of an accommodationist stance with both the Dock Labour Scheme and the Labour government left it ill-prepared for a sustained challenge from an organized membership. The TGWU did embark on an internal inquiry to investigate the members of the Unofficial Committee in the hope of disciplining them. Such a tactic failed, and once again the strike leaders took the offensive. The Unofficial Committee welcomed the inquiry; indeed, they expressed frustration that it was taking so long. As they stated in a pamphlet, *Reflections on the Strike,* "We await with limited patience the calling together of such bodies to enquire into the original dispute."[68]

The TGWU created a special committee to investigate the strike and the members of the Unofficial Committee. The new committee reported that seventeen men were "in breach of the rules and the constitution of the Union." Additionally, it "viewed with grave concern the visit of four members of the Unofficial Strike Committee to other ports." The criticisms of TGWU officials by the Unofficial Committee were "not sustained." It would appear that the TGWU could have easily suspended or ejected the seventeen from the union.

But after members of the Unofficial Committee gave "an assurance" that it was no "longer in existence," the special committee recommended "that no action of a disciplinary character be taken against the Members."[69]

This lack of forceful action cannot be explained by the "assurance" that the Unofficial Committee had been disbanded, however. Prior to the inquiry, the TGWU was bombarded with complaints against the Dock Labour Scheme's disciplinary clauses. From Hull came a July 5 resolution that the clauses "should be totally eliminated from the Scheme." This resolution echoed those from Bristol and Manchester.[70] Other port committees were angry that employers escaped censure under the scheme. Officials of Area No. 12 (Liverpool) complained that "there is no clause in the Paper [scheme] which allows men to report an employer." Many of the branches felt that there was an inordinate number of docker dismissals due to the scheme: "There is a strong feeling that far too many men are being dismissed for a variety of reasons and it is suggested that all clauses relating to dismissal should be deleted." Grimsby officials echoed their Liverpool counterparts: "Considerable criticism was leveled at the disciplinary clauses applying to employers. It was considered that at present it is far too difficult, and in some cases impossible, to take action against employers who are in breach of the Scheme." It was left to the Dundee Committee to equate the general unhappiness with the disciplinary clauses and the actions of the strike leaders. In a July 9 resolution the committee stated, "No disciplinary action should be taken against men involved, until full investigations have been made by every recognized Committee or Authority" within the TGWU.[71]

The point had been made: the country's dockworkers were angry and frustrated with the scheme. The London strike leaders' actions were therefore supported by other dockers and their officials. The strike leaders were seen merely as reflecting their members' interests and should not therefore be disciplined. So the report of the special committee was colored by an outpouring of resentment. TGWU officials realized that an open attack on the leaders would create a storm of criticism.

The TGWU was also faced with the judgment against Coe's gang. Deakin had publicly promised a further look at the case. Although the fourteen-day suspension still stood, the controversy continued about when the suspension should take place. The issue was not a trivial one. The union was forced to argue that the period of the strike should be incorporated into the suspension term. The NDLB and employers were upset with the idea of factoring in strike days with the suspension. The NDLB had tried to use its counsel, Sir Cyril Langham, to guide its resistance to the union's argument. In a string of meetings both sides jockeyed for position. Deakin became somewhat exasperated by the drawn-out proceedings by arguing that "he had not desired to seek a legal solution to the problem, but rather to approach it from a 'common-sense angle.'" Tipping the scales for the union side was Langham's finding that the original suspension date of the Appeals Tribunal of June 20–26 should stand.[72] In effect, the men would not lose any days because of the correlation of the suspension with the strike.

The NDLB met on July 13 and accepted the finding, in turn recommending that the LDLB do the same. Privately, Lord Ammon was particularly upset with the decision. In a note to his NDLB confederate, Stephen Parkin, Ammon declared: "I give it up. . . . A dreadful warning to some of us who are getting on in years." Some employers outside of London had seen the decision coming. C. L. Bennett, a partner in Bristol City Line of Steamers and a management member of the local Dock Labor Board, charged that if a decision was handed down to give the men what they wanted, "then I for one would much prefer not to be associated with the Board in the way that I am at present." For Bennett, the fault lay in the hands of TGWU officials. As he said, "The Officials of the Unions must take control and not be subject to the 'big stick' which is wielded by any unofficial body within the Union."[73]

There were bitter feelings all around. Employers felt that the strike was unnecessary and that the machinery of the Dock Labour Scheme had been undermined. The NDLB's decision to include the strike days in the suspension punishment for Coe's gang had alienated some employers, so much so that they threatened to boycott future local boards. The TGWU was perceived by the rank and file as being hopelessly out of touch with the members' wishes and concerns. By tying themselves to the disciplinary clauses of the Dock Labour Scheme and the Labour government, their motives and allegiance had become suspect. For their part, the TGWU and the Labour government regarded the Unofficial Committee as wreckers. The Unofficial Committee had refused to follow constitutional methods, instead encouraging dockworkers throughout London (and elsewhere) to challenge directly the TGWU leadership. Significantly, the Labour government was also distressed by the actions of the Unofficial Committee. Government officials regarded these actions and those of the striking dockworkers as damaging not just to the British economy, but to their special relationship with the labor movement generally. With a nation surviving on food rations and a balance-of-payments crisis, the strike was seen as politically inspired and as nothing more than an attempt to damage the weakened economy and provide fodder for critics of the government's nationalization policies.

The life of the Unofficial Committee had not come to an end, however. In the following six years, strikes were led by the group over such issues as the firing of older men, sympathetic action with Canadian seamen, union expulsion of three members of the committee, police arrests of strike leaders, and overtime. The group would remain a dynamic presence along the London docks, confronting the established union officials and putting forth the dockworkers' case.

Notes

1. Kevin Jefferys, *The Attlee Governments, 1945–1951* (New York: Longman, 1993), 42–46; Ina Zweiniger-Bargielowska, *Austerity in Britain: Rationing, Controls, and Consumption, 1939–1955* (New York: Oxford University Press, 2000), 99–150, 151–202; Leo Panitch, *Social Democracy and Industrial Militancy: The Labor Party, the Trade Unions and Incomes Policy, 1945–1974* (New York: Cambridge University Press, 1976).

2. "Schedule: Dock Workers (Regulation of Employment) Scheme 1947, Arrangement of Clauses," 7, LAB 8/2162.

3. "Complaints Received and Disciplinary Action Taken under Clause 16 (2) of the Scheme—12 months ended 26th June, 1948," National Dock Labour Board Meeting, July 13, 1948, BK 5/2, Minutes of the NDLB, PRO; "Annual Review, NDLB, 1948–49," BK 2/1218, PRO.

4.Joe Bloomberg, interview by author, August 5, 1996.

5. Minutes and Record of Special Meeting of Docks Group Committee, June 14, 1948, Transport and General Workers' Union—MSS 126/TG/3, Sack 30/31, Modern Records Center, University of Warwick (hereafter MRC); "LDLB—Appeal Tribunals, Re-Hearing, Case No. 404," June 17, 1948, NDLB, BK 2/72, Discipline, PRO.

6. Minutes of the London Dock Labour Board, June 9, 1948, LDLB, BK 2/269, PRO.

7. Minutes and Record of Special Meeting of Docks Group Committee, June 14, 1948; Report of J. H. Withal, June 14, 1948, LAB 10/783, 1948 Strike, PRO.

8. Memorandum: London Dock Strike, June 1948, Appendix A, NDLB, BK 2/72, Strike, PRO.

9. Minutes and Record of Special Meeting of Docks Group Committee, June 14, 1948.

10. Memorandum: London Dock Strike, June 1948, Appendix A.

11. "Strike in the Port of London over disciplinary action by the Dock Labour Board," June 23, 1948, W. J. Tull, Regional Industrial Relations Officer, Ministry of Labour, LAB 10/783, 1948 Strike, PRO; "LDLB—Appeal Tribunals, Re-Hearing, Case No. 404," June 17, 1948, NDLB, BK 2/72, Discipline, PRO.

12. Letter to Lord Ammon, Chair, NDLB, from Mr. Saunders, June 17, 1948, NDLB, BK 2/72, Strike, PRO.

13. Memorandum, Dock Strike—June 1948: Men on Strike and Ships Affected, June 30, 1948, NDLB, BK 2/72, Strike, PRO.

14. Memorandum, Strike in Port of London over Disciplinary Action by the Dock Labour Board, Industrial Relations Department, Ministry of Labour, 23 June, 1948, LAB 10/783, 1948 Strike.

15. Report of the Area No. 1 Secretary to the General Executive Council's Committee of Inquiry into the Unofficial London Dock Strike, TGWU, Transport and General Workers' Union, MSS 126/TG/3, Sack 30/31, MRC; "Confidential Report to A. E. Stillwell,

Minister of Labour and National Service, from L. J. Hull, Regional Industrial Relations Officer," June 23, 1948, LAB/10/783, 1948 Strike, PRO.

16. Joe Bloomberg, interview by author, August 8, 1996; "Confidential Report to A. E. Stillwell."

17. Secret Memorandum—Personnel of "No Name Organization," undated, LAB/10/783, 1948 Strike, PRO; Minutes of Local Board—London, April 27, 1948, LDLB, BK 2–269, PRO; "Sectional Committee Meeting (London)," May 24, 1948, MSS.360/13/01/24, National Museum of Labor History, Manchester.

18. Minutes of the Special Meeting of Docks Group Committee, June 19, 1948, LAB/10/783, 1948 Strike, PRO.

19. "Confidential Report to A. E. Stillwell." In a Ministry of Labour report to Stillwell it was claimed that Harvey "would like to forget this visit now." Ibid.

20. Ibid.; Memorandum, Dock Strike—June 1948: Men on Strike and Ships Affected, June 1948, BK 72, NDLB, PRO (quote); memorandum to Mr. Tennant from Ness Edwards, June 20, 1948, LAB/10/783, 1948 Strike, PRO.

21. Minutes and Record of Special Meeting of Docks Group Committee, June 19, 1948, Transport and General Workers' Union, MSS 126/TG/3, Sack 30/31, MRC.

22. Ibid. The avoidance of giving free air time to the Unofficial Committee was based on the experience of unofficial strikes in 1945: "A definite decision was taken by the previous Board of Governors on this matter in special relation to unofficial strikes in 1945 and the present Board of Governors maintains the same view." Letter, "Dear Mr. Deakin from Simon of Wythenshawe, Director General, BBC," June 28, 1948, ibid.

23. The snoek fish was almost universally hated by the British public. Paul Addison, *Now the War Is Over: A Social History of Britain, 1945–51* (1985; reprint, New York: St. Martin's, 1993), 38–39; Zweiniger-Bargielowska, *Austerity in Britain,* 229.

24. "Press Conference, June 16, 1948," Ministry of Food Press Conferences, MAF 102/133, PRO.

25. Memorandum to Clement Attlee, Prime Minister, from Ness Edwards, Parliamentary Secretary, Ministry of Labour, June 18, 1948, Prime Minister's Correspondence, PREM 8/1086, PRO.

26. Peter Weiler, *Ernest Bevin* (New York: St. Martin's, 1993), 183; "Cabinet Conclusions," June 23, 1948, June 24, 1948, CAB 128/13.

27. Minutes of Cabinet Meeting, June 17, 1948, CAB 128/12 (quotes); James E. Cronin, *The Politics of State Expansion: War, State, and Society in Twentieth-Century Britain* (New York: Routledge, 1991), 161–71.

28. Minutes of the Cabinet Emergencies Committee, June 21, 1948, CAB 134/175, PRO. All quotations in this and the next four paragraphs are from this source.

29. "Labor Cabinet Meeting, 10 Downing Street," Cabinet Conclusions, CAB 128/31, PRO.

30. *Daily Mirror,* June 21, 1948, 1, 8; ibid., June 22, 1948, 1.

31. *Daily Mirror,* June 22, 1948, 2; *Daily Herald,* June 21, 1948, 2.

32. *Hackney Gazette and North London Advertizer,* June 23, 1948, 3.

33. "Note of Meeting between Deakin and Strike Committee—Bros. Dickens, Riddell, Cowley, Saunders, Higgins, and Starker," undated, MSS 126/TG/3, Sack 30/31, TGWU-MRC.

34. *Daily Mirror,* July 23, 1948, 8.

35. "Confidential Report to A. E. Stillwell."

36. Ibid.

37. "Unofficial Dock Strike: Course of Events," undated, MSS 126/TG3, Sack 30/31, TGWU-MRC; "Cabinet Meeting, June 24, 1948," CAB 130/38, PRO.

38. *Unofficial Stoppages in the London Docks: Report of a Committee of Inquiry, Ministry of Labour and National Service* (HMO, 1951), 7.

39. Bloomberg interview, August 5, 1996; interview, George Pye, August 14, 1996.

40. *Daily Worker,* June 23, 1948, 1.

41. "Cabinet Meeting, June 24, 1948"; Cabinet Conclusions, June 24, 1948.

42. *Daily Herald,* June 24, 1948, 1.

43. *Daily Mirror,* June 26, 1948, 1; *Daily Herald,* June 26, 1948, 1; *Daily Worker,* June 26, 1948, 1 (quote).

44. "Unofficial Dock Strike: Course of Events"; *Daily Mirror,* June 23, 1948, 1.

45. Letter to Anthony Eden from Anthony Nutting, June 23, 1948 (first quote); letter to Clement Attlee from Anthony Eden, June 24, 1948; letter to Francis L. T. Graham-Harrison, private secretary, Prime Minister, from A. W. Petersen, Home Office, July 2, 1948 (second quote); all in Prime Minister's Correspondence, PREM 8/1086, PRO.

46. Keith Laybourn and Dylan Murphy, *Under the Red Flag: A History of Communism in Britain, 1849–1991* (Thrupp, Gloucestershire, Eng.: Sutton, 1999), 127–31; Nina Fishman, "No Home but the Trade Union Movement: Communist Activists and 'Reformist' Leaders, 1926–1956," in *Opening the Books: Essays on the Social and Cultural History of British Communism,* ed. Geoff Andrews, Nina Fishman, and Kenneth Morgan (London: Pluto Press, 1995), 117 (quote).

47. "Cabinet Meeting," June 24, 1948 (quote).

48. "Circular #52, June 18, 1948, NDLB Circulars, BK 6/1, PRO (first quote); "Unofficial Dock Strike: Course of Events" (second quote).

49. Memorandum to A. E. Stillwell from M. MacLachlan, June 24, 1948, LAB/10/783, 1948 Strike, PRO.

50. Memorandum of Area No. 2 Meeting, undated, MSS 126/TG/3, Sack 30/31, TGWU-MRC; Report to Arthur Deakin from R. Chick, Area Secretary, Area No. 2, July 16, 1948, MSS 126/TG/3, Sack 30/31, TGWU-MRC (quote).

51. Report to Arthur Deakin from R. Chick (first quote); "Unofficial Dock Strike: Course of Events" (second quote).

52. *Daily Mirror,* 28 June, 1948, 1.

53. Minutes of the Special Meeting of the Liverpool and Birkenhead District Committee, June 27, 1948, MSS 126/TG/3, Sack 30/31, TGWU-MRC.

54. *Daily Mirror,* June 28, 1948, 1; *Times* (London), July 28, 1948, 4; *Daily Worker,* June 28, 1948, 1.

55. By the afternoon of June 28, the Ministry of Labour reported 8,659 men out in Liverpool and Birkenhead, with "65 ships affected," while 2,532 were still at work. "Docks," undated memorandum, LAB/10/783, 1948 Strike, PRO; Minutes of the Special Meeting of the Liverpool and Birkenhead District Committee, June 28, 1948, MSS 126/TG/3, Sack 30/31, TGWU-MRC.

56. "Circular 2321, Make-Up of Meat Ration," June 24, 1948, MAF 100/257—Circular Files, PRO (first quote); Report from the Ministry of Food on the Dock Strike: Position as at 4 P.M., June 28, 1948, Prime Minister's Correspondence, PREM 8/1086, PRO (second and third quotes).

57. "Cabinet Conclusions," June 28, 1948, CAB 130/38, PRO.

58. Memorandum, Dock Strike—June 1948: Men on Strike and Ships Affected; Keith Jeffery and Peter Hennessy, *States of Emergency: British Governments and Strikebreaking Since 1919* (London: Routledge, 1983), 190–95; Steve Peak, *Troops in Strikes: Military Intervention in Industrial Disputes* (London: Russell Press, 1984), 92–94. For further discussion, see Roger Geary, *Policing Industrial Disputes, 1893–1985* (Cambridge, Mass.: Harvard University Press, 1985), 67–115, and John W. Duncan, William E. J. McCarthy, and George P. Redman, *Strikes in Postwar Britain: A Study of Stoppages of Work Due to Industrial Disputes, 1946–73* (London: G. Allen and Unwin, 1983).

59. London Dockworkers' Strike: Memorandum by the Parliamentary Secretary to the Ministry of Labour, June 27, 1948, Prime Minister's Correspondence, PREM 8/1086, PRO (quote); Memorandum to Clement Attlee from F. L. T. Graham-Harrison, Private Secretary, June 27, 1948, PREM 8/1086, PRO. At a June 28 meeting of the LDLB, gridlock occurred over the request "to supply adequate labor for the loading and discharge of ships and the operation of essential services." The LDLB referred the issue to the NDLB for "guidance." Minutes Local Board—London, June 28, 1948, LDLB, BK 2-269, PRO.

60. "Cabinet Conclusions," June 28, 1948; Minutes of Cabinet Emergencies Committee, June 28, 1948, CAB 134/175, PRO.

61. *Times* (London), June 29, 1948, 1.

62. "STRIKE at Port of London over Disciplinary Action by the Dock Labour Board," William E. Thomas, Conciliation Officer, Industrial Relations Department, Ministry of Labour and National Service," June 30, 1948, LAB 10/783, 1948 Strike, PRO (quote); *Daily Mirror,* June 30, 1948, 1.

63. *Daily Mirror,* July 1, 1948, 1 (first quote); letter to S. C. Parkin, NDLB, from William H. Cullis, Managing Director, Severn Ports Warehousing Company, June 30, 1948, NDLB, BK/72, PRO (second quote).

64. *Daily Mirror,* July 1, 1948, 1.

65. "STRIKE at Port of London over disciplinary action by the Dock Labour Board."

66. *Parliamentary Debates (Hansard),* 5th ser., vol. 452, June 29, 1948, 2009; *Daily Worker,* June 30, 1948, 1.

67. "Cabinet Conclusions," June 29, 1948, CAB 128/13, PRO (first quote); letter to Lord Ammon, Chair, NDLB, from George Alfred Isaacs, Minister of Labour and National Service," August 8, 1948, NDLB, Welfare, BK 5/30 (remaining quotes).

68. *Reflections on the Strike,* London Port Workers Strike Committee, BK 2/72—Strike, PRO.

69. Report of Committee of Inquiry, August 24, 1948, MSS 126/TG/3, Sack 30/31, TGWU-MRC.

70. Minutes of the Special Meeting of the Hull Docks District Committee, July 5, 1948; Minutes of Special Meeting of the Bristol Transport Committee, July 8, 1948; Minutes of the Special Meeting of the Manchester Dock Trade Committee, July 5, 1948; all in MSS 126/TG/3, Sack 30/31, TGWU-MRC.

71. Letter to Deakin from J. Butcher, Branch Secretary, Liverpool, Area 12, July 8, 1948 (first quote); letter to Deakin from P. G. Gripp, District Officer, Area No. 10, Grimsby, July 8, 1948 (second quote); Minutes of Special Meeting of Docks Group Committee, Area Office Glasgow, July 9, 1948 (third quote); all in MSS 126/TG/3, Sack 30/31, TGWU-MRC.

72. Minutes of Meeting between NDLB and Arthur Deakin and Dickie Barrett, July 5,

1948 (quote), and "Decision of Appeals Tribunal: Opinion of Sir Cyril Langham (Ministry of Labour)," June 27, 1948, both in BK 2/72—Strike, PRO. Employers were unhappy with Langham's "Opinion"; see letter to H. T. Parkin, NDLB, from E. C. Parsons, Hays Wharf and Dock Co., July 1, 1948, BK 2/72—Strike, PRO.

73. Note to S. Parkin from Lord Ammon, undated, and letter to Stephen Parkin from J. H. Bennett, partner, Bristol City Line of Steamers, July 3, 1948, both in BK 2/72—Strike, PRO. Parkin had earlier warned Bennett that the decision might go in the men's favor.

6 Rivalry: New York

The 1948 London and New York strikes had clearly introduced an insurrectionist mood along the respective waterfronts and in the union halls. In New York, dissident behavior had become more prevalent. A culture of open opposition had been born. Neither violence nor the absence of democracy within the ILA prevented a key group of New York longshoremen from challenging the union leadership and its criminal allies during the postwar period. The Back Pay Committees were evidence of the new set of relations. The opposition, an amalgam of longshoremen and outside supporters, gradually grew to confront openly the ILA leaders. The "outside" organizations were the Communist Party of America and the Xavier Institute of Industrial Relations, the latter run by Catholic labor priests. Although bitterly opposed to one another, the two organizations provided the only outlets for a frustrated rank and file. As Father John Corridan, the principal priest working the docks, explained: "The only constant information dispensed on the waterfront comes from either the Communist Party or from this school."[1]

Neither group could operate effectively without a core of union activists to support them. At certain points in the confrontation it was union leaders at the local level that became the catalyst for challenging the ILA hierarchy. In 1948, Gene Sampson of Local 791 seemed to have potential but many saw him only as a pretender for the ILA crown. In 1951 other local leaders would emerge as opponents to Joe Ryan's rule. Johnny Dwyer, leader of Local 895, became the focus of opposition after 1951. Dwyer became the point man of the American Federation of Labor's efforts to replace the ILA with a new union.

Dwyer was more than just a local union leader; he was intimately connected with what became known as the Xavier Labor School.

Labor priests have long held an important position in the American labor movement and a vital role in Catholic working-class communities. Their prominence accelerated during the Great Depression as their parishioners endured increasing hardship and unemployment. The labor priests were concerned not only about economic issues but also about the rise of the Communist Party. Catholic labor schools were developed during the 1930s to counter such influences among the laity. One such school was the New York City Xavier Institute of Industrial Relations, run by Jesuit priests. Father John Corridan, S.J., was associate director of the school from 1946 to 1955. His professed mission in life was to improve the working conditions of longshoremen along the New York waterfront and to rid their union of gangsters. His visibility was such that he was the model for the character played by Karl Malden in the Oscar-winning film *On the Waterfront*.

Organizing on the docks along Manhattan's West Side, Father Corridan represented the dual crusade for improved working conditions for the downtrodden New York City longshoremen and opposition to Communism. He fought simultaneously against corrupt union bosses, shipper employers, and Communist agitators along the waterfront. Father Corridan was relatively successful in placing the issue of atrocious working conditions and mob control of the International Association of Longshoremen (ILA) before the country. Corridan increased public awareness of his deep fear of Communist opportunism on the New York waterfront and of the acute corruption of the ILA. Though he increased the visibility of these problems, he was sorely disappointed in his efforts to counter criminal control of the ILA.

The establishment of the Xavier School was one manifestation of the Catholic Church's "Social Action" crusade of the 1930s. The catalyst for such a movement was of course the Great Depression and the rising strength of the Communist Party. A series of papal encyclicals formed the basis for the Catholic attack. In 1931, Pope Pius XI issued his encyclical *Quadragesimo Anno* calling for "social justice" and stating that "riches . . . ought to be distributed among individual persons and classes that the common advantage of all . . . will be safeguarded." The role of the state was important in promoting "social justice." Although performing a "subsidiary function," the state was expected to encourage responsible trade unionism and employer associations.[2] The American priesthood and other Catholics were quick to respond to the encyclical. Although there were significant differences between the responses of many of the groups and their leaders, including Father Charles Coughlin, the Association of Catholic Trade Unionists, and Dorothy Day, the Jesuits quickly established labor schools to educate Catholics about the twin evils of capitalist exploitation and communist infiltration of the American labor movement. The Xavier School was one of the schools that emerged during the period 1932–45.[3]

The institution was founded in 1936 as the Xavier School of Social Studies, but it soon switched its attention to the labor movement. Renamed the Xavier Labor School, it concentrated its efforts on organizing Catholic workers in New York City. The growing influence of the Communist Party in the city, particularly among transit workers, stimulated the change in direction. As Father Philip E. Dobson, S.J., a Xavier priest, explained, "What prompted the decision . . . was the fact that the Communists seemed to be spending most of their money and their energies on the unions."[4] Xavier established courses to counter the Communist influence. One of the courses provided instruction in understanding parliamentary procedure. As Dobson pointed out, most workmen would "not recognize Communists or Communism in their unions unless Earl Browder rose to speak. . . . Thus the courses were designed to train constructive, well-informed, Catholic, American, union men, who knew what to say or do, how to go about it, and who could handle themselves under any circumstances."[5] Throughout the late 1930s and World War II, the target union for the Xavier School was the Transport Workers' Union (TWU). The TWU's Communist leadership and overwhelmingly Catholic membership made it an obvious focus for labor priests.[6]

Although the battle over control of the TWU would continue, after World War II the school shifted more of its attention to New York City's waterfront workers. By 1948 the Communists were in rapid retreat in the TWU, thus allowing the school to turn its attention to the waterfront. The shift coincided with the arrival at Xavier of Father John Corridan in 1946. Corridan was born in New York City in 1911, the son of Irish-born parents. Corridan's father died in 1921, leaving the family to struggle on. Although taking part-time jobs, Corridan managed to finish high school and enroll at New York University. He eventually found a job on Wall Street as a "correspondent." At the age of twenty he read Rene Füllöp-Miller's *The Power and Secret of the Jesuits* and promptly decided to join the order. After fifteen years of "intensive training" he was assigned to Xavier.[7]

Corridan was no stranger to Catholic labor schools. In 1941 he had been assigned to the Crown Heights Labor School in Brooklyn.[8] As with other labor priests, Corridan viewed his work at Xavier as the recruitment of Catholic activists. He related his vocation to that of Christ's disciples as fishers of men. The words in the Gospel of St. Luke, "Launch out into the deep, and let down your nets," had a special resonance for him. As he explained, "That's part of the job of any priest. He is looking for good men—and women too—who will truly serve God."[9] The appointment of Corridan as associate director galvanized the school to reach those Catholic workers laboring at the bottom of the pile, namely, the Irish and Italian-American longshoremen on the West Side of Manhattan. Such a group of workers seemed ripe for organization and salvation.

Under the tutelage of Father Philip Carey, Father Corridan reached out to these longshoremen. Xavier had established classes in economics, sociology, labor law, public speaking, and labor history. The purpose of the classes was to create a cadre of activists that could confront and challenge both the corrupt ILA leaders and Communist militants. Such a tactic held large risks for activists and priests alike. The organizing had to be achieved in a painstakingly slow fashion—the dangers of physical violence or the inability to obtain work were constant features of such organizing. On one occasion shots were fired into the front room of one activist, Joe Cuerro. Cuerro was an army veteran and had come under fire on the battlefield, but as he related to Father Carey, "When you have your little fellow of nine in bed with you and see him shivering with fright then you know what fear really meant." Xavier eventually banned Cuerro from the meetings to protect him from further harm.[10]

Most contacts with longshoremen were made away from the prying eyes of mobsters and union officials. Corridan related the common experience of meeting sympathizers "in basements and alleyways." Innovative tactics were used to get information out to the rank and file. Leaflets advertising the classes were left in locales frequented by longshoremen. Father Philip Carey claimed leaving leaflets in toilets "served a double purpose, it gave a man freedom from fear while he was reading it and number two it gave him sufficient time to reflect on its contents."[11]

At first, Corridan appeared at the docks also but he discovered that such a tactic was of little use. Sympathetic longshoremen avoided being publicly seen with Corridan because of fear that the hiring bosses would later refuse them work. Cognizant of this reluctance, Corridan instead concentrated on making the public aware of the working conditions of the longshoremen and the corruption of the ILA. His opportunity to challenge the existing conditions came after a series of wildcat strikes on the waterfront between 1948 and 1951.

The 1948 strike specifically rallied Corridan to the cause of the longshoremen and affirmed his belief that the federal government should clean up the waterfront. Just before the 1948 strike broke out, Corridan traveled to Washington, D.C., where he warned Cyrus Ching, director of the Federal Mediation and Conciliation Service, of the tense situation on the docks.[12]

Throughout the strike Corridan remained very active. On his return from

Washington, Corridan quickly produced a pamphlet entitled *The Longshoremen's Case.* While the New York newspapers were reporting that the men would accept the agreement, Corridan argued otherwise. He successfully gauged the rising temper of the men and their determination to strike. *The Longshoremen's Case* was distributed along the waterfront on the first day of the strike, detailing the criminal control of the docks and Communist efforts to infiltrate the union. The target of his attack, and one he would continue to assail, was the shape-up. As Corridan pointed out, "Men are hired as if they were beasts of burden, part of a slave market of a pagan era." Drawing on the Catholic critique of capitalism's innate unfairness, Corridan described the shape-up as "pure Adam Smith laissez-faire. It's free enterprise with a vengeance." Corridan predicted that the supposedly ungodly nature of the hiring system would lead to a destruction of moral and Christian character. The inequities of the shape-up made it "easy to understand the corrosion of the man's character. . . . Living from hand to mouth can do something to man's ideas of fairness. One's ideas of justice fade where injustice is rampant." Such a system and dangerous work conditions also led to a form of martyrdom. Corridan exclaimed, "If John L. Lewis could say that the nation's coal is stained with blood, then the docks are spattered with the blood of longshoremen." Corridan called on the federal government to establish a "Commission of Inquiry to investigate and solve this cancerous condition in a free society."[13]

The theme of Christian justice would continue to frame Corridan's call for reform of waterfront working conditions. Just as important, Corridan's activities reflected well the "social action" component of the Catholic Church's call on the central state to alleviate economic injustice. Corridan used the encyclicals of *Rerum Novarum* (1891) and the *Quadragesimo Anno* as his standards, but a more pragmatic foundation was also evident.[14] The lack of political will by employers, local politicians, and ILA officials to reform conditions forced Corridan to look to state and federal authorities for action against gangsterism along the New York waterfront. As he explained to Rev. R. A. McGowan of the National Catholic Welfare Conference, "If ever a situation called for government intervention, the Port of New York does. Neither employers nor the union have the slightest intention of correcting the present abuses. Everyone admits the situation is dangerous, but no one will take the lead because of the vast political ramifications."[15]

Just as important as Corridan's disdain for gangsters was his intense dislike for the Communist Party. The 1948 strike cemented Corridan's belief that if conditions on the waterfront did not improve, then the Communists would take advantage. Corridan had publicly expressed his fear in a Labor Day speech in 1948. Corridan described "Communist control" as "stench" rising out of the waterfront.[16] The Back Pay Committees fueled Corridan's fear of the spread of Communism among the longshoremen. In a letter to U.S. Senator Wayne Morse, Corridan explained that the Communist Party was "given a ready-made issue when the union leadership failed to press for the men's just claims." "The vast majority of the men," Corridan continued, were "unaware that their lawyers were pro-Communist."[17] Corridan was concerned that some Brooklyn longshoremen had gravitated to the Communist Party. As Corridan told Reverend George G. Higgins of the National Catholic Welfare Conference in a letter on December 2, 1948, "Unfortunately the Commies made some headway in the strike among the Italian locals. . . . We'll do our best to get some opening before these men are permanently captured."[18]

The Communist Party was a direct competitor for the longshoremen's allegiance. It focused on the longshoremen as potential recruits because of their bad working conditions and an inattentive ILA. Its recruitment campaign was also part of a larger strategy to reach out to basic industry workers. Following William Z. Foster's ascendancy to the leadership of the CPUSA, a reinvigorated policy of industrial concentration was adopted. The point was to direct resources toward gaining footholds in basic industries such as "steel, auto, mining, *maritime* [my emphasis], electrical and railroad." American Federation of Labor (AFL) unions were also viewed as potential targets. The Party had traditionally aligned itself with CIO unions but saw the "Right-led unions" of the AFL as possible recruitment targets. Party officials recognized that they had mistakenly ignored the AFL workers. As one Party official, John Williamson, stated, "the Party generally continues to underestimate and even ignore the A.F. of L. workers."[19]

Sustaining the concentration policy was a defensive posture. The Party leadership had identified "dangerous tendencies" within the American labor movement. The key "tendency" was the action by labor leaders to "tie the workers to Wall Street's war policies." As the cold war began to heat up, labor leaders were perceived as reducing their members' economic interests in exchange for stabilizing the capitalist economies. Red-baiting throughout the CIO and AFL unions was seen as a harbinger of a higher form of fascism. The key strategy for the Party was to encourage rank-and-file movements, gain control of union leadership positions, and hold back the red-baiting. The 1948 longshoremen's strike was seen as evidence of rank-and-file resistance. John Williamson described the 1948 strike as a "significant struggle" and one that required the attention of party cadres. The aim therefore was to encourage such rebellious action and thereby capture the trade union leadership.[20]

One of the CPUSA's Industrial Concentration Clubs focused on the Brooklyn longshoremen. Audrey West, a member of the club, handed out Party literature during the shape-up. Accompanied by other Party members she traveled along Columbia Street, one of the major thoroughfares along the Brooklyn docks, giving out copies of the *Daily Worker.* When confronting Italian-American longshoremen, the group also handed out *Unità del Popolo.* There was generally an enthusiastic response from these longshoremen. West remembers that "they would grab for the *La Unita.* They wanted that paper."[21] Such work could be potentially dangerous as local mobsters looked on. As West explained, Jerry Anastasia "would be lounging against the building, watching us [but] he didn't stop us." She continued, "My personal opinion was that he didn't think we really mattered. I think it was contempt for the workers, you know, that they weren't going to do anything, anyway. . . . He had them controlled, you know. If they wanted to work and live, they had to do what he wanted."[22]

The job of organizing was not without its perils. Harold Mailman, another Communist organizer, remembered that many of the Italians would merely knock "the papers from my hands, nothing major." But on another occasion a fork lift driver tried to "knock him down."[23] The organizers adjusted to the potentially dangerous situation by making Audrey West a regular member of the club. With women in the group, it was calculated that physical attacks would be less likely. As West pointed out, "I'm sure they'd as soon slit my throat as anybody else's if I got in their way. . . . But I was told very plainly that my being there was very important because . . . the Mafia wouldn't attack us."[24]

Once the whistle was blown for the men to begin work, the club moved onto the next pier or shape-up. Those longshoremen who had taken the literature "tucked it into their back pocket, or whatever." Timing was everything. If the group had not had time to hand out information to all the assembled longshoremen, those who "hadn't received the paper . . . just weren't going to pay any attention to us any more, so we always had to be on time. We had to get it [the paper] out before that whistle blew." Moving along the waterfront, the club members would finish by visiting the black local under the Brooklyn Bridge. Here the longshoremen were more receptive to the literature. Following the shape-up, the invariably large group of black longshoremen not chosen for work "would mill around a little bit and we would talk." The discussion between the two groups never went beyond a surface dialogue. When discussing discrimination "it would not be direct. . . . They didn't come out and say, 'We know why we're getting the short end of the stick—because we're black,' but it was sort of 'What do you expect? . . . This is what happens to black workers.'" The club did "hear" complaints about not having steady work or regular gangs, but the black longshoremen continued to regard them as "outsiders." West recalled, "Even though we came week after week for several years, we were to a certain extent outsiders. They welcomed us but they weren't going to let all their grievances out."[25]

The lack of hostility displayed by black longshoremen reflected a shared sense of oppression. According to Mailman, the black longshoremen were well aware that "we were not there to exploit them, [or] hurt them." Instead there was an acknowledgment that the Communist organizers were genuinely "sympathetic to their plight." Such mutual recognition encouraged a dialogue between the Communist organizers and Cleophas Jacobs, head of Local 968. The organizers "were very close to Jacobs," even meeting him at his residence. Correspondingly, Jacobs invited Mailman and other organizers to Local 968 social events. They attended a "union dance . . . southern style where the longshoremen brought their own liquor and food." Once a firm connection had been established, Jacobs gave his blessing to the organizers' requests to visit the homes of the black longshoremen.[26] Such contacts melded well with the new directions of the Communist Party. Throughout 1949 the party engaged in an internal campaign against "white chauvinism." While the Party had previously supported African American political and economic equality, the new impetus in 1949 was fueled by anticolonial movements in Africa and elsewhere. Besides trying to purge the party cadre of latent racism, the new policy promoted black activists to leadership positions and pushed more forcefully for civil rights gains.[27]

Mailman's visit to Jacobs's house and Local 968 was part of a larger effort to identify potential black recruits to the Communist Party. Such visits never went beyond merely discussing general grievances, however. Jacobs never fully trusted the Communist activists for several reasons. First, they were outsiders, with no institutional power. Second, the activists could not overcome Jacobs's antipathy to white people, whether potential allies or not. Finally, although glad of their support, Jacobs was wary that such a connection could damage Local 968 within the international union by giving Ryan and others the opportunity to red-smear his leadership and ultimately Local 968.

Just as problematic for the Communist organizers, there was no coordination between the club and others throughout the port. As West explained, "We knew that there were others," but fear of infiltration by the Federal Bureau of Investigation (FBI) made communication between the groups unacceptable. "The atmosphere of the Cold War" encouraged caution, West said, and "the less we knew about the other groups the better." Adopting the hierarchical Communist model, reports were sent to the Manhattan headquarters. The club "made decisions about very immediate tactics" but strategy came "from the top." The "Party leadership," West recalled, "had a much better overall picture of what was going on than we had." Another concern of the club was the lack of any connection with Party members who were longshoremen. It was common knowledge that some of the Brooklyn longshoremen were Party members, but because of fear of infiltration by the FBI the two groups never organized together. As West attests, "Our work was separate from theirs. We were not in touch with them. Again, whether that was wise tactics or not, I don't know." Even when meeting a Communist longshoreman, the organizers were warned to stay away. Harold Mailman, for example, attended a union meeting and attempted to engage in a conversation with a sympathetic longshoreman. The longshoreman was uncomfortable with Mailman's overture: the "guy said, 'Get away from me son.' He was a member of the Communist Party."[28]

Not only were the club members and Communist longshoremen isolated from each other. Just as important, the Communist longshoremen were also detached from their fellow workers. Any hint of Communist allegiance would be met by suspicion or gangster violence. The club members confined themselves to handing out leaflets at the respective shape-ups and occasionally visiting the homes of sympathetic longshoremen. Such limited action could only scratch the surface of what they wanted to accomplish. The members were also fearful of the "burgeoning anti-Communism" during 1948. West described increasing anxiety as the cold war gained momentum: "We were a little afraid of pushing the idea of joining the Party at times when people were fleeing the Party out of fear. The big flight from the Party didn't occur quite that early, but it was happening and there was an atmosphere among even the Party leaders of 'we have to protect ourselves.'" Even the longshoremen's families were given low priority. As West explained, "There was a sense that you would try to talk to the wives, but it really wasn't part of a greater strategy. . . . First of all you dealt with the men because they were the workers. They were on the point of the class struggle, and they were the people directly involved."[29]

For all the work, there was little successful recruitment: "I don't think that in the three or so years that we were on the docks that our group . . . accomplished any recruiting." Nonetheless, "ninety percent" of the men "accepted [a leaflet] and put it in their pockets and were interested in reading it." There may have been little impact for the men, but at least there was a presence of people around the docks who openly sympathized with their plight. Distributing leaflets, however, was not the best method to recruit members nor to create an oppositional movement. As West was forced to admit, there "was a difference between" taking leaflets "and taking action."[30] Mailman echoed West's pessimistic appraisal. True, the organizers had made inroads with Jacobs's local, but it "never got to the point where we gave help. [We were in] no position to fight the leadership, or change conditions."[31]

The recruitment policy was also hampered by outside forces that distracted the Communist leadership. William Z. Foster had grabbed control in 1945 and successfully purged the one-time leader, Earl Browder. Foster's brand of Communism was riven with paranoia. He feared that a postwar depression was in sight and that in turn it was nurturing "domestic fascism." Just as apocalyptic was his belief that war was imminent between the United States and the Soviet Union. By 1948, some of Foster's fears appeared to be warranted as the first show-trials of American Communists under the Smith Act were under way in federal court. Also distracting the recruitment efforts was the Communist Party's support of Henry Wallace's third party during the 1948 presidential election. The campaign was a disaster for the party, however. It alienated large sections of the labor movement, particularly its centers of strength in the Congress of Industrial Organizations (CIO). Just as important, the cold war in 1948 was heating up both at home and abroad. Communists in the labor movement were very susceptible to attack. The Taft-Hartley Act insisted that union leaders should identify whether they were Communists or not. Initially, the union movement opposed the anti-Communist clause, but after Walter Reuther routed his Communist opponents in the UAW and signed the pledge, the floodgates opened.[32]

The Communist Party was therefore distracted by events beyond its control. Anti-Communist hysteria was growing, and fears of an American-brand of fascism and world war took an enormous toll. So the Communist Party expended its limited resources pushing for peace, while many of its leaders were preparing to go underground to avoid prosecution. The organization of New York's longshoremen was therefore given low priority. Even when organizing began, it was not coordinated. Separate groups worked in Brooklyn and Manhattan, but they did not meet to exchange ideas or formulate a coherent policy for agitation. To a large extent they were left alone to fend for themselves.

Father Corridan, however, was more successful in his quest to build an oppositional movement among New York's longshoremen. He concentrated his efforts among the longshoremen of Manhattan's West Side. To counter the growing influence of the Communist Party and align himself with the economic concerns of the longshoremen, Corridan embarked on a campaign to support their overtime case. The case was a ready-made issue. The Supreme Court had ruled that the men were entitled to back pay because of the overtime case but the ILA, in alliance with the shippers, appealed to Congress to exempt the shipping industry from the Fair Labor Standards Act.

The blatant attack on the men's claims fueled Corridan's assault. In an article entitled "Overtime on Overtime: Longshoremen's Case," Corridan spelled out the issue to the general public. Corridan also used the opportunity to publicize the poor working conditions along the waterfront and the role played by the ILA in keeping its membership in line through violence and intimidation.[33] He found important allies in the journalistic field. In a series of Pulitzer Prize–winning articles, Malcolm Johnson, a *New York Sun* journalist, had dramatically revealed the criminal control of loading, the shape-up, and the ILA. Such treatment brought to the public eye the subterranean world of the New York longshoremen. Corridan provided Johnson a great deal of information and introduced him to longshoremen who agreed to provide information detailing kick-backs, threats, and theft on the waterfront, though retaining their anonymity.[34]

Corridan also urged Congress and New York State to investigate the corrupt ILA. Appearing before the U.S. House Committee on Education and Labor on June 15, 1949, Corridan contended that reform could "be brought only by a Federal and State investigation resulting in remedial action."[35] Much to Corridan's annoyance he had to share the congressional stage with Communist activists such as Mitch Berenson and the labor lawyer Julius Bagley. Both men had testified on the overtime-on-overtime issue in early 1949.[36] These rank-and-file militants had long been in the struggle against ILA domination. They had become particularly visible during the 1945 strike and subsequent rank-and-file campaigns.

The concern for New York longshoremen shared by the two groups led to an extraordinary encounter on January 24, 1950. Corridan met with Mitch Berenson among others and discussed the West Coast hiring halls for longshoremen. Berenson explained he was in favor of establishing three union hiring halls in Manhattan, Brooklyn, and New Jersey. In a memo of the meeting Corridan explained he "refused to cooperate with them in any way." Although dismissive of the militants, Corridan did acknowledge that "it would be OK if they wanted to drop in from time to time and talk things over."[37] Although both parties were obviously attempting to alleviate the same conditions, Corridan eyed Berenson warily and refused to overcome his disdain for Communist longshoremen.

Corridan's bitter feelings toward Communists at times clouded his judgment, as was the case with black longshoremen. African American longshoremen in Brooklyn had long complained of discrimination. Although belonging to Jim Crow Local 968, they were unable to have their own pier. This was a strategic disadvantage that forced them to go to work along the Brooklyn waterfront as extras. As the leader of Local 968, Cleophas Jacobs had appealed to Joe Ryan to ensure his members could have steady work as regular gangs. Ryan ignored this entreaty, prompting Jacobs to turn to the Protestant Council of New York for support and arrange hearings with the New York State Commission Against Discrimination.[38]

After the Protestant Council invited George Hunton of the Catholic Interracial Council to attend an organizing meeting with Local 968, Hunton turned to Corridan for advice. Although somewhat sympathetic to the plight of the black longshoremen, Corridan was generally dismissive of their concerns. Fueling this antipathy was his belief that Jacobs had Communist sympathies. As Corridan put it, "Jacobs has been palling around with the Commies." What also concerned Corridan was Joe Ryan's inability to resolve the problem of discrimination and his threats to remove Local 968's charter. Such action could only lead to Communist penetration: "If he [Ryan] should revoke 968's charter, the Negro longshoremen . . . may fall into the hands of the party." Corridan remained aloof from the controversy, partly because of Jacobs's supposed Communist attachment. He directed his efforts instead to Manhattan's West Side and only rarely delved into the Brooklyn longshoremen's world, whether white or black. In any event, Corridan was convinced that the issue was one of a congested labor market. Recognizing that "race prejudice" existed on the waterfront, Corridan nonetheless pointed out to Hunton that "the disturbance has its roots in the overcrowded supply of men in relation to work opportunities in which both white and colored suffer."[39]

Corridan concentrated his efforts on constructing an oppositional movement within the ILA. Through a long period of agitation Corridan strived to build up momentum to challenge the ILA and end the shape-up. Such efforts, however, were slow going. Corridan experienced difficulty in overcoming the longshoremen's traditional suspicion of outsiders purporting to represent their interests. Corridan's fortunes would change for the better, however. A wildcat strike in 1951 would bring to the public's attention the conditions of the New York longshoremen and the need for reform. Corridan would ride the wave of rebellion and successfully encourage reform by state and federal politicians. The 1951 strike mirrored that of 1948. The ILA leadership negotiated an agreement and the ILA members supposedly voted to accept it. While Ryan was happy with the agreement, the rank and file thought otherwise and began walking out on October 15, 1951.

Again, it was the "Mother Local" 791 that initiated the walkout. The strikers wanted a larger increase than the twelve cents offered, in addition to an improved vacation and welfare scheme and one shape-up a day. They were also frustrated by the way the vote was tabulated. The charge was one of fraud. Local 791 was joined by Manhattan Local 895 and Brooklyn Local 808.[40] Ryan tried to use his usual tactic of condemning the strikers as being misled or having Communist connections. He charged that Local 791 strikers "won't listen," and in a subtle snub to Gene Sampson he declared, "They have no leader I can deal with." Ryan's continued membership in Local 791 precluded his charging that local with Communist involvement. No such restriction applied with the Brooklyn strikers, however, and he described them as "strictly Communist-inspired."[41]

The accusation of Communist involvement had little, if any, substance. The locals involved in the initial walkout shared one unifying element: they had each voted against the agreement. True, each local had its reform elements, but the agreement was seen as another betrayal. The strikers were a disparate bunch. Gene Sampson, Ryan's chief ILA rival, led Local 791 men out. The other Manhattan local, 895, was led by Johnny Dwyer. Dwyer was born in New York and raised in Greenwich Village, "close to the waterfront." For a short while he was a hiring boss and generally "hired neighborhood people." Pressured to hire some ILA favorites, which would mean having to fire somebody, Dwyer refused. Consequently he lost his job as hiring boss and "from that day" began "his career to fight" corruption within the ILA. As an official of Local 856, Dwyer witnessed first-hand the corrupt practices of union officials, and he was determined to fight for reform. He garnered support from the Association of Catholic Trade Unions, but more important, he aligned himself with Father Corridan. He attended some of the Xavier labor classes taught by Father Corridan and Father Carey, although as Dwyer admitted, his principal source of instruction was the daily struggle of work on the waterfront: "really learning it from the docks, that's where you're learning it, the school of hard knocks." Dwyer did share Corridan's antipathy toward Communists: "I was anti-Communist, we used to chase them off the waterfront."[42]

The members of Brooklyn Locals 968 and 808 were also a disparate lot, but they too were joined by voting against the agreement. Black Local 968 had established itself as an anti-Ryan force along the Brooklyn waterfront. Local 808, like Local 791, called for an end to ILA connivance with shippers at contract time. Led by Frank Nowracki, Local 808 was solidly in the reform camp and, significantly, outside the criminal control of the Anastasia brothers. By October 18, the third day of the strike, other locals joined the strike. Ryan was becoming increasingly desperate and threatened violence against the strikers. He accused Harry Bridges, the ILWU leader,of stirring up the conflict, especially in Brooklyn. Ryan insisted that on October 18, "We will meet Bridges' strong-arm squads with our squads tomorrow morning. . . . If there's any violence it will be Bridges' fault."[43] Instead, it was left to the notorious Tony Anastasia to attempt to break the picket lines in Brooklyn. In a bruising display of intimidation, Anastasia personally tried to "push" strikers back to work at the Brooklyn army base. After attempting literally to shove men back to work, he announced, "I am Anastasia. . . . This is one place you gotta work." When the assembled men ignored him he "sent in seventy-five of his men into the base." Such blatant strike-breaking infuriated the strikers. Salvatore Brocco, a hatch boss, openly challenged Anastasia. Jumping onto a truck, he yelled: "Anyone who calls us a Commies is a damn liar. We are patriotic. We have worked this base before the war. Gene Sampson . . . is our man and a better leader than Joe Ryan." The accusation of Communist leanings had obviously upset Brocco. The Korean War and the resultant antipathy toward Communists had nurtured widespread disdain for the CPUSA along the Brooklyn waterfront. By accusing Brocco of Communist sympathies Anastasia had overstepped the bounds of the political compact. Initially, Brocco reluctantly acquiesced to Anastasia's order to return to work. "Glaring" at Anastasia, Brocco announced, "Get those stooges out of there and we'll go in." "Anastasia grinned" at Brocco's entreaty and ordered his seventy-five men off the pier, while three hundred strikers resumed their jobs. Anastasia "then stepped into a limousine . . . and made a hasty retreat." Anastasia's victory was short-lived, however, because the men again left their jobs at noon.[44]

Having openly defied Anastasia without retribution, those Brooklyn men still working began to join the strike. Flying squadrons of strikers were of critical importance in spreading the walkout. Moving along the Brooklyn waterfront, two hundred cars and trucks "roamed the waterfront," their occupants pulling out those men who were continuing to work. Sampson also threatened to send a motorcade to Staten Island and the Jersey docks. The only weak areas in Manhattan were the piers above Forty-second Street and those on the East River. These piers were controlled, respectively, by the "pistol local" 824 and Mike Clemente's Local 856 on the East River. Patrick J. Connolly, known as "Packy," controlled Local 824 and was a close ally of Ryan's. Ryan had earlier rewarded Connolly's allegiance by appointing him executive vice-president of the international, a position Sampson had long coveted. According to journalists, Connolly was being groomed as Ryan's successor; consequently Sampson's power within the union would be further threatened.[45]

Ryan continued to use his tried-and-tested tactic of red-smearing the members of the opposition but his maneuver only galvanized them. Sampson used the issue to bolster his own position and he decried Ryan's accusation: "I am sick and tired of these references to Communism that emanate from Ryan's headquarters. . . . These men who refuse to work are more patriotic than any of their critics. If the critics were half as patriotic and honest we would not have this situation." The Association of Catholic Trade Unionists

(ACTU) jumped into the fray. James McElroy, the ACTU's secretary-treasurer, explained that the issue was a "red herring" and that the strikers were "definitely anti-Communist." Echoing the argument of Father Corridan, McElroy charged that the strike "was essentially a rank-and-file clean-house movement." Ryan's tactic of labeling internal and external critics as Communist inspired had a hollow ring. It also had little effect on federal agencies. The FBI in particular was singularly unimpressed by his charges. As one FBI agent reported, "Joe Ryan, whenever he is confronted with internal union difficulties, usually blames it on the Communists." Although Communist Party members handed out copies of the *Docker's News,* an FBI report held that "the consensus of all well-informed sources is that the Communist influence in connection with this strike is negligible and that Communist activity so far has been limited to disseminating literature designed to spread the strike."[46]

Sampson was emboldened by the spreading strike, but for it to be an effective challenge to Ryan, and for the shippers to reopen negotiations, the port as a whole needed to be closed down. On October 19, Sampson called on all oppositional forces to attend a meeting in the Manhattan Center on West Thirty-third Street. The following day Sampson, Dwyer, Nawrocki, and others attended the meeting. There were calls from the floor that either Sampson or William Lynch, a Local 791 officer, should lead the strike. Wary of directly challenging Ryan's leadership, Lynch insisted "that no single man should 'front' for the strike." Such a sentiment was not universally shared by the meeting. From the floor came cries of "Give us some leadership, tell us what you want us to do." Also from the floor the point was made that only a few locals were in attendance at the meeting and for the strike to succeed the "entire port would have to be drawn out." It was agreed that each local should organize flying squadrons to maintain the momentum of the strike and bring out those longshoremen still working. One of the more dramatic episodes in the meeting was Nawrocki's charge that Anastasia "goons" had threatened him with violence. Acutely aware of the peril he was in, and mindful of the fate of Pete Panto, Nawrocki told those attending the meeting, "If anything happens to me, I hold the Anastasia brothers responsible."[47]

The following day, October 21, men from Sampson's and Dwyer's locals formed a "motorcade" and succeeded in bringing out men on the East River and, even more important, Jersey City and Hoboken. Thus by the end of the day, work continued on only a smattering of piers in Manhattan and Brooklyn and on those on Staten Island. Buoyed by such success, the motorcade reformed on the morning of October 22 and convinced the remaining Brooklyn and Staten Island longshoremen to join the strike. The morning was not without incident, however. Frank Nawrocki's car was attacked outside the

Hamilton Avenue pier of Gerardo Anastasia. The car windows were smashed by rocks and bottles and Nawrocki was roughed up. Anastasia was arrested for felonious assault, as was Frank Russo, a delegate of Local 327.[48]

With most of the port's longshoremen on strike, Gene Sampson met with Ryan to convince him to lead the strike. Such an overture could not have been appreciated by many of the strikers and just reaffirmed their suspicions that Sampson was playing his usual role as the "loyal opposition." Sampson explained that the majority of the men were on strike, and that it would be in the best interests of all concerned for Ryan to take the reins and reinstitute contract talks with the shippers. Ryan was in no mood to accept such an offer. Unlike the situation during the 1948 strike, in this one Ryan was determined to hold off the challenge of the insurgents by ignoring their demands. Instead, he argued that the contract had been voted on and that any action to settle the dispute must be made by "Federal officials."[49]

Ryan appealed to President Truman to settle the strike. The plan of the Truman administration was again to use the officers of the Federal Mediation and Conciliation Service. Spurring on such action was the spread of the strike to Boston. On October 22, Cyrus Ching dispatched three federal mediators to New York City, but he was not optimistic that such action could end the conflict. Unlike the 1948 strike, this conflict had split the union, pitting strikers against the union leadership and, in some cases, other longshoremen. Clyde Mills was Ching's point man and he arranged a meeting with both union factions. Once the meeting began, it degenerated into personal attacks and accusations. Journalists reported that "angry shouts could be heard from the mediation room." The strike committee continued to claim that the vote had been rigged. Boston strike leaders supported the strike committee by charging that the conflict was a "rebellion against New York mobsters who have a stranglehold on the ILA and against a group who sold us out by accepting an entirely unsatisfactory contract."[50]

The mediators faced an uphill battle and by October 25 admitted defeat. They dodged their brief, however, by publicly criticizing the strikers and demanding that they return to work. Clyde Mills announced to reporters, "This situation is intolerable and must be ended immediately. . . . We see no possibility of solving it, and there is no alternative but to withdraw." His remarks brought an immediate rebuke from Sampson, who declared that such an "intolerable" statement was "biased." Sampson said, "We are found to be guilty while the conditions we are fighting are found to be just." Sampson and his committee then severed all further ties with the mediators.[51] It was left to President Truman personally to ask the strikers to return to work. Declaring that the strike was having a "direct and immediate effect on our defense effort" during the Korean War, he pleaded with the men to "return to work at once." Although the strike was an intra-union dispute, Truman could have invoked the Taft-Hartley Act and declared a national emergency. With such a declaration he could have ordered the men back or instituted an injunction to do so. That he did not take these options says as much about the advice he received from John R. Steelman to steer clear of the conflict as it does about Truman's own reluctance to act. Steelman, Truman's principal advisor on labor matters, was instrumental in keeping the government from invoking the Taft-Hartley Act. Steelman was convinced that the dispute would eventually be settled as the strikers tired and returned to work.[52] Further influencing Truman not to take action were promises by the strike committee to work military ships in the harbor. By October 30, therefore, army and navy bases in Brooklyn, Staten Island, and Jersey City were unaffected by the strike.[53]

The lack of an aggressive response by the government surprised Father Corridan. Corridan had been encouraging strikers in the Chelsea and Greenwich Village sections of Manhattan. He ran prayer sessions to bolster the men's confidence. In one prayer, he said, "God grant that our government will order you back to work in honor. May God protect and preserve you this day."[54] Obviously, Corridan believed that Truman would order a return to work using the Taft-Hartley Act.

By October 30, the strike had lasted for fifteen days. For the most part the port had come to a standstill, and Boston longshoremen had joined the strike. The situation had become a stand-off. Ryan continued to refuse to recognize the strikers' demands for a reopening of the contract discussions, while the strikers for their part appeared determined to stay out until their demands were met. Truman's administration had failed to extract a compromise agreement and had left the field of battle. It seemed as though the intra-union struggle would be a fight to the finish. The stakes were extremely high for all concerned, not least the financial effects on New York's economy. The Commerce and Industry Association charged that $250,000,000 worth of cargo was trapped in the port, and just as damaging, the port was losing $25,000,000 a day in business. That lost business, they argued, was going to other ports in the form of transferred shipments. The association called on both Truman and New York's Governor Thomas E. Dewey to solve the crisis.[55]

At this juncture the New York State Board of Mediation entered the conflict. Its chairman, Merlyn S. Pitzele, invited the two sides to meet with him on October 30. Pitzele met with committees representing both Sampson and Ryan in an effort to hammer out a peace agreement. Pitzele was successful in getting the two sides to agree to a ten-man negotiating committee for each, and that Ryan would recognize Sampson as the strike leader. Pitzele was unable, however, to move the sides further together and was forced to ask Governor Dewey to appoint a fact-finding board. Dewey in turn ordered Edward Corsi, the state industrial commissioner, to name a three-member Board of Inquiry.[56]

On November 2, Corsi appointed the board. The members were Professor Martin P. Catherwood, the dean of the New York State School of Industrial and Labor Relations, Cornell University; Msgr. John P. Boland, a member of the State Board of Mediation; and Dean Alfange, a lawyer and previous ALP candidate for governor. The timing was significant. By November 2, the strike had been on for nineteen days, making it the longest in the port's history.[57]

Not till November 5 did the board begin its work. As with other state and federal agency efforts, the principal goal was to get the men back to work. The inquiry immediately focused on how the vote had been taken on the disputed agreement. Peter Johnson, the attorney representing the strike committee, charged that the "spontaneous stoppage . . . is the finest commentary on the manner in which the vote was taken." Johnson claimed that "many of the locals never had an election," and in some cases when men turned up at the locals to cast their ballots they were informed "you have already voted." Once the board began to interview union staff who administered the vote it became clear that the balloting was riven with problems. First, the ballots were not numbered, so no clear record of who had voted could be assessed. When asked what guaranteed that "ballot stuffing" had not occurred, Louis Waldman, the ILA attorney, exclaimed that it was "the integrity and honor of the people who run the locals." Second, the vote tallies were phoned in by the locals to Ryan's secretary, Veronica Hennessy. Hennessy testified that she knew the "voices" of all the local officials who telephoned their respective results, therefore avoiding any confusion or "spurious vote call." Unfortunately, Hennessy's declaration could not be verified because the locals never received an "official letter" confirming their vote. Third, it was made plain that the wage committee was dominated by Ryan appointees, further tainting the agreement and subsequent vote.[58]

The strike committee offered a series of proposals to end the strike and, more specifically, to reform the union. The principal demand was for a sweeping democratization of the ILA. The committee argued that "the rank and file member is not a voice crying in the wilderness. He is not even a voice." Thus when asked to vote on an agreement the membership suffered from "general ignorance" of its conditions and was denied an informed choice. The ILA was then a mere "feudal estate dedicated to the enrichment of a chosen few." Specific proposals called for expanding the Wage Scale Committee to include a majority of "non-office holding members" and asked that the ILA membership elect these rank-and-file members. When voting on the agreement there should be central sites for balloting, and voting machines should be used. Each member voting should have also have his membership book stamped to that effect. Once the vote was tabulated it should be made public, showing the total vote and how each union local voted. The committee then outlined proposed reforms of the grievance procedure. The committee astutely blamed the lack of a workable grievance procedure for the constant unofficial strikes on the waterfront, thus shifting the blame for the 1951 walkout to Ryan and his allies. To ensure that its proposals would be carried out, the committee insisted that those locals where "incumbent officers" had not held an election for five years should hold elections forthwith. But in the most dramatic move of all, the committee demanded the resignation of Ryan and the entire executive council. Finally, the committee declared that the "negotiations for the 1951 Contract be continued."[59]

The strike committee's proposals went to the heart of its frustration with the ILA. Tired of being manipulated during negotiation time, the committee members clearly expressed their anger. They resented the lack of democracy within the ILA and how it had created an atmosphere of "general ignorance" by the membership. The committee members therefore demanded a sweep of Ryan and his allies from office. Only then, they believed, could the ILA at last represent the true interests of the members. It was obviously a tall order to get the board to dismiss Ryan et al., but the point had been made that the leadership was all that stood in the way of democratizing the ILA. In addition, if the proposals were carried out it could result in a decrease in the number and severity of "work stoppages."[60]

While the strike committee presented its proposals, events around the port continued to take on an explosive and dramatic character. Members of Local 824 continued to work the ocean liners by Hell's Kitchen, leading to tense confrontations with pickets from Local 791 and others. Ryan continued to encourage back-to-work movements, even threatening Sampson with removal as business agent from Local 791. New York City also witnessed a dramatic march on City Hall by foreign traders from the Commerce and Industry Association (CIA). Earlier the New York Board of Trade had expressed its "mystification" with Mayor Vincent Impellitteri's silence over the dispute. Impellitteri was trying to maintain a low profile to avoid antagonizing the two contending political forces of Sampson and Ryan. Frustrated with his inactivity, on November 8, two hundred members of the CIA marched to City Hall to demand a meeting with the mayor. The situation was further strained when the mayor's secretary, John Tierney, informed the CIA executive vice president, Thomas Jefferson Miley, that he was "surpris[ed] that a group of business men should come over here like a bunch of Communists." After Miley reported Tierney's comments to the marchers, there were calls to storm City Hall. Wiser heads prevailed, but the strike and its impact had resulted in frayed nerves all around.[61]

Also on November 8, New Jersey Superior Court Judge Thomas J. Stanton issued a restraining order against New York City strikers picketing Hoboken and Jersey City piers. By lunchtime the roving New York pickets left the waterfront. New Jersey longshoremen began to drift back to work that afternoon. For the first time the flying squadrons had been curtailed, leading to a serious break in the striker ranks.[62]

The restraining order had a profound effect on the trajectory of the strike. It threatened the solid nature of the strikers' response. The strike committee was under tremendous pressure to call off the strike. The injunction had broken the strike on the Jersey waterfront, and it would be only a matter of time before the ILA or shippers obtained one to cover Manhattan and Brooklyn. Martin Catherwood and his Board of Inquiry seized on the opportunity to end the conflict and quickly set up meetings with the strike committee. The committee agreed to advise a return to work, while the board agreed to carry on its investigation of the strike. On Friday, November 9, the strike came to an end.[63]

At last, Ryan confronted institutional opposition within the ILA. Sampson, Nawrocki, and Dwyer were ILA officials, making them a potent oppositional force. Once the strike ended, these leaders withdrew into the background but the effects of their actions did not evaporate. The strike had brought to the surface the continuing problems of ILA malfeasance and sweetheart contracts. Two groups in particular were looking for a change in the industrial order. First, there were the shippers, who had become increasingly disillusioned with the ILA leadership. The shippers had traditionally paid large sums to ILA officials to keep the peace. The strikes in 1945, 1948, and 1951 highlighted the inability of Ryan to control the rank and file and in turn the shippers began to lose confidence in him.

The second group was comprised of New York State officials, whose attention was captured by the disruptive effect of the strikes. For Governor Dewey of New York the waterfront seemed ripe for a high-profile investigation. Spurring on Governor Dewey was Martin Catherwood's Board of Inquiry. As promised, it continued its investigation of the ILA and waterfront working conditions. Its final report, in January 1952, was a scathing critique of ILA practices and employer connivance. Although the board admitted its purpose was to concentrate on "labor-management relations," it was "clear" that "criminal activities" affected every aspect of employment relations along the waterfront and how business was done throughout the port. Such "criminal activity," the board warned, would "force a substantial part of shipping. . . . to be diverted to other ports with injurious consequences to the economy of the City and State of New York." Just as problematic, the substantial number of men with criminal records who held "key positions" in the union had "create[d] a state of fear on the part of union members and employers and curtails such freedom of expression and of action as are necessary and desirable in order to bring about the needed reforms of the waterfront." The sole purpose of so many criminal union officials was merely to "enforce a strong-arm system for domination of the waterfront." The linchpin of this control was the "shape-up," which bred insecurity among the longshoremen and encouraged a quiescent and malleable union membership. The board had thus adopted many of the critiques put forth by the strike committee and reformers, including Father Corridan. The board then outlined its recommendations, which included ending the "shape-up," having more regular meetings of union locals, and establishing a coherent system of elections of officers of locals. To encourage such reforms the board called for the appointment of an "Industrial Commissioner" to meet with both sides (ILA officials and the strike committee) "to assist in implementing the Board's recommendations."[64]

The ILA, which had promised to abide by the board recommendations, immediately balked, insisting that the board had overstepped its authority and that it had not investigated the Communist influence among disruptive elements around the port. The ILA did not like the proposal for an "Industrial Commissioner" either, describing the office as an "overseer or commissar." Such statements prompted an angry response by Dean Alfange, a board member. In a statement released to the press, Alfange charged the ILA leadership with engaging in a "callous and shameful attempt" to ignore the board's recommendations. He described as "unadulterated camouflage" the ILA contention that the board had "failed to investigate" Communist involvement in the union. Alfange found it strange that Joe Ryan had had no problem with the board's stepping in and settling the strike, but once "his official family felt secure in the tenure of their office, they accuse the Board of usurpation." In a stinging conclusion, Alfange stated, "The ILA is not a typical labor union. It is saturated with gangsterism and racketeering. . . . Mr. Ryan would do well to understand that his tenure of his office is no stronger than the public opinion that supports him; and so would his advisers."[65]

Alfange's anger was clearly understandable. The board had saved Ryan from disgrace by getting the men back to work. Alfange's frustration was matched by that of shippers and associated industries in the New York City area. The 1948 and 1951 strikes had created a groundswell movement for reforming the ILA. The rank-and-filers and their allies had been successful in bringing to the public eye not only their poor working conditions, but also the corrupt leadership of the ILA. Although the rank-and-file leaders were generally in a state of flux, changing over every issue, the strikes and attendant reform campaigns had captured the attention of both federal and state governments.

It would be New York State that would at last challenge Ryan and his allies. The New York Board of Inquiry had certainly cleared the path for Governor Dewey. It had spelled out the problems of corruption within the ILA and the economic effects of this corruption on New York City's financial and trading prowess. Of course Dewey had earlier made a name for himself as a gang buster in the 1930s, so an investigation of the New York waterfront was timely. Dewey set up the New York State Crime Commission, which held hearings between 1951 and 1952. The hearings became a sensation in New York City and throughout the country. A string of ILA officials were cross-examined and they claimed a universal lack of memory or knowledge about membership figures, union dues payments, bribes from shippers, and criminal activity on the waterfront. When asked about the fact that 30 percent of the ILA officers had criminal records, Ryan replied disingenuously, "No sir, I don't know that." Commissioners asked Ryan about his payments to politicians, the hiring of general organizers with criminal records, the lack of democracy within locals, and payments made to him for vacations and golf club memberships. Throughout his testimony Ryan either feigned ignorance or asserted his right to certain expenses from the ILA's general fund.[66]

Although asked, John Corridan refused to testify before the commission. He believed that much of the information he had garnered of waterfront conditions had been shared with him in confidence. As he explained, "any testimony" he would give "would weaken the belief of people around the waterfront in my trustworthiness." Although he did not testify, Corridan provided the commission members with information off the record. He also privately shared his plans for reforming the waterfront, which included creation of a hiring hall, registration of all longshoremen, and institution of a seniority system.[67]

Corridan also received letters from longshoremen and their families criticizing his actions. After Corridan appeared on television, one longshoremen exclaimed, "You are either a liar or a dope." Corridan was encouraged to "get on the Milton Berle show, you sure was funny." A longshoreman's son accused Corridan of being a "disgrace. . . . We had enough of this with Father Coughlin." But many other letters were supportive. One Hoboken longshoremen thanked Corridan for his work and stated that the "longshoremen are with you in your fight." The men could not openly support Corridan: "But of course they have to sing dumb or else no work. So to live they have to keep quiet." This qualified support was repeated by another longshoreman, who congratulated Corridan yet asked, "But why should I stick my neck out?"[68]

One longshoreman explained how when he did "stick" his "neck out" he found himself alone: "It was an awful feeling to see so many men so spineless—and looking at me as though I was crazy." Anthony Silvio, a Hoboken longshoremen, thanked Corridan for his "recommendations" to the "State Crime Commission." Silvio was concerned that the revelations arising from the commission hearings had tainted many of his fellow longshoremen—"Especially family men who are decent, honest men who are willing to work hard for their families only to have the world point a finger at them calling them thieves, thugs and convicts." So while the hearings had the potential of calling attention to the lack of democracy within their union, it also publicly smeared longshoremen with criminal association.[69]

These differing responses to Corridan suggest the problems he faced. While many dockworkers were grateful for Corridan's efforts, others saw him as an annoying meddler. The suspicion of Corridan would continue to plague his reform activities. The rank-and-file was therefore split in its reaction to "outsiders" purporting to represent its best interests. As will be seen, even when presented with a clear choice, many, if not most, of the dockworkers preferred to stay with the ILA. Outside allies could never overcome deep-seated suspicion of their actions or intentions. Political reformers, both within and outside the ILA, were regarded by many longshoremen as opportunists merely looking for an angle to further their own selfish prospects.

Beyond Corridan's contribution, another noteworthy aspect of the investigation was its sheer scale. The overwhelming evidence of corruption on the waterfront and the critical role played by the ILA in furthering such activity brought to the public eye the need for reform. The commission heard from over seven hundred witnesses, and four thousand pages of testimony were recorded. It was by far the most thorough of all investigations and made abundantly clear the need to clean up the industry and the union.[70] Reform followed quickly. Governor Dewey released a scathing report and called for a joint authority with the state of New Jersey to oversee the New York harbor. A Waterfront Commission was to be established to oversee employment centers; the shape-up system was coming to an end. Dewey was not altogether supportive of the measure. He was wary of government intrusion and the creation of a "new governmental agency." But in his address to the state legislature, he was forced to admit that the survival of the port, and New York's economic health, depended on stable industrial relations on the waterfront.

While recognizing that the Waterfront Commission could not be expected to provide "the whole answer," he hoped "that the cancerous conditions will be cured."[71]

The creation of the two-state agency required congressional approval. At the July 22, 1953, hearing of the House Committee on the Judiciary, Corridan laid out once again the insidious criminal control of the shape-up and urged for "national security" purposes to have "racket-free handling of cargo out of the world's greatest port." Corridan had planned his attack well. Earlier, in front of the Senate Committee on Interstate and Foreign Commerce, Corridan stated that no reform could "be accomplished without Government intervention. . . . There is no will within the industry; there is no will within the union." In August, Congress ratified the two-state compact providing at last for the end of the hated shape-up and the establishment of a Waterfront Commission to oversee hiring. Many of the militants who were Communist or had Communist sympathies were barred by the commission from the waterfront.[72]

Corridan was encouraged further by the initiative of the American Federation of Labor (AFL) to expel the ILA. Embarrassed by the public revelations of criminal control of the ILA, the AFL executive board was determined to reform the union. As early as the 1940 AFL convention, the federation had begun to address cautiously the issue of corruption in its affiliated unions. The sticking point was the issue of autonomy. Since its founding the AFL had recognized the freedom of its affiliates to run their own affairs. After prodding by David Dubinsky of the International Ladies Garment Workers Union (ILGWU), however, the 1940 convention agreed that the executive council had the authority to encourage removal of corrupt officials.[73] The resolution gathered dust until the 1952 crime commission hearings. Then Dubinsky urged the AFL president, George Meany, to use the resolution as a weapon against the ILA. Meany agreed, and insisted that, in light of the hearings, the ILA should explain what it intended to do about the voluminous evidence of racketeering in the union. Meany had known Ryan for decades but it was clear to him that the ILA "was in the hands of racketeers and they were extorting money from the dock workers." While it was important to encourage the AFL and Meany to act, it was also desirable to offset any further investigation of affiliated unions. In-house cleaning was therefore more of a defensive measure, a mere holding action.[74]

The AFL established April 30, 1953, as the deadline by which the ILA had to clean up the union. The AFL ordered the ILA to comply with four recommendations: eject union officials who had accepted payments from employers; get rid of those who had criminal records; end the shape-up; and install "recognized democratic procedures" within the union generally.[75] The ILA basically ignored the AFL's entreaty. Although it admitted that problems existed within the union, it did not provide a blueprint for reform. Indeed, when it came to the issue of Ryan's acceptance of money from the shipping companies, the ILA contended that these funds were mere gifts, which incensed the AFL leadership. Additionally, the ILA canvassed its members concerning the shape-up. The longshoremen were asked to vote on the issue on May 8, 1953. The ILA used the opportunity to publicly attack Corridan. In a pamphlet entitled *The Waterfront Alert,* the ILA charged that Corridan was merely an opportunist. Citing Corridan's television appearances on New York City news programs, the pamphlet described him as a "TV ham." Father Corridan was also smeared as a careerist whose main "desire [was] to be the WATERFRONT ARBITRATOR." Although a majority of longshoremen voted to retain the shape-up, the total vote of 7,020 for and 3,920 against retention did not impress the AFL.[76] At its annual convention in September 1953, the AFL took the extraordinary step of expelling the ILA and creating a rival union, the ILA-AFL, known later as the International Brotherhood of Longshoremen (IBL). At last an institutional alternative was now available for the New York longshoremen.[77]

Joe Ryan was the first casualty of the AFL's campaign. Ryan was already under indictment for bribery after taking money from shippers and stevedores. The ILA leadership believed that the ouster of Ryan would take the heat off and maybe convince members who were thinking of jumping to the AFL that real reform was underway. It was left to Mike Clemente, the "union overlord" of the East River docks, to provide the coup de grace. Clemente called on Ryan to retire, which would offer the "only way to clean up the dirt on the waterfront." Although not happy about it, Ryan accepted the inevitable and announced his retirement in November 1953. A sweetener was added to the deal when the ILA agreed to pay him an annual pension of $10,000 for life. His troubles were far from over, however, and he was convicted of violating the Taft-Hartley Act for taking bribes from shippers. He was fined $2,500 and sentenced to six months in jail. He appealed to the United States Supreme Court but in February 1956 the conviction was upheld. Ryan paid the fine but successfully avoided prison after pleading ill-health. He continued to battle illness until on June 26, 1963, he died of cancer.[78]

In an effort to show a different face the ILA appointed Captain William V. Bradley, the Tugboatmen's leader, as the new president of the union. Such a strategy was not convincing to ILA insurgents or to the AFL. According to

Dwyer, "They pushed a clean face with Bradley" but it did not change the perception that the ILA was hopelessly corrupt and out of touch with its membership.[79]

The ILA decision to oust Ryan could not stop the AFL's intention to eradicate the union from the waterfront. Johnny Dwyer acted as the local leader of the AFL group. The AFL set up five temporary trustees: George Meany; Dave Beck, president of the Teamsters; Paul Hall, secretary-treasurer of the Seafarers Union; William Doherty, of the Letter Carriers; and A. J. Hayes, of the Machinists. George Boldanzi, a Teamster organizer,was also dispatched to support Dwyer.[80] Peter Johnson, the legal representative of the 1951 strike committee, was counsel for the group. Both Sampson and Nawrocki were absent from this new formation. Sampson had given up his position as business agent of Local 791 and become an AFL organizer. Unfortunately for Sampson, Local 791 members refused to follow him, leaving him isolated along the Chelsea docks. Nawrocki had been dismissed from the union pension board and was lying low.[81]

In reaction to the founding of the ILA-AFL, the ILA leadership immediately threatened strike action. It was a bold move, a test of strength. Its primary strategy was to offset the ILA-AFL initiative. If a strike was called the ILA-AFL members would be forced to cross the picket lines. Such an action held an emotional hazard, as well as publicly identifying participants to some of the gangsters on the waterfront. The strike warning also persuaded the New York Shipping Association to side with the ILA. The NYSA approached President Dwight D. Eisenhower and "urged" him to pressure the National Labor Relations Board (NLRB) to organize a quick representation election. After prodding by Eisenhower, the NLRB called the requested representative election, giving the ILA-AFL only seven rather than thirty days to prepare.[82] With strike action threatened, Eisenhower followed the lead of his predecessor and used the Taft-Hartley Act to establish a Board of Inquiry to investigate the dispute. Its October 5 report was pessimistic, arguing that in tandem with the "habitually suspicious" nature of longshoremen and union officials, the ILA-AFL challenge had created "an atmosphere of belligerence."[83] By December little had changed. The Board of Inquiry reported on December 4, 1953, that the "current position [w]as akin to guerrilla warfare. Bargaining is at a standstill. The issue of union representation overshadows all others."[84]

The ILA did more than just use intimidation and coercion to convince its members to reject the ILA-AFL. The ILA looked for allies within the labor movement and found an important one in John L. Lewis, president of the United Mine Workers. Lewis had become estranged from both the AFL and CIO leadership. As talk of a merger between the two labor movements gathered momentum, Lewis tried to create the impression that he would head a new labor organization. His support of the ILA was merely a spoiling tactic to remind labor leaders he was still a force to be reckoned with. He gave money and speeches to support the ILA's battle with ILA-AFL. While the ILA welcomed the money, it was the symbolic value of Lewis's support that was the key. The ILA distributed pamphlets stating, "We cannot be wrong. John L. Lewis is with us." William Bradley even traveled to Washington, D.C., and had his picture taken with Lewis.[85] With the vote coming up, the ILA distributed circulars arguing that a ILA-AFL victory would divide the union into the Teamsters' and the Seamen's respective organizations. Playing upon the longshoremen's traditional hostility to outsiders, the leaflets further pointed out, "The AFL Longshoremen's Union is controlled by Meany who was a plumber—Beck who was a truck driver—Hall who was a seaman." Dwyer and his longshoremen supporters were labeled "as a bunch of opportunists . . . [and] well paid stooges."[86]

The criticism of the Teamsters and Seafarers unions' intentions was a potent argument. For years the Teamsters had battled the ILA over jurisdiction of workers in and around the docks, and the charge that they would dominate the dock employment was a formidable accusation. Just as important, the shady reputation of the Teamster leader Dave Beck did little to assuage fears about his organization's intentions. Like Joe Ryan, Beck took from both his union and employers. For some New York longshoremen, therefore, there seemed little point in exchanging one corrupt union for another.[87]

The National Labor Relations Board held the election on December 22 and 23, 1953. The ILA garnered 9,060 votes, while the ILA-AFL received 7,568. The ILA-AFL immediately challenged the election. It targeted 4,405 of the votes cast, arguing that 2,400 ballots did not have the voter's name on the "eligibility list," 150 were supervisors and ineligible to vote, 650 had insufficient identification, and 1,100 voted at the wrong voting place (the remaining were challenged for a "variety of reasons"). The ILA-AFL were also upset over the quick call for the vote, describing its timing as being in "undue haste." The AFL argued that it was unfair that only seven days were given to prepare lists and notify longshoremen who were eligible to vote. Just as crucial, the AFL wanted to identify "phantoms" and keep them off the list. Consequently, the ILA-AFL charged that thousands of eligible men did not vote. Additionally, the ILA-AFL contended that widespread intimidation and coercion were evident throughout the two-day polling period. Finally, the ILA-AFL claimed that thirteen charges of unfair labor practices were pending before the NLRB and should have been dealt with before the election.[88]

With the ILA-AFL appeal pending before the NLRB, the ILA strike threat still remained. In response, the New York State Board of Mediation stepped into the controversy. Just as in the 1951 strike, the ILA maintained its hostility to the board. Board chairman Merlyn S. Pitzele met with Bradley, Connolly, and Teddy Gleason in a two-hour meeting and characterized their attitude "as one of complete non-cooperation." Pitzele also met with ILA-AFL members Johnny Dwyer, Paul Hall, and Peter Johnson. The three agreed to work with any state or federal inquiry; Pitzele in turn described them as giving their "full cooperation." The employers were hesitant. They were confused and unsure of which labor organization to recognize. The major question facing Pitzele was whether the ILA would act on its threat to strike. Although the presidency had been handed to Captain William V. Bradley, Pitzele observed that the other ranking officials, including Patrick Connolly and Teddy Gleason, were "identical."[89]

The matter was one of official survival. Pitzele remained convinced that the ILA was merely bluffing to maintain whatever legitimacy it had by forcing employers to negotiate. By negotiating with the ILA, the NYSA would send a clear signal to the longshoremen about who still maintained union power. Such an action would weaken the ILA-AFL's posture as the rightful representative of the men. The employers accepted the ILA assertion. John V. Lyon explained to Pitzele that because the ILA currently remained the only official representative organization, the NYSA had no choice but "to negotiate with them." For Pitzele, however, the ILA's bluff was tantamount to admitting a weak position. As he stated in his report, "A bluff can only be identified for what it is—a losing hand."[90] Pitzele would be proved wrong. Employers had already made clear they would continue to deal with the ILA. Complicating the picture further, once the NLRB called for a second election the ILA called a strike in early 1954. The employers preferred to work with ILA because they perceived the ILA-AFL as potentially more demanding during contract negotiations.

The strike began on March 24, 1954. The strike immediately put the ILA-AFL on the defensive because its members were forced to walk through the ILA picket lines. The ILA-AFL declared the strike "phoney" and ordered its members to continue to work. For the next month a series of violent confrontations occurred throughout the port. The newly installed Waterfront Commission reported daily assaults on "AFL longshoremen." These ranged from direct assaults on men as they tried to enter the piers, to cases of ILA pickets overturning cars. ILA-AFL men were also threatened at home, and their car tires were slashed. During some of the confrontations even mounted policemen were attacked by ILA pickets who threw stones and nails under the hooves of the police horses. Interestingly enough, the ILA pickets invariably outnumbered the ILA-AFL men trying to work. At least on the streets, the ILA held the upper hand. Employer intransigence was just as threatening to the ILA-AFL. Many stevedores refused to hire them for employment. Throughout the port many of the major stevedores (Universal, Jarka, American Stevedore, Bay Ridge, and McGrath) insisted on hiring only ILA men. The ILA-AFL gangs were confined to a few North River piers operated by Dwyer's Local 807 and to U.S. Army bases in Brooklyn and Staten Island.[91]

For Dwyer the daily scenes of confrontation were having a bad effect on the morale of the ILA-AFL men. He was also threatened, as he said, "Not to my face, sometimes on the telephone. I'm sure they'd love to get me outta the way, but I was just lucky." Although the AFL was footing the bill, Dwyer knew that the men generally were under enormous pressure from the ILA. As he pointed out, "I'm sure a lot of the Italians in Brooklyn were scared." These same men were told daily, "If you vote the wrong way [for the ILA-AFL] you'll be out of job." Thus their "livelihood" was "threatened," and as Dwyer said, "that's enough to change a guy's mind."[92]

The second election was set for April 1954. Dwyer was not sure how the men were going to vote: "you never know what they're going to do when they go in the polling booth." The result was again an ILA victory. In an extremely tight race the longshoremen voted for the ILA 9,110 to 8,791.[93] The election defeat stunned Corridan. The apparent gain of the establishment of the Waterfront Commission had been countered by a vote against the AFL. There were many reasons for the ILA win, among them intimidation as well as support for the ILA by the miners' leader John L. Lewis. More important perhaps was the perception by many longshoremen that the Seafarers and Teamsters unions were intent on stealing their jobs. For Dwyer the vote was not unexpected. As he explained, "A lot [of the men] were strictly ILA all the way." Although many of the longshoremen were "scared," Dwyer believed that the election had been "fair."[94]

Dwyer continued his efforts to challenge the ILA. The ILA-AFL was transformed into the International Brotherhood of Longshoremen (IBL), and Meany continued to bankroll the organization. But the momentum had been lost. Dwyer and Hall maintained an office and published a weekly newsletter, *The Waterfront News,* in both English and Italian. A third and final representative election was held in 1956 but again the majority of New York's longshoremen voted for the ILA. Teamster encroachment drove many longshoremen to vote ILA. In 1955, Beck had made public his intention to get AFL backing to take control of the IBL, or in his words, "assimilate it" into the teamsters' organization. Such moves only confirmed longshoremen's suspicions of Beck's imperial intentions to dominate the New York waterfront. George Meany, now head of the AFL-CIO, reaffirmed his commitment to the IBL by stating, "One thing is certain, that the AFL-CIO will never desert the longshoremen who want a decent trade union."[95]

Dwyer then tried to obtain a job on the waterfront but when he did, the company moved its operation to another pier. The point had been made: Dwyer was not welcome. As he pointed out, the ILA leaders "were not going to let me work on the waterfront, no way . . . and they tell the companies not to hire me." But Dwyer remained optimistic. His IBL cohorts continued to work on the waterfront. As he explained, "Nobody lost their jobs." But it was the effect of the long campaign to oust the ILA that gave Dwyer hope: "We came close, gave them a scare anyway, and I think they're [longshoremen] better off today with what we tried to do."[96]

Dwyer tempered his optimistic appraisal once the AFL-CIO decided to accept the ILA into the fold in August 1959. A special AFL-CIO Executive Council Committee reported that the union had undertaken extensive reforms and that many of the international officers with criminal records were gone from the organization, as were those who had taken payments from employers. Important as these reforms were, the AFL-CIO had also become wary of the process. More than $1 million had been expended but the majority of the longshoremen remained loyal to the ILA. As Meany later recalled, """We spent more than a million dollars to give these people a new union, and it didn't work. It was pretty difficult because, despite all the corruption, there was a certain loyalty to the old union on the part of the workers, especially the old fellows." The three failed representative elections were also part of the mix. The 1954 ILA election victory had forced the NLRB to certify it once again as the sole collective bargaining agent for New York's longshoremen. The AFL-CIO Executive Council Committee in turn recommended that "the ILA be admitted to affiliation with the AFL-CIO as an International affiliate." The committee's report stated that the IBL should first accept this finding before the AFL-CIO convention vote on the reaffiliation of the ILA. Dwyer tried to block the IBL from accepting the recommendation. In an impassioned speech to the 1959 IBL convention, Dwyer charged that little had changed in the ILA and the "mob" still controlled the union. As he argued, "How indeed can the House of Labor, through its sages, expect the ILA to live up to any promises against discrimination, when the history of the ILA, even up to this very moment, is replete with assassination, vengeance and economic contrition against any and all who have stood in the path against this motley herd of Jackals posing and bulldozing in a manner best exemplified by Edward G. Robinson and Humphrey Bogart." Dwyer's plea failed, however, and the IBL accepted the ILA's reaffiliation, clearing the way for the AFL-CIO to vote to accept the ILA at the 1961 AFL-CIO convention. According to Dwyer, the IBL was suffering from exhaustion and the AFL-CIO was veering toward negotiations with the ILA. Thus, once it seemed the AFL-CIO was losing confidence that it would ever beat the ILA, "some of the guys at the top [of the IBL] figured they should start making deals to get back in [the ILA]."[97]

For Corridan, the lack of support by the rank and file hurt the most. As he explained later, "The rank-and-file dockworkers have lost this fight, and they won't make another for a long time to come." Corridan took the defeat personally and equated his position with that of the men: "I've lost. . . . The mobsters won. They're still on the docks."[98]

Corridan had reason to be depressed. The ILA had survived and would continue to control the membership through intimidation. In a 1960 report, the Waterfront Commission found extensive criminal control within the union and continuing pilferage of union funds. Such a state of affairs left Corridan further demoralized and his already heavy drinking degenerated into alcoholism. No longer able to gather momentum for further reform, Corridan moved away from his dock work and eventually died in 1984 at the age of seventy-three.[99]

Although unable to rid the ILA of criminal control, Father Corridan had been extremely successful in bringing to the public's attention the atrocious working conditions of New York's longshoremen. Numerous congressional and state committees and commissions had investigated the longshoremen's world. Just as important, the abusive shape-up had been abolished. A hiring hall had been established and the longshoremen were no longer victims of kick-back demands and loan sharks. Corridan had also been successful in ridding the waterfront of Communists. But the victory was hollow. The curbing of any oppositional movement could only strengthen the conservative forces within the ILA. The Xavier School continued with its classes but the momentum had been lost after the ILA's electoral victory.

The tumultuous years of 1951–59 saw the rise and fall of rank-and-file leaders. Dramatic confrontations between these leaders and the ILA hierarchy were a constant feature of the period. Just as frequent was the changing composition of this rank-and-file leadership. True, Father Corridan and Communist agitators were invariably in and around the movement, but others shifted in and out. Vincent Longhi and Mitch Berenson, while active in the 1948 strike, were absent in 1951. The local trade union leaders also moved in and out of the oppositional movement. In the three major strikes of 1945, 1948, and 1951, the strike leaders were different. Only Gene Sampson remained a vocal opponent to the ILA leadership, but his posturing still was that of the "loyal opposition." Once the strikes became too threatening to the established leadership, Sampson tended to back off and stand on the sidelines. When given an institutional alternative with the ILA-AFL, Sampson was deserted by Local 791 members. It was left to Johnny Dwyer to take up the baton. With such a divergent leadership it is not surprising that the members were wary of those who purported to represent them. Even when given the opportunity to rid themselves of a corrupt leadership, it was more a case of staying with the devil they knew. The sordid reputation of Dave Beck did little to help the reputation of the reformers. Beck's demand that the membership rid the ILA of corrupt officials rang hollow. Once Beck made clear his union's intention to gain control of the IBL, it merely reaffirmed deep-seated suspicions of his predatory designs.

On the west side of Manhattan today, the world of the labor priest appears as a phantom, while the piers have all but disappeared. The legacy of Father Corridan is still evident as retired longshoremen lounge along the avenues, sharing their stories and feeling thankful for having survived such a turbulent and dangerous occupation. The longshoremen's medical centers in Manhattan and Brooklyn testify to a union leadership forced by a small cadre of Catholic and Communist activists to listen to the dockworkers. But having said that, one must also recognize that the men themselves stood up in 1948 and 1951 and confronted the ILA leadership. Wildcat action was the only weapon they possessed, symbolizing both power and powerlessness.

The rebellion between 1945 and 1959 also found its echo in London, where rank-and-file resentment and anger were just as potent as in New York. The only difference between the confrontations was that in London the nation-state played a major role in influencing the rebellion. Indeed, in London the conflict took on a more political shape, as the Labour government was determined to stamp out the rank-and-file movement, even going to the extreme of prosecuting the leaders for conspiracy.

Notes

1. Letter to Hon. Christopher C. McGrath, House of Representatives, from John Corridan, June 6, 1949, Records of the Xavier Institute of Industrial Relations, series 2—Father John M. Corridan, S.J. (hereafter XIIR), box 10, folder 15, Fordham University Archive. Jesuit priests from the Xavier Institute played a major role in galvanizing public opinion to clean up the ILA. See Colin J. Davis, "'Launch Out into the Deep and Let Down Your Nets': Father John Corridan, S.J., and the New York Longshoremen in the Post–World War II Era," *Catholic Historical Review* (January 2000): 66–84.

2. David J. O'Brien, *American Catholics and Social Reform: The New Deal Years* (New York: Oxford University Press, 1968), 17, 19–20.

3. For studies that examine Coughlin and Day see Alan Brinkley, *Voices of Protest: Huey Long, Father Coughlin and the Great Depression* (New York: Vintage Books, 1983); William

D. Miller, *Dorothy Day: A Biography* (San Francisco: Harper and Row, 1982). See also Dorothy Day's *The Long Loneliness: The Autobiography of Dorothy Day* (New York: Curtis Books, 1952). Aaron I. Abell estimated that twenty-four labor schools had been formed by Jesuits, while diocesan authorities established thirty-two. Abell, *American Catholicism and Social Reform: A Search for Social Justice* (Notre Dame: University of Notre Dame Press, 1963), 278–79. The more radical anti-Communist organization was the Association of Catholic Trade Unionists; see Douglas Seaton, *Catholics and Radicals: The Association of Catholic Trade Unionists and the American Labor Movement, from Depression to Cold War* (Lewisburg, Pa.: Bucknell University Press, 1981); Neil Betten, *Catholic Activism and the Industrial Worker* (Gainesville: University of Florida Press, 1976); Philip Taft, "The Association of Catholic Trade Unionists," *Industrial and Labor Relations Review* 2 (January 1949): 210–18.

4. Philip E. Dobson, "The Xavier Labor School, 1938–39" (undated, unpaginated manuscript). I would like to thank Joshua Freeman for providing me with this source.

5. Ibid.

6. For the Communist influence in the transit industry and the Catholic Church's antagonistic response, see Joshua Freeman, *In Transit: The Transport Workers Union in New York City, 1933–1966* (New York: Oxford University Press, 1989).

7. Allen Raymond, *Waterfront Priest* (New York: Holt, 1955), 4–5.

8. Ibid., 59.

9. Ibid., 259.

10. Interview with Father Philip Carey, New Yorkers at Work: Oral History, Robert F. Wagner Labor Archives, Tamiment Library, New York University (hereafter NYAW).

11. Letter to Hon. Christopher C. McGrath from John Corridan; interview with Father Philip Carey.

12. John Corridan, Memo—"My Visit to Washington, 1948," XIIR, box 10, folder 18.

13. Father John Corridan, *The Longshoremen's Case,* XIIR, box 11, folder 33.

14. Much of the "social action" movement stemmed from Pope Leo XIII's *Rerum Novarum,* which reconciled the Catholic Church with the modern state: "Whenever the general interests of any particular class suffers . . . the public authority must step in to deal with it." O'Brien, *American Catholics and Social Reform,* 14. See also Aaron Ignatius Abell, *American Catholicism and Social Action* (Garden City, N.Y.: Hanover House, 1960).

15. Letter to Rev. R. A. McGowan, Director, Department of Social Action, National Catholic Welfare Conference, from John Corridan, June 29, 1949, XIIR, box 10, folder 4.

16. Letter to Hon. Christopher C. McGrath from John Corridan; "Labor Day Speech, 1948, Father John Corridan," XIIR, box 11, folder 30 (quote). For the anti-Communism of labor priests, see Joshua Freeman and Steve Rosswurm, "The Education of an Anti-Communist: Father John F. Cronin and the Baltimore Labor Movement," *Labor History* 33 (Spring 1992): 217–47, and Monsignor Charles Owen Rice, "Confessions of an Anti-Communist," *Labor History* 30 (Summer 1989): 449–62.

17. Letter to Hon. Wayne Morse, U.S. Senator, from John Corridan, 1949, XIIR, box 10, folder 15.

18. Letter to George G. Higgins, National Catholic Welfare Conference, from John Corridan, December 2, 1948, XIIR, box 10, folder 4.

19. Henry Winston, "The Meaning of Industrial Concentration," *Political Affairs* (August 1952): 28 (first quote); William Weinstone, "An Important Chapter in the Party's

History of Industrial Concentration," *Political Affairs* (September 1949): 76–80; John Williamson, "The Main Direction of the Party's Trade-Union Work," *Political Affairs* (February 1951): 66–67; idem, "Two Conventions of Labor: The Situation in the Trade Union Movement," *Political Affairs* (January 1949): 30 (second quote).

20. The party leaders were convinced that AFL and CIO leaders had adopted "profascist leanings." Robert Thompson, "Two Paths for American Labor," *Political Affairs* (March 1950): 12; Williamson, "The Main Direction," 61; idem, "Two Conventions of Labor," 27.

21. Audrey West, interview by author, August 5, 1995.

22. Ibid.

23. Harold Mailman, interview by author, June 12, 1998.

24. West interview.

25. Ibid.

26. Mailman interview.

27. James R. Barrett, *William Z. Foster and the Tragedy of American Radicalism* (Urbana: University of Illinois Press, 1999), 243–45; Joseph R. Starobin, *American Communism in Crisis* (Cambridge, Mass.: Harvard University Press, 1972), 130–35.

28. West interview; Mailman interview.

29. West interview.

30. Ibid.

31. Mailman interview.

32. Maurice Isserman, *Which Side Were You On?* (Middletown, Conn.: Wesleyan University Press, 1982), 214–56; Barrett, *William Z. Foster,* 226–51; Starobin, *American Communism in Crisis,* 121–213.

33. John Corridan, "Overtime on Overtime: Longshoremen's Case," *America,* April 2, 1949; idem, "Overtime on Overtime—Conclusion," ibid., July 28, 1949.

34. Malcolm Johnson, "Father Gangbuster—Mystery Man of the Waterfront," *Argosy,* March 1952.

35. John Corridan, "The New York Longshoremen's Problem," XIIR, box 10, folder 4.

36. "Testimony of Julius Bagley and Mitch Berenson," House Committee on Education and Labor, *Amendments to the Fair Labor Standards Act of 1938, Vol. 1,* 81st Cong., 1st sess., 1949, 600–625. One of the best sources that describes Berenson is Arthur Miller's autobiography, *Timebends: A Life* (New York: Grove Press, 1987).

37. John Corridan, Memorandum—1½ hour talk with longshore commies, XIIR, box 10, folder 7.

38. *New York Times,* April 2, 1949, 31; *New York Sun,* March 30, 1949, 2. Jacobs also appeared before the U.S. Senate to state his members' concerns over discrimination. "Testimony of Cleophas Jacobs," Senate Committee on Labor and Public Welfare, *To Clarify the Overtime Provisions of the Fair Labor Standards Act of 1938, As Amended,* 81st Cong., 1st sess., 1949, 488–91.

39. Letter to George K. Hunton, Catholic Interracial Council, from Paul W. Rishell, Chairman, Economic Justice Commission, Brooklyn Division of the Protestant Council, June 8, 1949, and letter to Hunton from Corridan, June 10, 1949, both in XIIR, box 11, folder 11.

40. *New York Times,* October 16, 1951, 1, 26, October 17, 1951, 1, 28.

41. Ibid., October 16, 1951, 26.

42. Interview with John Dwyer, November 21, 1980, NYAW.

43. *New York Times,* October 17, 1951, 1, 28.

44. Ibid., October 18, 1951, 1, 22. Anastasia's public antics were his last in the strike. Embarrassed by both public tirades and the eventual failure to keep the men at work, Ryan ordered him to "lay off" of any further strikebreaking displays. *New York Times,* October 19, 1951, 16.

45. Ibid., October 20, 1951, 1, 8, October 24, 1951, 21.

46. Ibid., October 19, 1951, 16, October 20, 1951, 8; "FBI Report—Longshoremen's Strike at the Port of New York, October 25, 1951," Maritime Folder, box 168, Papers of Harry Truman, Harry S. Truman Library (quotes).

47. *New York Times,* October 21, 1951, 1, 68.

48. Ibid., October 22, 1951, 1, 15, October 23, 1951, 1, 20.

49. Ibid., October 22, 1951, 15.

50. Ibid., October 25, 1951, 1, October 23, 1951, 20 (quotes).

51. Ibid., October 26, 1951, 15. When cutting the ties with the mediators, Sampson declared, "We are finished with this mediation board and will not meet with this board again."

52. Ibid., October 27, 1951, 1, 22. As late as October 28, Steelman believed the strike would end that day. Ibid., October 29, 1951, 1. See also Muriel L. Beach, "A Case Study of Government Intervention in National Emergency Disputes: Longshore Industry of the Port of New York," 11–12, Vernon Jensen Papers, box 3-4067, Kheel Center, Cornell University.

53. *New York Times,* October 29, 1951, 45, October 30, 1951, 1.

54. Budd Schulberg, "Waterfront Priest," *Commonweal,* April 3, 1953, 646.

55. *New York Times,* October 25, 1951, 1.

56. Ibid., October 31, 1951, 1, 25, November 1, 1951, 1, 24, November 2, 1951, 1, 48. Commissioner Corsi used the 1941 State Labor Law to institute the panel. It was only the second time it happened since the passage of the act. Ibid., November 6, 1951.

57. Ibid., November 3, 1951, 1.

58. Ibid., November 7, 1951, 23, November 8, 1951, 19.

59. "The 1951 Strike Committee's Select Proposals to Improve Maritime Relationships in the Port of Greater New York and Vicinity," Jensen Papers, box 17-4067 (quotes).

60. Ibid.

61. For the daily confrontations between longshoremen from Local 824 and strikers, and for Ryan's attempt to oust Sampson from Local 791, see *New York Times,* November 3, 1951, 32, November 4, 1951, 1, 37, November 5, 1951, 1, 53, November 6, 1951, 1, 25, November 7, 1951, 1, 33. For the march on City Hall by the Commerce and Industry Association see ibid., November 8, 1951, 1, 19.

62. Ibid., November 9, 1951, 50.

63. Ibid., 1, 50, November 10, 1951, 1, 7.

64. *Final Report—Board of Inquiry on Longshore Industry Work Stoppage, October–November, 1951, Port of New York,* New York State, Department of Labor, January 22, 1954, Jensen Papers, box 18-4067.

65. Statement of the International Longshoremen's Association, AFL, on the Report, dated January 22, 1952, of Industrial Commissioner Corsi's Board of Inquiry, signed President Joseph P. Ryan, Jensen Papers, box 9-4067; "Reply by Mr. Dean Alfange, Member of the New York State Board of Inquiry into the Longshoremen's Strike of 1951, to

the Recent Statement by Mr. Joseph P. Ryan, President of the International Longshoremen's Association, with Respect to the Board's Report," July 10, 1952, ibid.

66. "Testimony of Joseph Ryan," New York State Crime Commission—Public Hearing No. 5, Port of New York (Waterfront), 3606–3730, New York City Municipal Library.

67. Raymond, *Waterfront Priest,* 195–97. Cardinal Spellman had summoned Corridan to a private meeting on November 4 to answer charges that he had started the 1951 strike. Corridan denied the charge but Spellman persisted by demanding why Corridan had said a prayer before the strikers asking that "God grant that our government may order us back to work in honor." Corridan replied that the strike was coming to an end, and to allow the men to "return to work with their heads up" and not by "crawling on their bellies in front of a victory of the mob element within the port," the government should provide a way for the men to return to work. Such a way was found after the rebels agreed with the Board of Inquiry to return to work. Spellman accepted Corridan's argument and no action was taken against the labor priest. Ibid., 148, 154–57.

68. Unsigned and undated letter to Father John Corridan (first quote); letter to Corridan from "The Son of a Longshoreman," May 13, 1953 (second quote); undated letter to Corridan from Patrick Cleary; undated letter to Corridan from Edward Slinkauski, all in XIIR, box 11, folder 1 (third quote).

69. Letter to Corridan from Peter C. Kenney Jr., March 5, 1952, and undated letter to Corridan from Anthony Silvio, XIIR, box 11, folder 1.

70. "Message of the Governor in Relation to Creation of the Waterfront Crime Commission—Extraordinary Session," New York Legislative Docs., 176th Session, 1953, vol. 10, #93. The five volumes of the crime commission hearings are a wonderful revelation of industry connivance in allowing Ryan and his goons to run the ILA. See New York State Crime Commission—Public Hearings, Port of New York (Waterfront), vols. 1–5, New York City Municipal Library. See also Joshua B. Freeman, *Working-Class New York: Life and Labor since World War II* (New York: New Press, 2000), 162.

71. "Message of the Governor in Relation to Creation of the Waterfront Crime Commission—Extraordinary Session."

72. "Testimony of Father John Corridan," House Committee on Judiciary, *New Jersey–New York Waterfront Commission Compact,* 83d Cong., 1st sess., 1953, 99 (first quote); "Testimony of Father John Corridan," Senate Committee on Interstate and Foreign Commerce, *Waterfront Investigation. Part 1: New York–New Jersey Waterfront,* 83d Cong., 1st sess., 1953, 565 (second quote).

73. The specific resolution stated that if an international union "evaded its responsibility" then the "Executive Council shall be authorized to apply all its influence to secure such action as will correct the situation." Dubinsky had used the resolution as a pretext for reentering the AFL. Helping his case was a violent assault against him in a hotel bar by Joe Fay, vice-president of the Operating Engineers Union. Fay had drunkenly demanded that Dubinsky drop his resolution, and when Dubinsky declined the suggestion Fay attacked him with his fists. David Dubinsky and A. H. Raskin, *David Dubinsky: A Life with Labor* (New York: Simon and Schuster, 1977), 159–64; Philip Taft, *The A.F. of L. from the Death of Gompers to the Merger* (New York: Octagon, 1970), 426 (quote).

74. Archie Robinson, *George Meany and His Times: A Biography* (New York: Simon and Schuster, 1981), 189; Paul Buhle, *Taking Care of Business: Samuel Gompers, George Meany, Lane Kirkland, and the Tragedy of American Labor* (New York: Monthly Review Press,

1999), 159; John Hutchinson, *The Imperfect Union: A History of Corruption in American Trade Unions* (New York: Dutton, 1972), 295–97.

75. Dennis Howard, "Waterfront Underground: A Clean-Up Is Under Way on the New York Docks," *Jubilee: A Magazine of the Church and Her People,* May 1953, 23 (quote); Report and Recommendations of the AFL-CIO Executive Council Committee Respecting Affiliation of International Longshoremen's Association (Independent) for Affiliation with the AFL-CIO, August 17, 1959, series 5541, box 8, Philip Taft Papers, Kheel Center, Cornell University; Vernon Jensen, *Strife on the Waterfront: The Port of New York since 1945* (Ithaca, N.Y.: Cornell University Press, 1974), 105–11.

76. *Waterfront Alert,* undated, XIIL, box 10, folder 13; Jensen, *Strife on the Waterfront,* 106.

77. Report and Recommendations of the AFL-CIO Executive Council Committee; Jensen, *Strife on the Waterfront,* 110–11. David Dubinsky, who initiated action against the ILA, did not support the idea of expulsion. He believed that such action would "remove whatever influence you have over them; the only ones who benefit from that are the crooks." Dubinsky and Raskin, *David Dubinsky,* 165.

78. Jensen, *Strife on the Waterfront,* 124; *New York Herald-Tribune,* February 28, 1956, 4; *New York Times,* June 27, 1963, 33.

79. Jensen, *Strife on the Waterfront,* 124; Dwyer interview.

80. "Waterfront Priest Analyzes Dock Strike," *New York Herald-Tribune,* October 4, 1953, 2.

81. For Sampson and Nawrocki's dismissals from the ILA pension board, see *New York Times,* January 11, 1952, 8.

82. The Department of Labor reported that Chairman Lyons of the NYSA wanted the NLRB election "expedited" because his organization wanted to know "not later than December 1, with which union they were to deal." *National Emergency Disputes Under the Labor Management Relations (Taft-Hartley) Act, 1945–65, Bulletin No. 1482* (GPO: March, 1966).

83. *Report to the President on the Labor Dispute Involving Longshoremen and Associated Occupations in the Maritime Industry on the Atlantic Coast,* October 5, 1953.

84. Ibid., December 4, 1953.

85. Once Lewis fell in behind the ILA he had lunch regularly with Dave Beck of the Teamsters and David McDonald of the Steelworkers Union. The point was made that perhaps an alternative to the AFL-CIO was being created. Melvyn Dubofsky and Warren Van Tine, *John L. Lewis: A Biography* (New York: Quadrangle, 1977), 493; Jensen, *Strife on the Waterfront,* 127–28.

86. *Stand By for the Vote,* ILA leaflet, undated, Jensen Papers, box 1-4067.

87. As one-time leader of the Western Conference of teamsters, Beck consorted with known racketeers. His activities with notorious union-busters, such as Nathan Shefferman, president of Labor Relations Associates, went as far as pilfering union funds to pay for the new Teamsters headquarters in Washington, D.C., in the late 1940s. Beck's relationship with trucking companies was also tainted by corruption. The Fruehauf Company, for example, presented Beck with gifts such as a boat, automobiles, and loans. Hutchinson, *The Imperfect Union,* 180–81, 231–32.

88. Report to Governor Thomas E. Dewey from New York State Board of Mediation, December 28, 1953, series 5541, box 8, Taft Papers.

89. Ibid.

90. Ibid.

91. "Interim Report on Current Work Stoppage," Waterfront Commission of New York Harbor, March 25, 1954, series 5541, box 8, Taft Papers.

92. Dwyer interview.

93. Ibid. (quote); Jensen, *Strife on the Waterfront,* 105–36; idem, "Hiring Practices and Employment Experience in the Port of New York," *International Labor Review* 77 (April 1958): 345–48; Raymond, *Waterfront Priest,* 214–50.

94. Dwyer interview (quotes).

95. "Waterfront News," October 19, 1956, Jensen Papers, box 1-4067; Hutchinson, *The Imperfect Union,* 300 (quote).

96. Dwyer interview.

97. Robinson, *George Meany,* 190 (first quote); Report and Recommendations of the AFL-CIO Executive Council Committee (second quote); John Dwyer, "Merger or Mockery," Jensen Papers, box 1-4067 (remaining quotes). Peter Johnson had helped Dwyer write the speech. Dwyer interview.

98. Raymond, *Waterfront Priest,* 260.

99. *Special Report of the Waterfront Commission of New York Harbor to the Governors and the Legislatures of the States of New York and New Jersey, December 1960* (New York: Waterfront Commission, 1960); Father Philip Dobson, interview by author, July 1994, Fordham University Infirmary.

New York longshoremen at a shape-up in 1951. Note the horseshoe shape the group forms. (*New York Times,* October 28, 1951. Courtesy Associated Press)

Longshoremen's union head Joseph P. Ryan enters Pier 92 after skirting picketing strikers during the 1951 strike. (*New York Times,* October 28, 1951. Courtesy Associated Press)

USING PERSUASION ON LONGSHOREMEN

Anthony Anastasia, in leather jacket, pushes a reluctant striker back to his job at the Brooklyn Army Base. The longshoremen returned to work but later walked out again. (*New York Times,* October 18, 1951. Courtesy Associated Press)

FIRST VIOLENCE IN WILDCAT DOCK STRIKE HER

Frank Nawrocki, longshoremen's business agen shows damage to his car after a free-for-all at the Hamilton Avenue pier, the first violence in the wildcat dock strike. (*New York Times,* October 23 1951. Courtesy Associated Press)

POLICE-ESCORTED DOCK WORKERS BREACH WILDCAT LINES HERE

Nonstrikers, left, on their way to unload the liner *Queen Elizabeth,* skirting hooting insurgents. (*New York Times,* October 30, 1951. Courtesy Associated Press)

DISCUSSING STRIKE WITH BOSTON DELEGATION

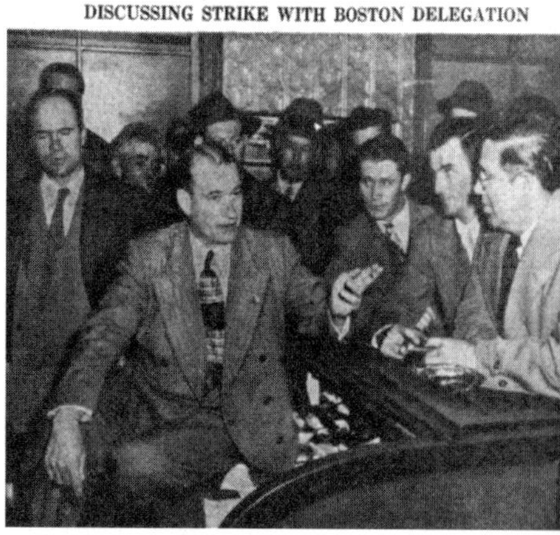

John J. (Gene) Sampson (seated on desk), leader the insurgents, discusses the strike with Boston delegates Francis J. Roache, Joseph Feeney, and Arthur La Coste. On the extreme left is Peter Johnson, legal advisor to the strikers. (*New York Times,* October 29, 1951. Courtesy Associated Press)

7 Rivalry: London

In London, as in New York, turbulence was a distinct characteristic of labor relations on the waterfront. Between 1949 and 1954 a series of explosive events took place that pitted the rank-and-file movement against trade union leaders and central governments alike. For the men, deepening alienation from their union leaders led to ever-increasing tension and estrangement. The issue of union control over the respective memberships was at the forefront of these struggles. For their part, the National Association of Stevedores and Dockers (NASD) and the Watermen, Lightermen, Tugmen, and Bargemen's Union (WLTBU) tried to maintain control of their members by using the oppositional movement to put forth their own agenda. Such an approach was encouraged by industrial relations law that precluded strike action. Lacking this important weapon in their arsenal, these two organizations were content to allow the unofficial movement periodically to fight their case. The Transport and General Workers' Union (TGWU), however, refused outright to recognize the validity of the rank-and-file movement. TGWU leaders perceived any vibrant oppositional movement of dockworkers as a serious internal threat. As in the 1948 zinc oxide strike, unofficial leaders were seen as disloyal wreckers.

In 1949, a series of issues and events that included a strike protesting the forced retirement of aged workers and a sympathy strike action with Canadian seamen came to the fore. Once the strikes ended, the rank-and-file leaders did not disperse as they had in 1948 after the zinc oxide strike. Rather, they maintained a permanent organization that directly challenged trade union officials. Once again the trade union leadership and the government scrambled to regain control of the situation. In an effort to maintain their authority, TGWU leaders decided on draconian action, purging some of the rank-and-file leaders from the union. This led to further dissension and conflict within the union and on the London docks. Consequently protest strikes broke out, showing that the rank-and-file movement had not faltered.

As the movement matured and gained confidence it became clear to the government that trade union disciplinary action had achieved little. In a dramatic display of force, the government shadowed the London rank-and-file leaders (and their Liverpool counterparts). When it became clear in 1951 that a strike was looming, and as the organizers were meeting in London, the government decided to act. As the rank-and-file leaders met in a London pub, it was raided by Special Branch officers and seven dockers were arrested on conspiracy charges. The case became a cause célèbre. It showed how far the government (and indirectly, the union) was prepared to go to maintain control. Such efforts were for naught, however. Neither the government nor union leadership understood that the attempt to muzzle the leaders would not end the movement's vital role as protector and guarantor of the dockworkers' interests. Rather, the drastic actions merely confirmed the rank-and-filers' belief in their unofficial leadership and reinforced their conviction that the established union leadership was not just out of touch with their interests, but too closely connected with a government that tried mightily to restrain the dockers' wages and working conditions.

In the weeks that followed the 1948 zinc oxide strike, a period of uneasy quiet descended on the London docks. The men continued to labor hard but bristled at the continuing autocratic power of the NDLB and the LDLB. The disciplinary measures of the Dock Labour Scheme continued to be applied. The dockworkers resented the perceived arbitrariness with which suspensions were meted out to those who had supposedly transgressed the rules of the scheme. The docks remained therefore a site of competing postures and attitudes. It would require only a spark for the fires of confrontation to break out once again.

In early April 1949 such a spark was ignited. In November 1948, the NDLB had ordered its constituent labor boards to "comb" their registers for "ineffective" workers, that is, those it considered too old or infirm to carry on their responsibilities. Using sliding criteria of "failing health" and "permanent physical incapacity," the boards were asked to "dismiss" such men from the registers. J. Hogger, the London Port manager and an NDLB official, reported to Ministry of Labour officials that the decision was predicated on an overmanning in the docks. Hogger explained "privately—he would not wish to be quoted," that "London had been carrying an excess of around 3,000 [men] for some time."[1]

As the LDLB was "combing" its register, the NASD held a meeting on March 6, 1949, to discuss the issue. Those attending the meeting "unanimously rejected" the policy and agreed to fight the dismissals. Dickie Barrett protested the treatment meted out to the aged men and called on the LDLB to rescind its dismissal order. The NASD's determination to fight the issue was known by both the NDLB and the government. Hogger warned Ministry of Labour officials on April 4 that a "crisis is likely to develop in the next two or three days." Hogger blamed "Communist elements" who "may start their usual disruptive campaign" to sabotage the London docks.[2]

The LDLB rejected Barrett's demand and on March 28 dismissed thirty-three men as being too "feeble" to continue working on the docks. On April 10, the NASD called an official strike to protest the dismissal of the "ineffectives." The following day 5,900 stevedores went out on strike. By April 12, the stevedores had been joined by TGWU dockers, increasing the number of men out to 14,238.[3] What had started out as clearing house policy had quickly degenerated into a conflict between the NASD and the LDLB. Just as problematic was that dockers quickly joined the strike. As the strike unfolded, the TGWU found it difficult to contain its members' actions; as with the 1948 strike the rank and file followed a different path from that of their leaders. The Labour government for its part witnessed a rapid deterioration in critical export and import shipments. Once again the government held a posture of being an ally to the TGWU while simultaneously working out a strategy that would ease the effects of the strike on trade.

How and why the dispute occurred says much about dockworker resentment against the Dock Labour Scheme, as well as against employers. The decision to dismiss the "ineffectives" struck a responsive chord among the men. A TGWU profile of the dismissed men certainly reveals the absence of regular work because of injury or old age. Of the 33 men, 22 were eighty years old or older, while 3 were over ninety. The men shared an array of physical characteristics including being considered "feeble," a "danger to himself," "unable to care for himself," "deteriorating," and at "risk of sudden collapse."[4] Thus there was a fundamental clash of principles. The TGWU leaders saw the men as a danger to themselves and others working nearby. Although sympathetic to the men who were being dismissed from employment, the leaders believed that the men's weakened condition could have tragic consequences.

Most of the strikers agreed that the men were not able to perform their work skillfully or well, but with no retirement plan in place, they were enraged that the workers were to be simply discarded. Maurie Foley, a docker, spoke for many when he said that the "ineffectives" should at least be given something for their years of hard work: "we considered the best way you were gonna get rid of people was at least give 'em some fodder—you can't send them into completely bloody poverty after a lifetime's service to the industry." The issue created a common feeling of trepidation. Foley continued, "The men were looking at themselves—what going to happen to us, someone going to chuck us out when we're 65 or 60, or if we can't breathe in the winter chuck us out?" The same docker explained that the deep feeling that erupted on the issue had a special political dimension. King George was on his death bed during the strike and was being attended by a contingent of doctors. During a strike meeting to discuss the issue, Foley remembered his dockworker father stood up, "very emotional" like, and asked, "Sack 'em, why don't you give 'em the same as you're giving the King, give them six fucking doctors, look after 'em?" It was a desperate cry, grounded in the notion that "you don't punch a bloke in the gut after serving the industry faithfully all his life."[5]

While the NDLB may have accepted the dismissal of men based upon age or physical capacity, the dockworkers did not so readily concede the point. Shifting expectations following World War II also played a role in the men's thinking. The prewar practice of taking what was given had been undermined by the war. As Foley remarked, "We were not going to have it now, it was the post-war era."[6] The war had deeply affected the dockworkers' attitudes to injustice and how it could be challenged. The discarding of old and infirm men from the register was seen as not just cruel but unwarranted, unless supported with some mechanism to provide for them financially. Both sides had a strong case. The newly formed attitude that the men had some rights and should not be summarily dismissed was a worthy one. In many cases when dockworkers could no longer physically function, the work gang would cover for them, or they would be given light work around the docks. But the TGWU and NDLB officials' belief that the men had outlived their usefulness also had validity. In general, aged men did not have special rights; there were no seniority provisions. To provide attendance pay to men incapable of performing work was perceived as unconscionable.

These divergent views contributed to a clash of ideals and to a short strike. Once the strike was underway it quickly spread throughout the port. Simultaneously the "No-Name" or "Unofficial Committee" was reconstituted to fight the issue. A collection of representatives from the 1948 strike got together and quickly established representation from the stevedores, dockers, and lightermen. Later in the strike, clerks would also join the effort. For the clerks it was a matter of trying to catch up to the unfolding events. Ted Dickens, a docker, was the key leader of this re-formed committee. Dickens had been one of the TGWU dockers forced to pledge not to maintain the Unofficial Committee. Indeed, he had kept his vow but once the "ineffectives strike" broke out he became one of the main instigators for joining the NASD out on strike. Dockers had enormous respect for Dickens. He was known as a facts and figures man. As another docker, Ted Kirby, put it, "He would have facts and he only dealt that way." There was "never a smile, never stopping like some of the other speakers and putting a crack over and making everyone laugh, there was none of that, and he'd say 'look this is their life and why should we laugh at their life,' and that was Ted."[7]

With men out on strike, the government once again instituted emergency measures to combat its effectiveness. An Emergencies Committee was created and chaired by Home Secretary J. C. Ede. On April 12, Ede reported to his cabinet colleagues that perishable food would not be "directly threatened until April 23." Ede was particularly concerned by the strike because of its official nature. As he put it to the cabinet, the strike "had set a precedent in the post war period." Just like many of his colleagues, Ede blamed Communist agitators on the NASD executive board. Minister of Labour George Alfred Isaacs was also intent on holding the line against the NASD's demand that the thirty-three men be fairly treated. As he pointed out in a memorandum to Prime Minister Attlee and the cabinet, "In my view, this strike must be firmly resisted and there is no room for concessions of any kind." Isaacs said further that the "Government should take emergency powers" as it did with the 1948 strike. Isaacs also informed Attlee that "close touch has been maintained with the TGWU" over the issue.[8]

Attlee carefully weighed this advice. The hard line taken by his cabinet was reflected by Attorney General Sir Hartley Shawcross's suggestion that the strike ringleaders, both official and unofficial, should be prosecuted. He promised Attlee he would "look into it." The cabinet members were, however, wary of instituting criminal proceedings during the strike. The general feeling during the April 13, 1949, cabinet meeting was that if "prosecutions were launched . . . they might have the effect of stiffening the attitude of the rank and file."[9] During the meeting the participants exhibited a siege mentality. The NASD was perceived as being "under Communist influence." The purpose of the strike then was to disrupt the economy and the Marshall Plan. The cabinet felt that the "organizers of the strike . . . aimed at dislocating essential services and impeding the delivery of Marshall Aid." The government shared with the TGWU an almost pathological suspicion of the NASD's motives. Rather then seeing the dispute for what it was, a rebellion against the perceived arbitrary and unjust power of the NDLB, the government saw conspiracy where the strikers' intention was "to bring about strikes in other ports and to keep the stoppage going for at least eight weeks." Consequently, the cabinet "endorsed" the mobilization of troops to "begin work" by April 20. Additionally, Isaacs was encouraged to give a radio broadcast outlining the "illegal character" of the strike.[10] For Isaacs, the strike, although official, was indeed illegal and had violated the Conditions of Employment and National Arbitration Order, commonly known as Order 1305. The order had been instituted during the war and extended through the postwar period. It specifically stated that before striking, a union must first notify the minister of labor of a dispute and allow twenty-one days for arbitration. The Trades Union Congress (TUC) had agreed to extend the order to facilitate more stable industrial relations and hopefully contribute to the postwar economic recovery.

The NASD decision to strike had clearly ignored Order 1305. Well aware of this, Isaacs had demanded a public explanation from the NASD. Isaacs and Barrett exchanged telephone calls and telegrams over the issue. Emboldened by the knowledge that the NASD had not followed the proper procedure, and urged on by the cabinet, Isaacs made his radio address on the evening of April 13. He explained that he had met with the NASD executive board that afternoon and he was "in no doubt" that the union officials "are fully aware they are breaking the law." Isaacs insisted the strike was clearly "illegal," and in a thinly veiled red-baiting jab he exclaimed, "The Government cannot, and will not, allow these disruptive elements to have their way." Isaacs then made good on his threat to use severe methods to ensure the loading and unloading of ships: "We have plans to deal with this situation and . . . they will, if necessary, be used."[11] As in 1948, the government was girding for a showdown and was prepared to use emergency powers and send in the troops to move perishable cargoes.

The NASD, under threat by the Labour government for defying Order 1305, and facing a heavy fine, decided to step back. On April 14, the morning after Isaacs's radio address, the NASD held a mass meeting in Victoria Park. Industrial relations officers of the Ministry of Labour reported that four thousand stevedores were present. Barrett was the "principal speaker." He explained that the government had declared the strike illegal. He asked the meeting for a resolution to return to work and allow him to "submit 21 days notice in order to make it legal." Barrett clearly envisioned the struggle as one of a process: "It is not the finish. It is one further stage, because it is upon your fight today that determines the question forever of the elderly men and the injured and whoever they of the National Board deem fit to be removed." With that the men voted to return to work on Saturday, April 16. The same afternoon the lightermen met at Canning Town Hall and agreed to follow the NASD men back to work. The following morning, Friday, April 15, the TGWU held a mass meeting at the West India docks. A resolution was passed to return to work, but a second one instructed the union leaders to speed up negotiations for pensions, so as "to avoid any undue hardship to our old fellows."[12]

By Saturday, April 16, the port was operating at "top speed." As in 1948, the dockworkers enjoyed abundant overtime following the strike. In a glaring headline, the *Times* reported that the men were "EARNING DOUBLE PAY." The work was somewhat unusual because April 18 was Easter Monday and therefore a public holiday, making the loading and unloading of ships that much more frenzied.[13]

Barrett and representatives of the Lightermen's Union visited Isaacs in his office on April 21. Their intention was to carry out the mandate of fighting for the dismissed men and giving the government the required twenty-one days' notice. Isaacs rejected Barrett's tactic of trying to activate Order 1305 and insisted that a dispute no longer "exists between yourselves and the employers." Isaacs justified this stance by stating that the Joint Council of the Port Industry had already "decided to give further consideration of the matter." Additionally, the NDLB had "also set up a committee" to look at the pension issue. In essence, then, the subject was still under consideration by two bodies, in both of which the NASD had representation (Barrett sat on both). Barrett was being urged to settle the issue along proper channels, namely, the Joint Council and the NDLB. The employer sides of both entities would ultimately reject the idea of dockworker pensions.[14]

The government and trade unions had little time to catch their collective breath when later in the month another dispute threatened to bring the London men out again. The issue this time was one of international solidarity. The Canadian Seamen's Union (CSU) was battling for its survival against encroachment from its American counterpart, the Seafarers' International Union (SIU). Aided by the Canadian Communist Party, the CSU had fought long and hard through the 1930s and 1940s. It had won an important strike in 1946, garnering a substantial pay raise and changes in working conditions including the eight-hour day, paid vacations, and union recognition. Canadian shipowners were determined to roll back many of these CSU gains. Using red-baiting tactics, they looked to the SIU to rescue them from the CSU. As one historian has put it, "The communist issue provided the pretext; the SIU the means." The shipowners then recognized the SIU claims to represent all North American seamen. The shipowners in 1948 subsequently demanded a 15 percent wage cut, which the CSU refused to accept. The shipowners then began to sign agreements with the SIU in 1949 forcing the CSU into a strike.[15]

As the strike wore on, the CSU called on other seamen and dockers around the world to support its struggle. While the battle raged throughout North America, Canadian seamen working ships tied up in Bristol went on strike in protest. They quickly established picket lines around their ships. Bristol dockers decided to honor the picket lines and refused to unload the ships. Local union officials and representatives of the regional Dock Labour Board tried using persuasion and then threats to force the men to work the ships. The men at first stood firm and went out on strike on May 2. After being threatened by employers with disciplinary action, however, they went back to work the following day.[16] But on May 14, the Bristol men went out on strike once again. They were joined by Liverpool dockers on May 26. At this point the NDLB stepped in and charged that the strikers would be dismissed from the Dock Labour Scheme. By early June, the Bristol and Liverpool strikers went back to work.[17]

London had escaped most of this disruption, but on April 4, Canadian seamen set up picket lines around two ships, the *Beaverbrae* and the *Argomont*. London dockworkers refused to handle the respective cargoes. Fearing a strike, the shippers and the LDLB agreed to move the two ships away from the docks until the dispute with the CSU could be resolved. Throughout the rest of April and up to June, shippers occasionally tried to get gangs to work the ships but were unsuccessful in getting men for the job.[18] Once the strikes in Bristol and Liverpool were settled in June, London became the focus of attention.

It would not be long until a confrontation followed. The NDLB was determined that the *Beaverbrae* and the *Argomont* be loaded. The NDLB had the full backing of the Labour government. Minister of Labour Isaacs had encouraged Attlee to act aggressively against the London men, especially once the other strikes had finished: "If we miss this opportunity of the collapse of the Bristol and Avenmouth strikes, it will be some time before another opportunity arises." Attlee in turn informed Lord Ammon to stand firm and the NDLB ordered stevedores to begin loading the ships. The stevedores again refused. Dockers who were subsequently ordered to take their places also refused. It was a "simple" matter of rolling confrontation. As docker Joe Bloomberg testified, they had been allocated to the ship and refused, thereafter "we became involved . . . as simple as that."[19]

In some sense it was not as simple as Bloomberg thought. Some London dockworkers had kept a close eye on the unfolding events in Bristol and Liverpool. Ted Dickens and other rank-and-file leaders were convinced that events in these ports would visit them in London. Dickens, along with Joe Cowley, Bill Jackson, Jack Dash, Pat Coleman, Ted Kirby, and Jack Prynn, published a leaflet condemning the action of the Bristol and Avenmouth employers. Referring to the use of troops in these ports, the leaflet pointed out, "INTIMIDATION having failed, DECEPTION having failed, now FORCE is to be used . . . to break their stand." The leaflets called on the London dockworkers to "stand firm with our harassed brothers." In a prophetic declaration, the leaflet continued, "If it goes unchallenged and is permitted to succeed in Avenmouth, then it could happen in London."[20]

As the London dockworkers refused to unload the *Beaverbrae* and the *Argomont,* Dickens and his small group reconstituted itself as the "Lock-Out Committee." It expanded to include not just dockers and stevedores but also lightermen and clerks. Most of the expanded Lock-Out Committee were branch officials. According to Ted Kirby, it was just a question of the branches "picking out the leading lights" to serve on the committee.[21] There were twenty-four members of the committee, representing every craft within the port, and every major dock. A NDLB investigation attempted to identify both the ring leaders and the followers on the committee. The docker leader was Dickens, of course, whom the NDLB recognized as "undoubtedly the big figure behind all this trouble." His lieutenants or "stooges" on the committee included Harry Constable, who had played a key role in the 1948 strike. Charles Saunders was classed as a "Communist" who was "always being associated with unofficial movements in dockland." Tim Cronin was also identified as a Communist and described as a "practiced speaker. . . . Knows his stuff." Victor (Vic) Marney, a "robust type," was said to be "always with a complaint." The report believed, however, that Marney could be controlled by the TGWU "if he was 'noticed' such as appointed a T.U. Officer. No fool." Joe Bloomberg was a hard man to categorize. The report sized him up by noting, "Political opinion doubtful. He has certainly been speaking as a Communist. . . . Not considered one of the brainiest. Quite a reasonable man to talk to on occasions."[22]

Other docker representatives were dismissed as mere opportunists or "followers." Harry Van Loo was described as someone who "simply cannot resist an opportunity to get up and speak." Van Loo had applied for official positions and was "awaiting result of further application for a T.U. Officer's job." Two clerks, Gordon Smith and Steven Smith, joined the committee. The NDLB had little information on the two although its report said of Smith, "No knowledge of him speaking in this trouble although there is nothing he likes better unless it is going to the 'dogs.'"[23] The "leading light" of the stevedores was Albert Timothy. He was described as a "robust dark visaged type." He was a "main speaker" and also a "bad tempered, loud mouthed type." Sydney Mott appeared "like Timothy, to have mixed parentage," but he was dismissed as a "simple, amiable fool." Liam O'Brien, a stevedore, was also labeled a troublemaker: "Loud mouthed, abusive type. . . . Always at a hand in, and behind, trouble but this time to the fore as a Member of the Lock-Out Committee."[24]

The NDLB report dissolved into petty portrayals when a Communist connection could not be made. Those on the committee with little experience and no leadership role to play were considered generally ignorant or having a proclivity for making trouble. They were said to be "Not a brainy type. Loud talkative type," "always ready with a grouse," "loud mouthed 'grouser' type," "states he is an athlete but does not look it," "argumentative type," and "fond of talking."[25] The derogatory descriptions of the Lock-Out Committee clearly show the disdain that the NDLB had for the men. Throughout, personal characteristics were invariably negative. The NDLB displayed a venomous attitude that was matched by the committee members.

For all the NDLB posturing, the strike continued to spread and by June 23 it had swept through the port, although certain docks such as Port of London and Tilbury remained working. TGWU officials tried once again to get the men back to work. In a novel twist, the officials called on four Labour M.P.'s, led by Bob Mellish, to address strikers in Poplar Town Hall in early July. One thousand dockworkers attended but defeated a motion to return to work. Two days later, on July 4, the Lock-Out Committee organized a march from "Custom House Fields (Royal Docks) through Poplar, Wapping and Stepney to Victoria Park" for a rally. Dickens, Cronin, and Timothy addressed the meeting of three thousand strikers. The point was made that since the 1889 strike, the union policy was one of not working ships "in dispute." Mingling with the crowd were industrial relations officers from the Ministry of Labour. They reported that many of the strikers were "confused" over the issue, but the men would remain out because of the fear of "accusations of blacklegging."[26]

Union officials continued to maintain that the strike was unnecessary because the dispute was between the Canadian seamen and the SIU. The strike leaders felt otherwise. They believed it affected all dockworkers and was clearly a case of international solidarity. Jack Dash, one of the members of the Lock-Out Committee, exclaimed that the conflict was a "question of international brotherhood." That there was no support from the TGWU just made the issue that much clearer to the strike leaders. As Dash pointed out, "This was the time of Deakinism, which was strongly McCarthyism." Thus it was no surprise that the union leadership opposed any involvement in the Canadian seamen's case. The CSU was clearly Communist-leaning if not controlled, making it unlikely that the established union movement would support its case. Another aspect of the dueling positions was that the strike leaders were well aware of the unsavory reputation of the AFL seamen's union and their ally, the ILA. Maurie Foley declared that he knew the "American seamen's union was made up of racketeers" and thus it was simply a case of supporting a militant organization against the bullying weight of the AFL and its "racketeering" affiliates.[27]

The strike was deeply troubling to both the TGWU and the Labour government. Once again they found themselves confronting a well-organized oppositional movement. Unlike the 1948 confrontation and the "ineffectives" strike, the Canadian seamen's dispute did not directly concern the wages and working conditions of the dockworkers. For the government in particular, the contest smacked of Communist manipulation to wreck the economy and undermine the Marshall Plan. Reports from the industrial relations officials seemed to confirm this. After troops had been sent into the docks, William Hull, an industrial relations officer, reported that Dickens asked a meeting of working dockers in the London dock: "The troops are going in to do your mates' jobs. What are you going to do about it?" Dickens's attempt to lead these men out added to the air of insurrection.[28]

It came as no surprise when cabinet ministers made public their anger that the strike was being led or controlled by sinister, outside forces. Home Secretary Ede blasted the strike leaders in a statement to the House of Commons on July 8: "The only reason why we are having to deal with the trouble . . . is that the Communists see in it a chance of fomenting unrest, [and] injuring our trade." For Ede, the government was also being challenged: "We are faced with a challenge to the whole authority of the State, and it must be met." As in 1948, Ede warned the strikers that a proclamation under the Emergency Act would be issued.[29] But as before, the government was frustrated by its lack of control. True, it could send in troops so a semblance of work was being carried out (in all, the government dispatched seventeen thousand servicemen and twelve hundred military vehicles into the port), but without experienced labor the job was merely a stop-gap measure. Just as annoying for government officials, the strikers and their leaders appeared immune from punishment. Alfred Barnes, minister of transportation, made this clear in a July 6 memorandum to Attlee. Barnes first blamed the rank and file for "readily listen[ing] to malcontents who try and exploit any cause of friction." The strike leaders "have no regard for the repercussions for their actions." Additionally, "despite all the losses which they cause, these unofficial leaders incur no penalty for their misdeeds."[30]

For the government, Communist influence or direction during the strike became a central issue. What remains to be proven is how accurate its assumptions were. One historian has recently argued that government statements, both public and private, prove that Communists were directing the strike. Additionally, Communist policy had changed from working with the Labour government to gain economic independence from the United States to taking a more combative stance. The formation of the Cominform in 1947 is judged to be evidence for such an argument. Spurring on the Cominform was the Truman Doctrine and the Marshall Plan. The Cominform was created by Moscow and included Communist leaders from eastern European satellites as well as from France and Italy; significantly the CPGB was not invited to sit on the new body. Clearly, Moscow had little confidence in the CPGB compared to its larger and more politically influential European cousins. The Cominform called for an end to working with Western democracies, who were perceived as hopelessly under the influence of the United States. The new ideology called for battling American imperialism, most notably the Marshall Plan, and for the creation of a peace movement.[31] There is, however, no evidence that the Lock-Out Committee (which included non-Communists) was following political instructions from either Harry Pollitt or the Cominform. The idea that over thirty thousand London dockworkers engaged in strike action because of some "sinister forces" within the Lock-Out Committee minimizes the antagonism of the strikers toward their trade union leaders. Additionally, police authorities had stated during the 1948 strike—that is, one year after the formation of the Cominform—that no Communist manipulation was evident in that action.

The organizational discipline of the Communist Lock-Out Committee officials did not necessarily stretch to following the dictates of Pollitt or any other higher official in the CPGB. As will be shown later, Communist dockworkers were a notoriously argumentative group and were particularly resistant to following orders either from fellow Communist dockworkers or from King Street officials. What is clear though is that Communist dockworkers were some of the most committed trade unionists. They carried out the mundane, day-to-day activities both in the branches and on the docks. Nurturing such commitment was their Marxist belief that the workplace was the battlefield and engine of change. How far they followed the dictates of the CPGB's leadership is therefore problematic and, at present, unproven.

Even non-Communist dockworkers felt insulted with the government red-scare tactics. Government red-baiting might have gone down well with sections of the public and the press, but it had little impact on the strikers. As one Ministry of Labour report made clear, "The idea of a 'red plot' does not make much impression on dockers." Indeed, when the issue was continuously raised by the government it merely angered the men and made them more determined to stick it out on strike. This was attested to by an army officer who commanded troops unloading cargo in the docks. Major General Robert Neville made clear to Attlee that the Communist issue had "been over-played." As Neville insisted, the "majority of the men are, of course, not Communists, but the amount of emphasis thrown on the fact that they have been duped by the Communists tends to make them 'bloody minded.'"[32]

The strike did more than highlight the government's impotence; it also led to a fracturing of its relationship with the NDLB. Lord Ammon was particularly incensed over the government's lack of verve in dealing with the strikers. Throughout late June and July he publicly attacked the government's lack of forceful action. On July 5 he wrote to Attlee expressing his fear that the strike leaders might let the men "drift" back to work but in a few months' time "we shall be faced with the trouble again." Instead, he argued, the militants "should be fought to the finish." Particularly angering Ammon were those Canadian seamen who had established picket lines around the *Beaverbrae* and the *Argomont*. In a rather extraordinary plea, he called on Attlee to bring to trial the "imported agitators" and "have them deported." Attlee immediately responded by stating that nothing the Canadian seamen had said or done could "justify" prosecution. As for deporting the troublemakers, Attlee made clear that they "are British subjects, and there is no power to deport a British subject from this country." Attlee was annoyed by Ammon's suggestion that the government was not doing enough. By July 5, the strike had been going on for thirteen days, but only approximately fifteen thousand of the twenty-four-thousand work force had quit work. Attlee had unleashed an emergency proclamation but its effect had been marginal. The government had been hesitant to use the proclamation to arrest any of the strike leaders for fear of encouraging the remaining dockworkers to go out on the strike. Attlee informed Ammon, "We must be careful to pick the right moment."[33] The government then adopted a wait-and-see attitude, which in turn infuriated Ammon.

Ammon was not satisfied with Attlee's response and he criticized the government's policy in the House of Lords. Ammon deplored the government's inaction and decided to take a more aggressive stance. Ammon's decision followed a frustrating meeting with the government's Emergencies Committee. Ammon insisted at the meeting that the strikers should be warned to return to work or lose their jobs. The Emergencies Committee informed Ammon that his caveat would not get the men back to work. Sir Frederick Leggett, a cabinet secretary, explained to Ammon that firing fifteen thousand men could not work because "eventually [employers would be] forced to admit the men back into employment." Leggett pushed for a more subtle approach, saying he "always found useful the Victorian hymn 'Lead kindly light.'" Ammon brushed aside Leggett's attempt to tread carefully with the strikers. In a caustic reply he declared Leggett's statement was just what "he had expected from the Civil Service mind." On July 18, he pushed the NDLB to release an ultimatum to the strikers to return to work on July 21 or forfeit their guarantee of employment. The threat also contained a warning that "failure to return to work will jeopardize the very existence of the Scheme." Such independent action deeply embarrassed the government.[34]

Ammon could not be placated by the meeting with the Emergencies Committee or by entreaties from civil servants to calm down. By July 22, it appeared that the strike was losing steam and the men wanted to go back to work. For Ammon to receive the men back without punishment being meted out was unacceptable. On July 22, he talked by telephone with a Press Association journalist and outlined his increasing anger and alienation from the government policy. He accused the government of "dithering and dallying" and losing the chance to effectively rid the dock industry of troublemakers. Ammon was afraid that a truce would be called, the strikers would return to work punishment free, and then in a few months the experience would be repeated, leaving the NDLB "in the unhappy position of being able to say 'we told you so.'"[35]

Attlee could no longer tolerate Ammon's individualistic course. Ammon had become a loose cannon, a maverick who could halt efforts to end the strike. On July 23, Attlee asked for Ammon's resignation—not from the NDLB, but from his positions as Captain of the Honorable Corps of Gentlemen-at-Arms and Government Chief Whip of the House of Lords. Attlee had initially tried to get Ammon to resign voluntarily but Ammon had refused. So Attlee wrote Ammon a letter asking him to resign, pointing out, "You have expressed criticism of the action of the Government to representatives of the Press, and this has been given, as you must have anticipated, wide publicity." Ammon remained defiant. In his reply to Attlee, although agreeing to step down, he insisted his actions were compatible with fighting the strike. As for his critical remarks to a journalist, Ammon stated he was merely "expressing incredulity" that the government hadn't done more to end the strike and punish the Lock-Out Committee. His unapologetic position had severely weakened the government's standing. It gave succor to those who believed that the government should have been more forceful in handling the dispute. The *Times* of London, for example, reporting on the schism between Attlee and Ammon, declared that "the Government, having poulticed and nursed the boil until it is red and swollen, and painful, are now refusing to have it lanced." Thus there was sympathy for Ammon's stand, although no explanation was given as to who should be "lanced" and what the consequences might be.[36]

Within a day the storm had passed, however. Harold Davis, the president of the CSU, had called on the Lock-Out Committee to end the strike. The CSU had been promised a hearing of its case by the Canadian Deputy Minister of Labour if it ended its strike. A Victoria Park mass meeting was held to discuss the changing circumstances. Ted Dickens led off by applauding the strikers for their support of the CSU: "The port workers of London are unshaken in their determination to uphold the principles of trade unionism and to maintain the highest possible standards of solidarity at all times." Dickens's statement was clearly aimed at the TGWU, which had argued that the Canadian dispute was not its concern. Dickens was arguing that the strikers were the legitimate representatives of "trade unionism," and their heightened sense of "solidarity" stood in stark contrast to the stance of the TGWU leadership. The resolution to return to work was passed, and the men agreed to return to work on Monday, July 25. As in 1948, the strikers did not believe they'd lost the fight. The *Times* reported, "It was not a meeting of defeated or repentant men."[37]

The Lock-Out Committee was determined to hold fast to its organization. The three strikes in 1948 and 1949 had convinced the committee members to create a more permanent organization, one that could easily move into position if strife loomed. But it was more important in this decision to be proactive, that is, to push for concrete reforms or gains in and on the job.

The creation of a more permanent body to represent London dockworkers was a galvanizing issue. George Cosey, a lighterman, believed it was inevitable that the rank-and-filers would like the committee to meet on a more "regular basis." The established unions on the docks were hamstrung by Section 1305. As the stevedores' union had discovered, when taking an aggressive stance, one could open oneself up to governmental and legal attack. For the Stevedores and the Lightermen Unions, therefore, parallel unofficial organizations were the only alternative in getting the case across. But according to Cosey, "There wasn't no agreement as such" between the Lightermen's Union and the "unofficial movement." It was more a case of officials turning a blind eye to the activities of the unofficial leaders and their tactics. In many respects, union officials could use the threat of the unofficial movement to obtain much-needed gains. The TGWU, of course, held a different view. The unofficial movement was perceived as a direct threat to its organization. The linkage between the TGWU and the Labour government was another factor to consider. As Cosey pointed out, the TGWU was "trying to back the Labour government up to the hilt." So "any stoppages or anything like that they [TGWU] frowned on as much as the employers did."[38]

The Lock-Out Committee then saw the urgent need to reform itself into a permanent organization. The established unions either were hostile toward taking aggressive action to maintain job control or felt hampered by Section 1305. The Lock-Out Committee presented its intentions to an August 7, 1949, Canning Town Hall meeting. The meeting began with a review of the events of the Canadian seamen's strike, but the thread throughout was to keep the committee in existence. Each of the speakers congratulated the committee for its outstanding work. Ted Dickens took the podium and spelled out the need to keep the organization going. He reasoned that the TGWU had lost whatever credibility it had left from the earlier confrontations. As Dickens put it, "We have got to bring our movement [forward] and to carry out the responsibilities and tasks that were originally set out by the pioneers of the movement." Because of his acute stutter, Joe Bloomberg's speech was short but to the point. He called for a complete overhaul of the NDLB. He charged that the union representatives, particularly Condon and Bird, were nothing more than "self-seeking careerists" and called for their removal. Arthur Deakin was the object of Victor Marney's speech. Marney scornfully labeled him as a dupe of the ruling class and perhaps the "worst enemy to us trade unionists than Hitler ever tried to be," a comment that was greeted with applause. The point, he said, was not to break away from the TGWU but to fight inside the union for better working conditions and wages. Marney then called for a basic wage of twenty-five shillings a week, and for industry pensions. The call should be, "Forward for the Dockers." The only way that dockers' demands could be met was to "give us the mandate to carry on. . . . We will not let you down." The resolution was carried and the Lock-Out Committee was transformed into the Port Workers Defense Committee (PWDC).[39]

Just as vital, the new committee decided to create a broadsheet, the *Port Workers' News.* Victor Marney agreed to be its first editor. The start-up costs were paid, with a "few bob left over," from the strike fund. The composition of the *Port Workers' News* was based upon that of the *Metal Worker.* The intention was to keep the members abreast of new developments, and the first issue, in October 1949, established its tone of agitation and humor. It put forth the idea of the Docker's Charter, which called for twenty-five shillings a week and an industry pension. The *Port Workers' News* also identified miscreants within their organization. Van Loo, in particular, was judged to have overstepped his brief and was believed to be using the committee to better his prospects for an unofficial position within the TGWU.[40]

Albert Timothy produced one of the more popular columns, entitled "Timmo." In it he highlighted stories from around the port that had a humorous edge. George Cosey, who worked on the paper, at times subbing for Marney as editor, described Timothy as "a big bluff, rotund man, looked like very swarthy features and always used to wear a trilby hat and a scarf tied up in a bit of cravat style." Cosey thought that Timothy's dark features were like those of a gypsy: "in fact you could have sworn he was a gypsy." Timothy wrote so well that Cosey had little if any editing to do: "[Timothy] was very shrewd and when he used to write I was editor of the paper [and] I never had to alter a word." According to John Cavanagh, a docker, there was no shortage "of willing hands" to sell the *Port Workers' News*. When selling the papers, whether outside the dock gates or in local pubs, "you had to apply tact," according to Ted Kirby. To help him in his efforts, Kirby had "the assistance of some muscle men." Such support ensured that he "was one of the biggest pushers" of the *Port Workers' News*.[41]

The trade union hierarchy and the government were also paying close attention to the activities of the Port Workers Defense Committee. The government had created the 1949 showdown by encouraging the NDLB to force the men to unload what were called the "blacked" ships. It had wanted to discipline the strike leaders during the conflict but feared that it would just inflame the rank and file. So the government was looking hopelessly misguided and outsmarted by the unofficial leaders.

The TGWU was smarting from its obvious lack of control over events. Deakin again tried to push the Communist issue as a way to shield himself from further blame. For Deakin, anti-Communism became part of a personal crusade to protect his political power within the TGWU. Nearly 20 percent of the TGWU's executive board were Communists, and Communist control at the branch level had increased during war. In late 1948 Deakin had successfully persuaded the Trades Union Congress to pass two anti-Communist statements.[42] The two 1949 strikes convinced him to press for the ouster of Communists within the TGWU. He explained to a July 21, 1949, meeting of the Docks National Committee that the Canadian "dispute was not one with which we had any concern." The TGWU "cannot dally with questions with another country." His remaining remarks focused on the oppositional leadership of the Port Workers Defense Committee. Deakin explained that he had "been too lenient" with these men and it was now time "they must face the music." His threat was clear to everyone at the meeting: it was the intention of the TGWU leadership to either discipline the supposed malcontents or rid the union of them. To nurture his anti-Communist crusade Deakin maneuvered a motion through the TGWU's July convention to ban Communists from holding union office. The close vote of 426-208 upholding the motion showed that many in the TGWU were uncomfortable with the issue.[43]

Deakin used the vote to attack Communist dockworkers in the Lock-Out Committee. In a July 25 circular to London's dock branches, Deakin again insisted that the Canadian seamen's strike was one with which the men "should never have become involved." The Lock-Out Committee had merely used the men "on the waterfront to further the purposes of international communism." In a December 28, 1949, circular to all TGWU branch secretaries Deakin reiterated his belief "that the strike was inspired and dominated . . . by the Communist International—the Cominform." Such a stance was clearing the way for an official union inquiry. The TGWU officials of London, Area No. 1, had played their part by calling for an investigation of eight of the strike leaders on December 9.[44]

Deakin had some ammunition with which to carry out his threat. First, Dickens, Constable, and Saunders had agreed after the 1948 strike that they would refrain from any more unofficial activity. Deakin was now preparing to use such pledges as a weapon against the three men. But even more dramatic was the fact that the August 7 Canning Town Hall meeting, in which the Port Workers Defense Committee was born, had been audiotaped.

The Port Workers Defense Committee had long felt it was under surveillance. It was common for members to search their meeting room before beginning, and they even covered their office telephone in an effort to muffle their voices. Considering the clumsy recording technology of the time, it was more than likely MI5 who did it and passed on the information to the TGWU. The Canning Town Hall recordings were an important document by which to present evidence against the rank-and-file leaders. One of the leaders had called for an extension of their organization, and personal attacks had been voiced. The tapes could "prove" that Dickens and the others had ignored their earlier pledge to stay away from unofficial organizational activity.

As with the 1948 inquiry, Area No. 1 officials charged the unofficial leaders with unconstitutional methods and actions. Area No. 1 officials wanted "to take such action . . . deemed necessary by way of securing full observance of the constitutional rules of the Union in the future." The eight ringleaders identified for investigation were Dickens, Saunders, Bloomberg, Dash, Constable, Cronin, Kirby, and Marney. Ostensibly, the men were singled out for signing a call for action during the 1949 Canadian seamen's strike, but it was obvious to those who were charged that the high number of Communists on the list meant there was a witch-hunt.[45] The specific evidence presented against the eight men was their signing of pamphlets calling for strike action, and the speeches and resolutions of the Canning Town Hall meeting.

Deakin presented the case against the men and in his initial exchange with Dickens the tone was set. Deakin charged Dickens with being a member of the Communist Party of Great Britain. Dickens did not deny it; in fact, he celebrated his membership. As he said, "I am proud of it." Deakin continued on with the Communist theme throughout the inquiry. In his cross-examination of Victor Marney, Deakin alleged that the committee had fomented trouble by inviting striking Avenmouth representatives to London. Once there, the Avenmouth men visited the houses of the members and saw rooms stacked with transmitter radios and banks of telephones. Marney was angered by Deakin's picture of subversive activity, which he described as "sheer rot." True, Marney sarcastically replied, he had taken the Avenmouth men into docker homes with "pictures of Stalin on the walls and . . . fellows with revolvers standing at the back of the door." He insisted that the portrayal of Communist conspiracy was "a lot of tripe." When Deakin turned his attack on Constable, an exasperated Constable demanded, "For the Lord's sake let it go." At times the proceedings degenerated into personal attacks with Dash accusing Deakin of being "an industrial prostitute." This encouraged Bloomberg to call a halt to the personal attacks: "For God's sake this is an industrial issue. I would ask all of you to refrain from bringing politics into it and keep it as an industrial matter."[46]

The men's combative posture was perhaps prompted by the realization that the inquiry was weighted against them. Therefore they had little to lose by taking an aggressive stand against Deakin. Van Loo attested to this in correspondence with Deakin. Van Loo explained that Dickens in particular had taken on the role of "martyr" to gain sympathy from London dockers. According to Van Loo this was part of a carefully orchestrated plan coming from the Communist Party headquarters in "King Street." Thus "as far as Dickens is concerned . . . the purpose [was] that he would so antagonize the Enquiry Committee that they would request his expulsion." The ultimate aim of Dickens extended beyond the dock gates and the TGWU corridors of power, however. Van Loo reasoned that Dickens wanted to use the proceedings "to defeat a Labor Government's return to power on February 23 [election day]." Van Loo's comments were ridden with hyperbole, but Deakin appreciated the information from his erstwhile antagonist, stating in his reply, "I have to say that I appreciate the points which you put in your communication."[47]

It never occurred to either Van Loo or Deakin that the men were not looking for "martyrdom" but held deep-seated feelings of persecution and truly believed they were the true representatives of the dockers' best interests. Van Loo's appraisal was more of an effort to ingratiate himself with Deakin and perhaps at last get a permanent union position. Deakin very well may have felt that Dickens et al. were following orders from the Communist Party, but he also was threatened by their actions. The authority of Deakin and other top officials had been continually undermined by the actions of the rank-and-file leaders. In turn, these leaders feared they would lose control. For TGWU dock officials, Dickens was perceived as the greatest threat. According to Ted Kirby, a large amount of "jealousy was applied against Ted." Kirby singled out Timothy O'Leary, assistant group secretary, Area No. 1, as being acutely embittered about the committee's hold on the men: "O'Leary hated our guts, because he saw us [as] a danger to him, because he was going to be an 'outer,' because he would be exposed for being stupid by allowing things to drift [along]." Joe Bloomberg remembered union branch and district meetings where O'Leary made it a point not to recognize the rank-and-file leaders.[48]

For the eight accused men the conclusion of the inquiry was never in doubt. A special committee singled out Dickens, Constable, and Saunders. The three men were found in breach of the rules because they had gone back on their "assurance" to stay clear of any further unofficial action. The committee declared that the three men "have no intention of conforming to the rules and constitution of the union." More damaging, the committee found that "they can find no place in the union" and recommended that they be thrown out of the TGWU. Although the committee members vacillated about the remaining leadership, they decided to bar them from union office until 1951. The special committee also tried to disassemble the Port Workers Defense Committee. The PWDC was condemned as "a subversive body." It was charged with "sabotaging the constitutional procedure and policy of the union." The PWDC was therefore labeled as a rogue organization. The *Port Workers News* also fell under the same banner of "subversive" activity. The special committee lumped the two together and recommended "that any continued association with" the PWDC or the *Port Workers News* "will call for disciplinary measures."[49]

The recommendations that the PWDC could be banned failed. It was plainly a question of denying free speech. Likewise, the attempt to prohibit involvement with the *Port Workers News* was on shaky legal ground. The ejection of Dickens, Saunders, and Constable stood, however. The three men appealed their "expulsion" from the union, but on April 17, 1950, the appeal was rejected. There quickly followed a protest strike, which became known as the "expulsion strike."

The strike followed the usual pattern of starting in the most militant sector of the port, the Royal Group of Docks. One thousand eight hundred fifty-six men from the Royals went out on strike on April 18, and they were joined by an additional 4,260 dockworkers from the India docks. Albert Timothy became the major leader and spokesman of the strike. The LDLB followed its usual tactic of threatening the strikers with the loss of their jobs if they didn't return to work. The ultimatum did nothing more than encourage others to join the strike. By Monday, April 24, men from the Surrey and London Dock joined the strike, making a total of 12,000 men out; and by April 26, 14,400 dockworkers were on strike.[50]

The men generally had seen the expulsion of Dickens, Saunders, and Constable as an attempt to muzzle the rank and file. While many did not agree with the Communist politics of the three men, they saw their treatment as blatantly unfair. Maurie Foley considered the expulsions "an attack on democracy" and believed that Dickens had been singled out "because of his political convictions . . . and we thought it was a step against democracy [within the union]." Dickens's expulsion certainly angered many dockers throughout the port. For Harry Browne, a docker, it was astounding that the union could dismiss Dickens, a "giant in the movement . . . one of the most knowledgeable men there ever was."[51] A *Port Workers' News* editorial on the expulsions caught the combative mood of the striking men. Deakin in particular was presented as the villain of the drama: "In one corner are Arthur Deakin, the shipowners and the representative of big business. In the other corner sit the three men who have been expelled, together with the rank and file dockers, stevedores, clerks and lightermen."[52]

The Labour government once again tried to lessen the effects of the strike. As before, its only weapon was to send in troops to work the trapped cargoes. The government was initially careful not to antagonize working dockworkers and had troops working only in the Royal Docks. Unlike in the Canadian seamen's strike, the government kept the LDLB and the NDLB out of the picture. The cabinet was well aware that both bodies would more than likely take a hard line and demand "the dismissal of the strikers." The government nonetheless was determined to hold fast. In all, 4,000 troops were working in the docks, while arrangements were finalized to bring in a total of 10,000 service personnel.[53]

The key organization throughout the dispute was the PWDC. It was perfectly situated as the leader of the rank and file. The PWDC had kept London's dockworkers apprised of the unfolding drama of the TGWU inquiry, the expulsions, and the subsequent appeals. The *Port Workers' News* was the key vehicle providing the information. Once the appeal was rejected, the PWDC called a meeting at the Connaught Fields, Canning Town. The three thousand men who attended (both TGWU and NASD members were present) agreed to strike until the three men were reinstated. At meetings held throughout the strike there were generally equal numbers of dockers and stevedores in attendance. As meetings were held, the resolutions for ending the conflict changed. The final resolution adopted called for a ballot of all members to decide what should happen to the three men.[54]

The strike did not last long, however. Many of the men were content with a protest strike but beyond staying out a few days, they felt little could be done. There were rumors that the three expelled dockers would merely switch their membership to the NASD. When it became clear that the three men would in fact join the NASD, thereby not losing their livelihood on the docks, there was a movement back to work. The PWDC tried to stay ahead of the return to work by calling a final meeting on Saturday, April 29. When a resolution was put forth to bolt the TGWU and join the NASD, confusion reigned. The PWDC had miscalculated the feelings of the men, and instead, a resolution to return to work on May 1 was adopted. The PWDC tried to get the men to impose an overtime ban in protest, but there was "no headway in spreading the ban" throughout the port. Consequently, the committee quietly shelved the idea.[55]

The TGWU had triumphed in ridding itself of the militant threat posed by Dickens, Saunders, and Constable. Union officials hoped that potential challengers would think twice before engaging in direct confrontation with the TGWU leadership. The three men had not left the docks, however. The PWDC continued its life as before and the *Port Workers News* continued its campaign of internal opposition. Although the PWDC's leadership and membership tended to shift, the circumstances that created it did not evaporate. As George Cosey explained, "It always throws up someone, someone comes to the fore." All it required was another contentious issue.[56]

In 1951, an issue arose that spawned not only further strike action but an amazing form of government oppression. As a strike that began in Liverpool seemed about to spread to London, the government decided to take drastic action against the principal leaders. The result was the arrest and trial of the strike leaders on conspiracy charges.

The Liverpool strike began over wages. Liverpool dockers were particularly angered over a 1951 wage increase negotiated by the Joint Council. The anger spilled over into strike action in early February 1951. The Liverpool men tried to spread their strike to London to make it more effective. Deakin promptly trotted out his usual anti-Communist rhetoric: "Well-known Communists and underground members of the Party associations with the unofficial Port Workers' Committees are seeking by usual means to cause unrest and having unofficial strike in dockland."[57]

Three Liverpool leaders—Joe Harrison, William Johnson, and Robert Crosbie—traveled to London to garner support, but they were frustrated with the lack of response by London dockers. The major problem was that in London, unlike in Liverpool, dockworkers were paid piece-rate and were consequently "quite happy" with the increase.[58] Led by Albert Timothy, the PWDC tried in vain to get the London dockworkers to support the Liverpool strikers.

Specifically, the PWDC called on the men to take sympathetic strike action. Timothy urged men at the Royal Docks to support the Liverpool men, while Harry Constable did the same at the West India docks. Each attempt was unsuccessful in moving the men, however. According to Jack Dash, the PWDC desperately tried to get the men out by marching "along the quaysides shouting out to those that were still at work." The spontaneous marchers used "invectives which would make Lady Chatterley's book look like choir boys," but again it failed to make the men budge. Such failures frustrated one Liverpool leader, Joe Harrison, who publicly pleaded, "Stand with us and don't send me back to Liverpool a broken-hearted man."[59]

The PWDC arranged to have a meeting with the Liverpool men on Saturday, February 10, at the White Hart Pub in Stepney. George Cosey was present at the meeting and described it as "tense" because the Liverpool men were frustrated that the PWDC "hadn't pulled their weight" in getting the London men out in support. Once the meeting began, the accusation that the London men had not done enough ensured that "tempers were going to start flaring." All of a sudden, "in marches plain clothes policemen dressed like school teachers." They arrested seven of the men on conspiracy charges. The seven men were Liverpool docker leaders Johnson, Harrison, and Crosbie and the London men Ted Dickens, Joseph Cowley, Albert Timothy, and Harry Constable. The specific charge was conspiracy "to incite dock workers to take part in strikes."[60] The government had shown its hand. The conspiracy charge was a serious one because it could result in long prison terms. The point was to rid the docks of the men once and for all.

The arrests galvanized the London dockers. Immediately following the arrests, George Cosey, Wally Jones, and Jack Dash met in another pub to develop tactics. They agreed to send out emissaries around the port on the following Monday morning, February 12, to call for a sympathy strike. By Monday afternoon, London dockworkers answered the call and went out on strike in protest. The quick turnaround was not lost on Jack Dash. As he testified, "so here was the situation[,] 800 [on strike] on Friday, [but] 12,000 on Monday."[61]

With the core leadership in the dock, new members stepped forward to take control. According to Dash there was "no permanent organization" but only individuals who on a daily basis discussed and adopted fighting tactics. The point was to maintain momentum of the protest strike. Docker Wally Jones took the lead in galvanizing the protest organization. It was agreed that it would be impossible to try and keep the men out on strike while the trial was still pending. The plan was to have "spontaneous" strikes when the men were in court. Thus the slogan was, "They're in the dock—we're out of the docks." So in tandem with the court appearances of the seven men at the Bow Street Magistrates Court, strike action broke out and protesting dockers marched on the court.[62]

What was so impressive was the large number of men who engaged in sympathetic strike action and attended the protest meetings. John Cavanagh, a clerk, remembered that the conspiracy case encouraged "thousands" of volunteer dockworkers to give their time to hand out leaflets at the protests. Cavanagh saw in the voluntaristic action an almost evangelical zeal. The rank-and-file movement was changing. No longer led by a small cadre of dockers and stevedores, now it was "just willing hands"—you "didn't have to be a committee member." Cavanagh was cautious, however. Immediately following the arrests he burned the PWDC minute books for 1949–51.[63]

The arrests had certainly galvanized the dockworkers,who saw them as a direct attack on their interests as workers and trade unionists. The Labour government was condemned as a bully. Banners held by protesting dockworkers outside the court attested to the feeling of persecution. Some read "RELEASE OUR SEVEN BROTHERS" and "DOUBLE-CROSS." Maurie Foley spoke for many when he charged that the seven men had been arrested on "trumped up charges." It was clear to Foley that the government was trying "to show an example to the rest of the workers of the country." Other workers engaged in public displays of support for the seven men. In a explicit show of solidarity, Festival of Britain workers on the South Bank came out on token strike.[64] The government was seen by many as being repressive and hostile to workers' rights.

The arrests also placed Arthur Deakin on the defensive. Some strikers and members of the PWDC were convinced that Deakin either engineered the arrests or at least knew they were in the works. Maurie Foley was convinced that both the TUC and Deakin "would have known of it [the arrests] before the government decided to take such drastic measures." Deakin was forced to respond to such accusations in a March 8, 1951, meeting of the TGWU executive council. Deakin insisted that he had no knowledge that action was to be taken. Indeed, he argued that he first heard of the arrests "from the newspapers." But Deakin clearly showed his sympathy for the police action when he stated, "If it can be proven that these seven men have been engaged since October, 1950, in a conspiracy, then they should have been dealt with long ago."[65]

The Communist membership of Ted Dickens and other movement leaders was certainly an activating issue. Dickens's activities throughout the two 1949 strikes, and his expulsion from the TGWU, had caught the attention of the CP leadership and he had risen through the CP ranks. In early 1950 he was nominated for and won a position on the party's executive committee, and he regularly attended meetings in the Communist Party headquarters, commonly known as the "Center," on Kings Street, London. Throughout 1950 and early 1951, however, his participation in the executive meetings was tangential. Only sporadically did he contribute to any of the discussions.[66]

Of course, his silence in executive meetings does not imply that Dickens was not in active discussions with the CP leadership regarding the situation on the docks and the oppositional movement that he and others had created. Dickens did make clear in a September 6, 1950, meeting with John Mahon, the CP London District secretary, that there had been little official contact with the CP leadership. As Mahon reported, Dickens stated "that the interview I had with him is the first he had had and that the Center has not had such discussions with him [either]." Dickens was in contact with the center after he was expelled by the TGWU and following his arrest in 1951, but whether his work with the rank-and-file committees was being directed by the top leadership is not altogether clear. Indeed, the movement encompassed more than one view or strategy for fighting the established union leadership. Dickens made clear to the party leadership that on occasion, decisions were made by the movement leaders without consulting many of the CP dockworkers. As was reported, the "result was that [at] times comrades would be arguing against each other in ignorance of the decisions already taken."[67]

Dickens was singled out by the party apparatchki to try and instill more discipline with his Communist dockworkers. He was initially uncomfortable with such a charge. On September 6, 1950, he "deplored the inability to devote time to obtaining a better political education." By February 12, 1951, Dickens reported he felt more secure because he had become "more tolerant to explain the political issues, [and had] more readiness to listen." He believed his strategy was successful because "the workers [were] coming to us more and more with their problems," and "they stand by us from time to time." The party leadership were not so convinced. On April 25, 1951, John Mahon implored Dickens to use his "Marxist knowledge" to reverse the "tendency to take decisions on feeling rather than a serious political analysis." Mahon explained that the "Comrades have to train themselves to take a more far-sighted view," and that Dickens "can help them do this."[68]

For Dickens and his fellow Communists, such a directive was difficult to embrace. Using a Marxist approach or language along the docks and in branch meetings could alienate non-Communist allies. Dickens and his dockworker comrades were outnumbered by non-Communists, not just in the oppositional movement's leadership but along the docks generally: the number of Communists totaled only 108 members out of a work force of 25,000.[69] John Mahon beseeched members generally "to get up on the soapbox in the canteen, in the Trade Union branch, and speak and fight for Party policy, confident that our policy sets in motion the process in the mind of the listener that will eventually bring him into the Party." But such a tactic could result in offending the members attending the branch meeting. John Cavanagh, a clerk and non-Communist, explained that the point was to steer away from politics in branch meetings because "it's [only] their place of work they're interested in." Even "simple" Communist rhetoric had to be avoided: "You might hear someone get up and say 'there ought to be direct action Mr. Chairman' and as soon as you hear 'direct action' [they'd] say 'hello where's he been I wonder,' you see he used the expression 'direct action.' You see what I mean, a simple word!"[70]

Even Communist dockworkers refused outright to be manipulated by "Center" cadres. George Cosey explained, "We never had much contact with the Communist Party; we held a card but that was as far as it went." Suspicion of outsiders, Communist or otherwise, was typical. Cosey explained, "I mean we didn't want no-one, . . . whether he's called himself a Communist or what he called himself, coming down telling us how to run the show—we knew how to run the show." The success of Dickens and other Communist militants was that they submerged an overt political expression of party loyalty. This was done partly as a response to the local conditions on both the docks and in the branch meetings. Just as important, it was also a reaction to the common suspicion of outsiders. The ability to meld tactical and community considerations gave a special cast to men like Dickens and Cosey. It also encouraged non-Communists' allegiance to the movement. Maurie Foley, a non-Communist docker, expressed this satisfaction when he stated that the movement had all types of political alliances, encompassing Conservatives, Labour Party members, and Communists: "you've got all bleedin' sorts of people meeting together." The simple formula was that "if it's a good idea take it, if it ain't take it out."[71]

With the arrest of Dickens and the others, dockers like Foley were furious because they perceived it as a direct attack on both Communists and the movement generally. On the surface Foley saw the arrests as a political offensive on known Communists, an attempt to "scare people telling 'em about these red bogeys." On a deeper level, the assault was framed by the larger issue of threatening the rank-and-file movement. As Foley put it, "It was an attack on democracy."[72] Dickens and his comrades had achieved a remarkable consensus. Their ability to address the day-to-day concerns of the dockworkers had won allies from a wide range of political persuasions. Politically connected to the Communist cause, Dickens and his cohorts were also dockworkers. Their fight was colored by the tension inherent in the blend of Marxism, work on the docks, and political alliances within the movement. Although it annoyed party functionaries like Mahon, Dickens's worker-centered approach nourished critical cross-political support. His trial at the Old Bailey, and the accompanying demonstrations by thousands of dockworkers, bore out his success at walking the thin line of party activist and worker.

The trial at the Old Bailey began on April 9, 1951. Simultaneously eight thousand dockworkers went out on token strike. Attorney General Sir Hartley Shawcross opened the proceedings by arguing that the seven men had been engaged in a conspiracy to destroy the country's trade. As he stated, "They were prepared to hold the nation to ransom and defy the law of the land."[73] The seven men and their lawyers tried to use the trial as a platform for attacking the government and the Dock Labour Scheme. It was made clear by the defense attorneys that London and Liverpool dockworkers felt alienated from their trade leaders. The point was sharply made that TGWU officials were "not elected but selected." The ground was laid that the dockworkers had no representation other than their rank-and-file leaders. The defense also took the position that the strike leaders were not doing anything illegal. Defense Attorney Rose Heilbron put it succinctly when she explained that the seven "men [were] sincerely seeking to improve the conditions of their fellow-men, without violence, but by means of the exercise of freedom of speech." She continued, "If it is legal to have strikes, then it is legal to persuade, encourage or lead."[74]

Ted Dickens clashed frequently with the prosecuting attorneys, eventually finding himself "gagged" and sent back to the dock. Albert Timothy, for his part, had a verbal duel with Shawcross:

> Shawcross: You were trying to get these dockers into a mood in which they would strike. . . .
> Timothy: They were already in the mood.
> Shawcross: You were quite prepared to strangle the nation by cutting its lifeline if necessary?
> Timothy: No!

William Johnson, a Liverpool strike leader, provided some comic relief in the proceedings when he responded to a question about the wage demand:

> Shawcross: If the employers would have offered you 25s wouldn't you have gone back to work with flying banners?
> Johnson: I have not got as fertile an imagination as you. We are only dockers.[75]

On April 17, the jury handed down its verdict, which resulted in a victory for the seven men. Although the men were found guilty of breaking their contracts by going on strike, they were found not guilty of conspiring to incite other dockworkers to join them. The decision infuriated Shawcross. He stated, "It seems impossible to reconcile the jury's verdict" of finding the men guilty on the first count but not on the second. Shawcross was deeply frustrated by the decision but was forced to drop the prosecution, and he entered "a *nolle prosequi* to the whole indictment." Outside the Old Bailey, the verdict unleashed joyous public celebration. The seven men were carried aloft by the dockers and marched along the street. One elder docker even kissed Dickens on the cheek. Thumbing their noses at the TGWU and the government, the men held a celebration later that night in the White Hart Pub, where they were first arrested.[76]

The victory was also celebrated by the Communist Party. John Mahon expressed his satisfaction at the September 11, 1951, London District Conference. Mahon congratulated specifically Dickens, Ernie Thomas, and Victor Marney for their "epoch making fight." He extolled the virtues of working with non-Communists on the common cause of democracy within the labor movement. He argued that the victory was won "because our comrades knew how to work with those not yet in the Party, and helped them to share the responsibility of leading the workers in the struggle." Although perhaps exaggerating the role of the party, Mahon nonetheless recognized that cross-political allegiances had won the day.[77]

To a large extent the acquittal ended the turmoil on the docks. The government was forced to abandon its plans to discipline the rank-and-file leadership. Its embarrassing failure to obtain a conviction soured any further attempts to rein in the unofficial movement. But by 1951, the government had changed. The newly installed Conservative Party government treaded carefully to avoid any direct confrontation with London's dockworkers. The London docks experienced a remarkable calm after the tumultuous years of 1948–51.

The Port Workers Defense Committee remained in existence, although it had lost much of its raison d'être. No major conflagration erupted that could arouse rank-and-file anger. The *Port Workers News* continued its life as an organ of contestation for the members' allegiance.

Not until 1954, nearly three years after the trial, did the organization once again take shape and assume the role of aggressive defender of the dockworkers' interests. The members felt that once again the union leadership had let them down; in turn, there were strong calls for an overhaul of the union hierarchy and, as in New York, there arose union jurisdictional problems.

Dockers "chair" the acquitted seven as they leave the Old Bailey after the 1951 conspiracy trial ended. From left to right are Joe Cowley, Albert Timothy, Harry Constable, Ted Dickens and, behind him, Bob Crosbie. (*Daily Worker,* April 18, 1951. Courtesy Daily Worker)

Trucks carrying goods for export waited to be unloaded at the docks during the 1949 dockworkers' strike. (*Times* [London], April 13, 1949)

The scene at the Royal Albert Docks shows idle cranes, deserted docks, and goods waiting to be loaded into vessels at the quayside. (*Times* [London], April 13, 1949)

A jubilant Joe Cowley is held aloft by Jack Dash following his acquittal on conspiracy charges. (Courtesy People's History Museum, Manchester, England)

The single issue that catapulted the men into conflict with their union, especially the TGWU, concerned overtime. For years the issue of what constituted "reasonable overtime" captured the attention of all dockworkers. Under the Dock Labour Scheme dockers were expected to work overtime when requested. The principal reasoning behind the order was to ensure that the loading and unloading of ships could continue beyond regular working hours. Although the dockworkers welcomed the ready overtime, the ambiguity of the term "reasonable" caused enormous problems. For employers, it generally meant that the men should work when requested to do so. For dockworkers, the "requests" felt more like orders. Heightening their sense of insecurity were the disciplinary measures attached to Clause 8(8)(*b*). Men were routinely fined and suspended for not agreeing to work overtime. The lack of flexibility and free time affected both married and single men. For married men it resulted in long absences from their families and, not least, cold meals. Single men also suffered interruptions of their daily and weekly patterns. Harry Browne, a docker, was always concerned that his Sunday soccer games would be disrupted, no mean fear for a good athlete and player. As he put it, "I didn't have a family but I played Sunday morning football."[78]

Other than daily upheavals caused by requested overtime, what really ignited the issue was its commonality. The vast majority of the dockworkers had experienced some form of turmoil associated with working overtime. As Harry Browne pointed out, there was "so much common ground on the issue. . . . I mean, why should people keep dictating to you how you're going to live. . . . We didn't want people to tell us we had to work morning, noon, and night every day of the week." Dockworkers strongly resented the imposition of overtime. It was not merely a case of their being used to casual work; it was also the inherent inflexibility of the system aligned with harsh measures that could be applied. As Browne succinctly put it, "Now from the war we're talking about seven or eight years of it, of people being suspended, punished, you know." "Being punished because one night they had to visit someone in hospital" seemed blatantly unfair. It really came down to men not wanting to be "told when to work it." Reasonable overtime had in effect become unreasonable. The men were not being obliged to work, but being forced. Surely, Maurie Foley reasoned, "it was up to the individual" whether he worked overtime or not.[79]

Although always percolating beneath the surface, the issue had never boiled up into outright war. By 1954, however, stevedore rank-and-filers pushed their executive committee on the issue. Accordingly, NASD president Dickie Barrett called for an overtime ban. Initially the ban seemed more like a bluff, but the stevedores enthusiastically supported it. At least the NASD was not alone once the Lightermen (WLTBU) joined the ban on January 25, 1954.[80]

The LDLB adopted a wait-and-see policy, fearful of antagonizing the NASD and perhaps bringing the dockers into the dispute. Barrett encouraged such a view by publicly stating that the stevedores and lightermen had become "content" with working normal hours: "The men seem to be content working from 8 A.M. to 5 P.M. and if the employers do not handle this carefully they might find it boomerang so that overtime is not worked at all." The NASD and WLTBU gained an immediate ally in the *Port Workers News*. Editorials and articles written by Ted Dickens supported the ban. Dickens, now a NASD member, blasted the notion of "reasonable" overtime and the TGWU resistance to fighting for an overhaul of the disciplinary measure associated with Clause 8(8)(*b*).[81]

Efforts by the NASD and WLTBU to bring the TGWU on board were for naught, however. The TGWU even refused any meeting over the overtime issue unless the NASD and WLTBU called off the ban. On July 10, 1954, Barrett gleefully pointed out to the TGWU that the ban had been successful because no one had been disciplined by the LDLB. As Barrett put it, although "thousands of men have been reported to the London Dock Labour Board no disciplinary action has been taken." For Barrett the overtime ban was a success because "the principle of voluntary overtime has been established." To a large extent Barrett's observation was correct. By June 30, 1954, over sixty-six thousand men had been reported for failing to work overtime, but none had been penalized.[82] The TGWU refused to budge, however, and seemed to determine to wait out the NASD and WLTBU.

The NASD reacted forcefully to its increasing isolation by calling for a mass meeting on October 1. Those attending the meeting favored a strike over the overtime ban but also over a meat-sorting issue. The task of meat-sorting was a new one and therefore a new guide for piece-work payment needed to be established. The NASD insisted that the issue be discussed along with the continuing controversy concerning overtime. The LDLB refused its request and negotiated a unilateral agreement with the NASD's erstwhile ally, the TGWU. For Barrett, such an action ignored the organization's right to be recognized over policy on the docks. Barrett and the membership were convinced that both the LDLB and TGWU were further trying to isolate them. The strike call was passed by a solid majority. On October 4, the stevedores, numbering 7,000, came out on strike and were joined by 3,000 TGWU dockers. By October 14, 21,000 stevedores and dockers were out on strike, and the lightermen and clerks pledged to join them in a few days.[83]

Deakin and his TGWU associates in the London docks scurried around trying to hold dockers on the jobs. Deakin once again used the red-smear card and blamed Communist agitators for the conflict: "This is another reckless attempt to involve the ports of the country in chaos."[84] As in earlier confrontations Deakin found himself on the defensive. His red-baiting may have made good newspaper copy, but it had little impact on the strikers or those dockers who continued to work. Again Deakin was at odds with his membership; consequently his lieutenants tried to keep him away from planned meetings. One vital meeting he missed was at the Albert Hall on October 13. Deakin was traveling south from Rotherham to attend the meeting. He was met at London's Marylebone Station and persuaded to stay away by the London Docks Group Committee. The committee members were convinced that Deakin "would not get a hearing" and that he would more than likely be "howled down and disowned by the Union membership."[85]

The strike had opened up old scars throughout the TGWU membership. One major consequence was NASD's attempts to expand its influence among northern dockers. Hull dockers in particular invited the NASD to organize them. The NASD accepted the invitation and began a campaign to attract disgruntled dockers. The NASD subsequently opened up offices in Hull and Birkenhead. Within weeks the NASD had organized two thousand dockers in Hull and eighteen hundred in Birkenhead.[86]

By October 11, the strike had gained momentum following a march through London's East End. In what the *Daily Herald* described as a "mile-long procession," dockworkers marched to Victoria Park. Victor Marney addressed the meeting as an "unofficial representative of the TGWU." Once the lightermen joined the strike the marches became even more impressive. In one procession over ten thousand dockworkers marched from the Embankment to Hyde Park. According to Maurie Foley, four "drummer and fife" bands accompanied the marchers. At the head of the procession were Dickie Barrett and the WLTBU leader, William Lindley. Adding to the carnival atmosphere, "most of the men all wore their war medals and I think this gave more guts to their march."[87]

As in the previous postwar strikes, the TGWU was absent from the struggle and fanfare of a strike of London dockworkers. In a TGWU Special Council session on October 24, Deakin repeated his charge that the strike was Communist-inspired. The strike was also taking a toll on Deakin's patience and revealed his increasing insecurity. Deakin expressed frustration with the "abuse" he had received during the dispute. He sounded petulant when he announced, "[I am] getting tired of it and was beginning to wonder whether it was worthwhile giving one's all in the interests of the dockers." Deakin's continual charge of Communist subversion and agitation had lost its ring, however. One member at the session complained that "too much" attention had been spent "on Communist activity," and it would be "better to create a better informed membership." Finally, it seemed, TGWU officials were taking notice that "criticism of or lines of communication were continuous and it might be well, therefore, to divert some of the moneys allocated to the Educational side for the development of proper lines of communication."[88] The proposed solution ignored the central complaint of the rank and file, namely, that officials were appointed, not elected.

The TGWU was certainly left isolated by its insistence that the overtime strike was unnecessary. William Lindley informed Deakin on October 27 that the WLTBU was joining the strike. Lindley justified his position by attesting to the sanctity of the eight-hour day: "To be compelled to work ten or twelve hours per day, even though the extra time is paid at overtime rates, makes a mockery of the established 8-hour day."[89]

By October 27, the strike was solid. All the sections of the London port were out. Joining them also were Liverpool, Hull, and Southampton. For Barrett, a solution to the crisis was simple, a recognition by employers and the respective dock labor boards that overtime was "voluntary": "But let them say they accept our view that it is voluntary and let us get the men back to work."[90] Complicating the issue was the decision by the TUC to suspend the NASD from the TUC Council. Reacting to TGWU complaints of NASD poaching, the TUC took the extraordinary step of suspending the NASD on October 26, during the height of the overtime strike. Although potentially damaging to the cause of the NASD and its militant TGWU allies, the suspension had little effect on the trajectory of the strike.[91]

While the strike continued, the Conservative government held a policy of providing mediation. Unlike the earlier Labour government, the Tories were far more cautious in their approach to the problem. The previous government's use of troops had clearly not solved the problem of recurring strikes. Another consideration may have been the financial costs of previous operations. The effective coordinating of loading and unloading of millions of tons of cargo took vast resources. The "ineffectives" and Canadian seamen's strikes of 1949 alone, for example, saw the use of 37,000 troops, and 1,845 vehicles. So the inability to stem unofficial strikes and punish their leaders was just as much of a financial failure as a political one.

Minister of Labour Sir Walter Monckton arranged a series of meetings with the NASD and the WLTBU, the TGWU, and employers. As Barrett had earlier suggested, it came down to merely recognizing that overtime was "voluntary." Deakin had tried to steer clear from the term but he could not maintain his stance. During negotiations with Monckton, Deakin expressed the view that overtime was "voluntary but necessary." Employers were disappointed that the NASD and WLTBU insisted on a nationwide recognition of "voluntary" overtime, but they also caved in and accepted the strikers' demand.[92]

With Deakin and the employers accepting the concept that overtime was voluntary, mass meetings of dockers, stevedores, and lightermen on Sunday, October 30, voted to return to work the following day. On November 1, London docks were busy sites of working dockworkers. In what must have seemed to many an ironic statement, Barrett publicly called on the returning London strikers: "Having achieved all this, I want you to do all the overtime you can to get this port back into working condition."[93]

The TGWU leadership once again was left to pick up the pieces of a shattered policy. It had ignored its members' concerns over the "reasonable" clause. Deakin did his usual acrobatic maneuver by blaming the unofficial leaders. In a circular issued to the TGWU executive council, he insisted that the rank and file "have been completely led up the garden." It would "appear," he continued, that "dockers . . . have lost their guts. To be dragooned and bulldozed by strong-arm methods is something I thought I would not have lived to see." Deakin nonetheless held off from any public statement attacking either the TGWU strikers or the NASD and the WLTBU.[94]

But the rank and file firmly believed it was an issue worth fighting. Indeed, in the aftermath of the strike, overtime was more negotiable throughout the port. The word "reasonable" had remained in Clause 8(8)(*b*), but its application was now in doubt, and the discipline cases arising from it had slowed to a trickle. The TGWU had lost more than just goodwill from its members; NASD encroachments into its northern ports directly threatened its docker membership.[95] The TGWU's insistence that the overtime issue was not one to pursue had alienated many dockers throughout the country. It was just one more example of a leadership seriously out of touch with its members' concerns.

But the TGWU survived the NASD challenge. It also enjoyed a period of relative calm following the 1954 strike because many of the militants within the unofficial organization began dropping away. Years of fighting and sacrificing had taken their toll. Ted Dickens suffered a heart attack that left him weak and he transferred to a clerking job. But he was virtually incapacitated by the attack and he left the industry, eventually dying in 1964. John Mahon gave a tribute at Dickens's funeral service and applauded his "unremitting and selfless participation in 40 years of class struggle in London's Dockland and East End." Echoing dockworkers' description of Dickens and his style, Mahon exclaimed, "There were no airs or graces in Ted's speech. He had the greater gift of getting to the heart of the matter in a few simple words all could understand, and when he spoke, goodness, sincerity and truth shone out from him like a light from the lamp." Others also fell victim to the job. Victor Marney suffered a "severe accident" that forced him to leave the docks. Wally Jones was less fortunate; he fell down a hatch and died.[96] It seemed to many that the unofficial movement had lost steam, but that was not to be the case. As George Cosey had predicted, someone would always come to the fore. In the late 1950s and 1960s, Jack Dash took on the responsibility of leading the rank-and-file movement.

The generation that had led the oppositional movement had succeeded in putting forth the rank-and-file concerns. But even more important, such efforts had resulted in victories. The disciplinary clauses of the Dock Labour Scheme were harnessed by the 1948 and 1954 strikes. The 1950 expulsions and 1951 arrests of the movement's leaders had failed to stem the rank and file's power. Indeed, the men singled out by both the TGWU and the Labour government continued to work in the London docks throughout the 1950s. Even more than in New York City, dockworkers in London were able to engage in direct confrontation with their union leaders, employers, and central governments and win.

To some extent the London dockworkers' victories were based upon common feelings of alienation and anger. In New York City, although resentment against union officials was prevalent, a work force that was fractured along ethnic and racial lines continued to act as a brake on concerted and unified action. As will be seen in the following chapter, racial fault lines became the issue that drove but also separated New York City's longshoremen.

Notes

1. Report, "Strikes over Discharges of Class C Dockers," to Industrial Relations Department, Headquarters, Ministry of Labour, from W. E. Thomas, Conciliation Officer, April 12, 1949, LAB/10/183, PRO; "National Dock Labour Board, Press Notice—London Dock Strike," April 12, 1949, BK 2/202, PRO.

2. Report, "Strikes over Discharges of Class C Dockers," to Industrial Relations Department (quote); Report to Industrial Relations Department, Headquarters, Ministry of Labour, from W. E. Thomas, Conciliation Officer, April 4, 1949, LAB/10/183, PRO.

3. Report, "Strikes over Discharges of Class C Dockers," to Industrial Relations Department; Report to Industrial Relations Department, Headquarters, Ministry of Labour, from W. E. Thomas, Conciliation Officer, April 10, 1949, LAB/10/183, PRO.

4. "Circular to Area No. 1 Docks Group from T. W. Condon, Area Secretary," April 11, 1949, BK 2/202, PRO.

5. Interview, Maurie Foley, MSS 371/QD7/DOCKS/2/12, Modern Records Center, University of Warwick (hereafter MRC).

6. Ibid.

7. Report, "Strikes over Discharges of Class C Dockers," to Industrial Relations Department; interview, Ted Kirby, MSS 371/QD7/DOCKS/ 2/6, MRC.

8. Memorandum by the Home Secretary, J. C. Ede—The London Dock Strike, April 12, 1949, and Memorandum by the Minister of Labour and National Service, G. A. Isaacs, April 12, 1949, both in Prime Minister's Correspondence, PREM 8/1085.

9. Letter to Atlee from Attorney General Sir Hartley Shawcross, April 13, 1949, Prime Minister's Correspondence, PREM 8/1085; "Labour Cabinet Meeting," April 13, 1949, Cabinet Conclusions, CAB 128/15, PRO.

10. "Labour Cabinet Meeting," April 13, 1949.

11. *Times* (London), April 13, 1949, 2, April 14, 1949, 4 (quotes).

12. Report, "Strikes over discharges of Class C Dockers," to Industrial Relations Department (first quote); Minutes and Reports of Docks National Committee, 1948–49, MSS 126/TG2, MRC (second quote).

13. *Times* (London), April 17, 1949, 4. Industrial relations officers reported, "All labor requirements have been met except in the lighterage section where the total number of registered lightermen has proved insufficient to cope with the increased rush of work." Report, "Strikes over discharges of Class C Dockers," to Industrial Relations Department.

14. Letter to Barrett from Isaacs, May 4, 1949, LAB/10/183, PRO. By late 1950 employers on the National Joint Council and the NDLB had rejected "any form of retirement allowance to men over 70 years of age." "January 8, 1951, Meeting, TGWU, Docks National Committee," Minutes and Reports of the Docks National Committee, MSS 126/TG2, MRC.

15. Peter Weiler, *British Labor and the Cold War* (Stanford: Stanford University Press, 1988), 231–39.

16. Letter to H. R. Priday, Area Secretary, TGWU, from J. R. Cross, Secretary, Port of Bristol Employers' Association, May 6, 1949, and letter to Cross from Priday. May 9, 1949, both in BK 2/75, NDLB, PRO.

17. Report—Industrial Disputes, 1949, BK 2/75, NDLB, PRO.

18. "London Dock Labour Board—Ships Affected by the Canadian Seamen's Strike," May 15, 1949, BK 2/75, NDLB, PRO.

19. Interview, Joe Bloomberg, MSS 371/QD7/DOCKS2/3, MRC.

20. "Appendix A—Leaflet Issued during Unofficial Stoppage Arising out of the Canadian Seamen's Dispute—TO ALL PORTWORKERS," MSS 126/TG/3, Sack 30/31, MRC.

21. Kirby interview.

22. "Canadian Seamen's Strike: Brief Particulars of Dock Workers Known to Have Been More or Less Prominent during the Strike," BK 2/76, NDLB, PRO.

23. Ibid.

24. Ibid.

25. Ibid.

26. William E. Thomas, Conciliation Officer, and William J. Hull, Regional Industrial Relations Officer, Report—Canadian Seamen's Dispute, July 4, 1949, LAB 10/904, PRO.

27. Interview, Jack Dash, MSS 371/QD7/DOCKS/2/10, MRC; Foley interview.

28. William J. Hull, Report—Canadian Seamen's Dispute, July 5, 1949, LAB 10/904, PRO.

29. "Statement Made by the Home Secretary in the House of Commons, on Friday July 8, 1949," LAB 10/904, PRO.

30. "Appendix A: List of Recent Industrial Disputes Involving the Services, 1949,"

PREM 8/1538, PRO; Cabinet: The Dock Labour Industry and the NDLB—Memorandum by the Minister of Transport, July 6, 1949, PREM 8/1534, PRO (quotes).

31. Phillip Deery, "'The Secret Battalion': Communism in Britain during the Cold War," *Contemporary British History* 13 (Winter 1999): 1–28. Deery does acknowledge that "the role of the communists was far from peripheral to, but not the root source of, the dock strike" (6). For discussion by another historian who provides no direct evidence of Communist involvement but believes that Communists did lead the strikes by following the dictates of the CPGB, see Willie Thompson, "British Communists in the Cold War, 1947–52," *Contemporary British History* 15 (Autumn 2001): 105–21. Thompson argues that "the party reversed the general posture of stable employer-employee relations which it had pursued ever since 1941 (though less extensively since 1945) and unleashed its industrial militants. In due course severe and damaging strikes broke out, particularly in the docks" (113). For a more reasoned appraisal that looks directly at the dock industry and the grievances of dockworkers that were the motors for rebellion, see Jim Phillips, "Decasualization and Disruption: Industrial Relations in the Docks, 1945–79," in *A History of British Industrial Relations, 1939–1979: Industrial Relations in a Declining Economy,* ed. Chris Wrigley (Brookfield, Vt.: E. Elgar, 1996), 165–85.

32. Hull, Report—Canadian Seamen's Dispute, July 5, 1949 (first quote); letter to A. F. A. Sutherland, Parliamentary Secretary, Minister of Labour, from E. S. Carr, Private Secretary, Prime Minister, July 16, 1949, LAB 10/904, PRO (Neville quotes).

33. Letter to Atlee from Ammon, July 5, 1949, BK 2/76, NDLB, PRO; letter to Ammon from Atlee, July 5, 1949, BK 2/76, NDLB, PRO.

34. "Notes of Meeting," July 19, 1949, BK 2/76, NDLB, PRO.

35. "London Dock Strike: Text of a Press Association Message Received from the Duty Officer, Ministry of Labour, at 11:35 P.M., July 22, 1949," LAB 10/904, PRO.

36. *Times* (London), July 22, 1949, 4.

37. *Times* (London), July 23, 1949, 4.

38. Interview, George Cosey, MSS 371/QD7/DOCKS2/8, MRC.

39. "'Appendix C, D, & E,' Extract from Notes of a Meeting of the London Central Lockout Committee held at Canning Town Public Hall, on Sunday, August 7, 1949," MSS 126/TG/3, Sack 30/31, MRC.

40. Cosey interview; *Port Workers' News,* October 1949, 4; ibid., November, 1949. George Cosey (lighterman) helped put the paper together. Although he was a Communist, the Communist Party did not provide any technical support for the paper.

41. Cosey interview; interview, John Cavanagh, MSS 371/QD7/DOCKS2/6, MRC; Kirby interview.

42. Nina Fishman, "The Phoney Cold War in British Trade Unions," *Contemporary British History* 15 (Autumn 2001): 97–98. Not one of the Communists on the TGWU Executive Council represented dockworkers. Noreen Branson, *History of the Communist Party in Brtain, 1941–1951* (London: Lawrence and Wishart, 1997), 179.

43. "Docks National Committee: Minutes and Record of the Statutory Quarterly Meeting, July 21, 1949," MSS 126/TG2, MRC (quote); Fishman, "The Phoney Cold War," 98.

44. "Circular: TO LONDON DOCK BRANCHES," from Deakin, July 25, 1949, MSS 126/TG/3, MRC; "Circular: TO GENERAL EXECUTIVE COUNCIL, PERMANENT OFFICERS AND BRANCH SECRETARIES," from Deakin, December 28, 1949, MSS 126/TG/3, MRC; Mem-

orandum to Deakin: CANADIAN SEAMEN'S STRIKE (London Docks Stoppage), December 9, 1949, MSS 126/TG/2, MRC.

45. Memorandum to Deakin: CANADIAN SEAMEN'S STRIKE.

46. "Transcript of Proceedings, Inquiry, Unofficial London Docks Strike, 1949," January 26, 1949, MSS 126/TG/3, SACK 30/31, MRC.

47. Letter to Deakin from Harry Van Loo, January 25, 1950, and letter to Van Loo from Deakin, January 31, 1950, both in MSS 126/TG/3, SACK 30/31, MRC.

48. Kirby interview; Joe Bloomberg, interview by author, August 8, 1996.

49. Unofficial London Docks Strike (1949)—Report of the Special Committee appointed under the terms of the decisions recorded in minute No. 1125 of the General Executive Council, Dated December 15, 1949, MSS 126/TG/3, Sack 30/31, MRC. Cronin was luckier than most; he was "warned as to future conduct." Cronin had resigned earlier from the Lock-Out Committee after the government's proclamation of a state of emergency.

50. J. R. Whitlock, "London Dock Strike, 1950," May 23, 1950, LAB 10/955, PRO; Edward Bolton, Regional Industrial Relations Officer, "Expulsion of Three Men from the TGWU-Strike," April 24, 1950, LAB 10/955, PRO.

51. Foley interview; interview, Harry Browne, MSS 371/QD7/DOCKS/2/5.

52. *Port Workers' News,* April, 1950, 1.

53. "Cabinet Conclusions," April 21, 24, 25, 27, 1950, all in CAB 128/17, PRO.

54. Whitlock, "London Dock Strike, 1950."

55. Bolton, "Expulsion of Three Men from the TGWU-Strike"; Whitlock, "London Dock Strike, 1950."

56. Cosey interview.

57. J. C. Potts, Conciliation Officer, "Stoppage of Work—Liverpool Docks," February 7, 1951, LAB 10/1019, PRO; *Daily Herald,* February 4, 1951, 1; ibid., February 5, 1951, 1 (quote).

58. Cosey interview.

59. Edward Bolton, Conciliation Officer, "Attempts to Provoke a Strike at London Docks," February 7, 1951, LAB 10/1019, PRO; Dash interview; *Daily Herald,* February 6, 1951, 1. Albert Timothy had exclaimed, "We want a straightforward resolution and no messing about." *Daily Herald,* February 6, 1951, 1.

60. Cosey interview.

61. Ibid.; Dash interview; Edward Bolton, Conciliation Officer, "Strike Following the Arrest and Prosecution of Seven Port Workers," February 15, 1951, LAB10/1019, PRO.

62. Dash interview (quotes); Bolton, "Strike Following the Arrest"; A. L. Nicholson, "Strike Following the Arrest and Prosecution of Seven Port Workers," February 21, 1951, LAB10/1019, PRO. At one of the court appearances strikers occupied themselves by playing with a giant balloon bearing the slogan "Our lads in the dock—no one in the docks." Policemen tried to "capture it" resulting in "jostling" with laughing dockworkers until "finally a police sergeant trapped it against a car." *Daily Herald,* February 21, 1951, 1, 3, February 28, 1951, 1.

63. Cavanagh interview.

64. *Daily Herald,* April 10, 1951, 5; Foley interview; *Daily Worker,* February 21, 1951, 2.

65. Foley interview; "Statement by the General Secretary to the General Executive Council at Its Session Held on March 8, 1951," Minutes and Reports of the Docks National Committee, 1950–51, MSS 126/TG2, MRC (quotes).

66. "Executive Committee Meeting," January 14, 1950, CP/CENT/EC/02/01, Labor History Archive and Study Center, John Rylands University Library, Manchester (hereafter LHAM). Dickens's silence was evident throughout the 1950 and 1951 meetings. Ibid., March 4, 1950, May 13, 1950, June 8, 1950, July 8, 1950, August 12, 1950, September 9, 1950, February 10, 1951, CP/CENT/EC/02/03, LHAM; ibid., March 10, 1951, April 14, 1951.

67. "Interview with Comrade Ted Dickens by John Mahon," September 6, 1950 (first quote), and Report of Meeting with Comrade Ted Dickens by L. Zaldman (second quote), May 26, 1951, both in CP/CENT/PERS/2/3, LHAM.

68. "Interview with Comrade Ted Dickens by John Mahon"; Letter to John Mahon, London District Secretary, Communist Party, from Ted Dickens, February 12, 1951, CP/CENT/PERS/2/3, LHAM; Letter to Ted Dickens from John Mahon, April 25, 1951, ibid.

69. "London District Conference," September 11, 1951, CP/LON/SEC/1/2, LHAM. London dockworkers had their own section, the Port of London Branch. "Dues Position as at August 23, 1952, CP/LON/ORG/1/6, LHAM.

70. "Address by John Mahon, London District Secretary, London District Conference," September 11, 1951, CP/LON/SEC/1/2, LHAM; Cavanagh interview.

71. Cosey interview; Foley interview.

72. Foley interview.

73. *Daily Herald,* April 10, 1, 5 (quote). The eight thousand strikers returned to work the following day. A. L. Nicholson, Conciliation Officer, Ministry of Labour, "Strike Following the Arrest and Prosecution of Seven Port Workers," April 9, 1951, LAB10/1019, PRO; *Daily Herald,* April 11, 1951, 5.

74. *Daily Herald,* April 12, 1951, 5, April 17, 1951, 5 (quotes).

75. *Daily Worker,* April 14, 1951, 1; *Daily Herald,* April 13, 1951, 5 (quotes).

76. *Times* (London), April 19, 1951, 3, April 20, 1951, 3; *Daily Herald,* April 18, 1951, 3; *Daily Worker,* April 19, 1951, 1.

77. "Address by John Mahon."

78. Browne interview.

79. Ibid.; Foley interview.

80. *Final Report of a Court of Inquiry into a Dispute in the London Docks* (London, 1954), 5–19. The TGWU tried to brand the NASD as a rogue organization and told its members to stay away from the conflict. Arthur Bird, National Secretary, "Circular to London Docks Officers and London Docks Branches," March 19, 1954, MSS 126/TG2/Box 33, MRC. The NASD and WLTBU in turn called on dockers to be sympathetic with their plight. R. Barrett and William Lindley, "Overtime—Compulsory or Voluntary," April 30, 1954, MSS 126/TG2/Box 33, MRC. Arthur Bird informed Deakin that Barrett's and Lindley's overtures to the dockers was "to let their conscience guide them as to whether or not they should support the ban." Letter to Deakin from Bird, May 4, 1954, MSS 126/TG2/Box 33, MRC.

81. *Financial Times,* February 3, 1954, 3; Ted Dickens, "The Overtime Ban—Splitters Exposed," *Port Workers News,* April–May, 1954, 1; *Port Workers News,* August, 1954.

82. Letter to Barrett from Arthur Bird, March 15, 1954, MSS 126/TG2/Box 33, MRC; letter to Bird from Barrett, July 10, 1954 (quotes), ibid.; "National and London Dock Labour Boards—Alleged Refusals to Work Overtime," June 30, 1954, BK 2–83, PRO. By September 1, 1954, the number of men reported had reached 80,855. "National and London Dock Labour Boards—Alleged Refusals to Work Overtime," September 1, 1954, ibid.

83. *Final Report of a Court of Inquiry,* 19–21; *Daily Herald,* October 5, 1954, 1, October 9, 1954, 1, October 14, 1954, 1.

84. *Daily Herald,* October 4, 1954, 1.

85. "TGWU Special Council Session—Docks Situation, October 24, 1954," MSS 126/TG/3, Sack 45/2, MRC.

86. Prior to the strike, Hull and Birkenhead dockers had been in revolt against the TGWU over the hand-scuttling of grain. The Hull men wanted available technology introduced to supplant the arduous hand-scuttling. Angered by TGWU indifference on the issue, the NASD was invited by Hull (and Birkenhead) dockers to organize them. *Times* (London), October 28, 1954, 8. The NASD policy was a risky one because it could entail sanction by the Trade Union Congress (TUC). Earlier in 1924, the TUC had found the NASD guilty of poaching TGWU members and had been duly thrown out of the trade union organization. In 1929, the TUC established the Bridlington Agreement whereby affiliated unions could be censored and banned if they engaged in poaching members. Not until 1944 was the NASD accepted back into the fold. Shirley W. Lerner, *Breakaway Unions and the Small Trade Union* (London: Ruskin House, 1961), 66–81.

87. *Daily Herald,* October 13, 1954, 1; Foley interview.

88. "TGWU Special Council Session—Docks Situation, October 24, 1954," MSS 126/TG/3, Sack 45/2, MRC.

89. Letter to Deakin from Lindley, October 27, 1954, MSS 126/TG/3, Sack 45/2, MRC. Lindley made clear that while the WLTBU recognized that overtime was "essential" in keeping cargoes moving, "at the same time [we] reserve the right of the individual to finish at the end of the day without being reported to, and disciplined by, the London Dock Labour Board" (ibid.).

90. *Daily Herald,* October 22, 1954, 2.

91. *Times* (London), October 28, 1954, 6; Jim Phillips, "Inter-Union Conflict in the Docks, 1954–1955," *Historical Studies in Industrial Relations* 1 (March 1996): 110–13.

92. *Times* (London), October 28, 1954, 8, October 29, 1954, 8, October 30, 1954, 6.

93. *Daily Herald,* November 1, 1954, 1.

94. "Docks Situation—The Members of the General Executive Council," November 1, 1954, MSS 126/TG/3, Sack 45/2, MRC. Deakin had promised reporters a "full statement" following the strike but never did provide one. *Daily Herald,* November 1, 1954, 1.

95. The controversy between the TGWU and the NASD would continue for another year. In 1955, the NASD attempted to hold onto its northern acquisitions. A failed strike and eventual TUC decision in the TGWU's favor ended its foray into northern ports. Trades Union Congress—Transport and General Workers' Union and National Amalgamated Stevedores and Dockers (and Vice-Versa)—Memorandum and Award by Disputes Sub-Committee, June 24 and 28, 1955, MSS 126/TG/3, Sack 45/3, MRC; Phillips, "Inter-Union Conflict," 116–17.

96. "Ted Dickens—A Tribute—John Mahon's Speech at the Funeral Ceremony, Friday, September 25, 1964," CP/CENT/PERS/2/3, LHAM.

8 The Fault Line of Race

While the interunion battles of the postwar period were being fought in London and New York, another form of confrontation was taking place on New York's docks. African American and Hispanic American longshoremen were challenging racist hiring practices along the waterfront and in the hiring halls. Between 1950 and 1962, black and Hispanic longshoremen followed a path of rebellion to gain a semblance of dignity on the job and in the union hall. As the general rank and file revolted during the period, these minority longshoremen waged their own distinct battle. Black and Hispanic longshoremen faced a struggle that was even more bitter than that of their white coworkers. They had to contend not only with employers and union officials, but with white longshoremen. As with the general rank-and-file revolt, minority longshoremen looked to outsiders for succor. Not all of them, however, followed a path of overt resistance. Some attempted to find an alternative method of obtaining regular work. These longshoremen paid kickbacks, eagerly volunteered to work at a moment's notice, or consistently made themselves available for overtime. For all of these black longshoremen the record was a mixed one. Sometimes they were successful in changing some hiring policies and union attitudes; at other times, however, they were ignored or chastised for their efforts. Just as complex as the differing experiences of black workers was the role played by employers in excluding blacks from the workplace. Too often, some historians see the union or white worker as the primary agent in excluding blacks from employment.[1]

Black longshoremen experienced discriminatory treatment every day. In 1961, a black longshoremen explained to the journalist Pete Hamill his position on New York City's docks: "The way it is now is not good, but I think it's getting better. The white guys think we're trying to take their jobs away from them. We're not. But if we can do the work, we ask that we be considered fairly. I want to work. I want to put money in the bank. For me the only way to do it is with [a] hook—down here on the waterfront. All I want is a chance to do that work and still have some kind of dignity—even if it means doing business with the boys." The "boys" meant white union leaders and mobsters. While black longshoremen experienced entrenched racism and understood the need to work with white coworkers and union officials, the officials saw a different picture. For one white union leader, Teddy Gleason, it was a question not of race, but of getting in line for the available work: "The newcomers believe when they come down [to the docks], the [white] old-timers on the waterfront should share . . . their work opportunities with these people whether they be Puerto Rican or whether they are colored. And if they are not put to work, they go back to the NAACP or State Division Against Discrimination [*sic*] and the first thing you know we are up on charges."[2]

Such differing interpretations underscore the complexity of life on New York City's waterfront between 1950 and 1961. While black longshoremen wanted equal access to jobs, whites saw them as trying to jump the queue. What white union leaders and longshoremen failed to acknowledge was that black longshoremen had always been a presence on the docks. Thus it was that black longshoremen were not necessarily getting ahead in line but were demanding their due. Black longshoremen attempted to maneuver their way through these treacherous waters while confronting an array of barriers that kept them from regular employment. A fortunate few enjoyed somewhat frequent work, while the majority were confined to fluctuating employment or handling odious cargoes. Most were denied access to easier dock jobs, such as those of the checkers and drivers, which remained the domain of white ethnics. Black longshoremen used two specific agencies to challenge discrimination on the job: a Jim Crow union local in Brooklyn and the New York State Commission Against Discrimination.

Biracial unionism had given African American workers the ability to navigate the shoals of racist hiring practices and hostile trade union structures. As Eric Arnesen has shown, African American longshoremen in late nineteenth-century New Orleans retained power over hiring and promotion through the institution of biracial union locals.[3] Such locals provided a semblance of protection while simultaneously ensuring a black voice at both the port and regional levels. For black New York longshoremen in the post–World War II era, the picture was not as hopeful. Although they retained a degree of institutional freedom with their Jim Crow Local 968, they were unable to control a pier and thereby guarantee steady work, which meant they were constantly searching for work. Nonetheless, Local 968 acted as a springboard for direct attacks on the black longshoremen's representative trade union and discriminatory employers. Additionally, black longshoremen throughout the port and from Local 968 looked to the New York State Commission Against Discrimination for redress of their grievances. They used the commission as a vehicle to publicize discrimination and, at times, even win some limited victories.

The experience of New York's black longshoremen was as varied as it was turbulent. From the colonial period to the present, black longshoremen had been a constant presence along the seven hundred miles of New York's waterfront, which stretched along the shores of Manhattan, Brooklyn, and Staten Island, and Newark, Jersey City, and Hoboken in New Jersey. Their employment fluctuated depending on local or national circumstances. Between 1840 and 1850, African Americans reportedly constituted a majority of the work force. Thereafter they suffered a decline, but rose again in and during World War I and World War II.[4] In the late 1940s, they numbered from 4,000 to 5,000, or 15 percent of the work force. Representing a significant minority of the work force did not guarantee them union power. Blacks were barely integrated into the union structure; there were no black union representatives at the New York district level. The only African Americans who served as representatives to the international union came from southern and southwestern ports.[5]

Black New York longshoremen had many types of experience on the job (although they usually all worked in a racist environment) and adopted different strategies to survive. They labored in a complex labor pool, where an array of ethnic and racial groups contended for work and power. A common characteristic among all workers, however, was the constant battle for acceptance and dignity. Above all, the black dockworkers shared with white longshoremen the intense desire to put food on the table. But separating them were entrenched and virulent attitudes that saw work in strictly racial terms. Work rejected by white longshoremen was considered the domain of black workers. Black workers, in turn, either directly challenged such definitions or grudgingly accepted them to guarantee a vestige of employment in a job market that was far from stable.

Just as vital were the divisions within the black labor force itself. Some black longshoremen fought a civil rights battle within the ILA. In this struggle, they looked to labor movement allies such A. Philip Randolph or middle-class reform groups such as the Urban League, the NAACP, or the New York State Commission Against Discrimination for support. But other black longshoremen took a different tack. They disregarded formal opposition within the union and instead opted to obtain employment on any terms possible. Thus there was a separation between those black longshoremen who actively challenged discrimination on the New York waterfront and those who tried to work within the racialist circumstances, hoping to get enough work to feed themselves and their families. The myriad of exclusionary practices aroused a fatalistic attitude in some black longshoremen. As one remarked: "You know what it is to be a Negro on these docks? It's to be a nigger again. To the boss, you're a nigger. To the guy next to you, you're a nigger. And to yourself, you're a nigger. That's the worst part of being a Negro on the docks."[6]

The New York waterfront was the site of competing ethnic and racial groups. Throughout the port, black longshoremen had different job experiences. The divisions encapsulated birthplace and union-local strength. Some black longshoremen in Brooklyn had been working on the waterfront prior to World War II, while men like Arthur ("Standby") McMillon were recent arrivals. More established blacks had to compete for work with the new arrivals from the South. Placing themselves for hire on a daily basis on the streets of Brooklyn and Harlem, the more casual black longshoremen undermined the position of their brothers throughout the port. Casual longshoremen like McMillon were ready to take any work offered, which was a stratagem for gaining more permanent status. McMillon had a union card, enabling him to search for work along the waterfront in Brooklyn, Manhattan, and, eventually, Newark, New Jersey.

Such a tactic did not mean McMillon was willing to accept second-class status, however. In a telling exchange with an Italian-American longshoreman, McMillon made clear his need to be respected. McMillon said that as he walked down the street with a "white guy," his companion turned around and "kicked me, playing with me." After making sure no other black longshoremen witnessed the kick, McMillon informed the white longshoreman: "I believe you like me, but don't do that no more. [I'm] not mad with you, [but] black people say white people got their foot up their ass for a long time." McMillon warned the man he was lucky no other black longshoremen were present because he would have got "a stick and knock[ed] your ass right out here." The white longshoreman "never did it no more." The point had been made: it was one thing to horse around, but certain rules of respectful behavior had to be observed.[7]

For African Americans, rampant discrimination by the hiring bosses and the ILA made for an insecure existence. Unable to dominate a pier, blacks had to shape-up as extras and only rarely as gangs. According to Howard Kimeldorf, in San Francisco during the 1930s and early 1940s the union local was controlled by left-wing elements who fought hard to retain a vibrant black membership, while in Portland, Oregon, a hostile white work force succeeded in barring entry to blacks even through World War II. The factors that enabled black longshoremen to work in New Orleans included enhanced trade union principles of brotherhood and raw numbers of black workers, which ensured strong job and union control.[8]

In New York, African Americans were reluctantly accepted in part because of their relatively high numbers and the fact that they handled certain disagreeable cargoes such as bananas that had been refused by white ethnics. Such factors led to a combination of biracial unionism and free-floating black and Hispanic members. Just like the Italians and Irish who created ethnic locals, blacks were forced either to organize or to accept whatever work was available. Unlike their white counterparts, however, black locals were set apart by embedded racism and their inability to control a pier to ensure regular employment.[9]

In the postwar period African American longshoremen actively challenged their second-class status. Such confrontations were largely contextualized by anger and frustration with the union leadership. Long dominated by gangsters, the union had traditionally negotiated sweetheart contracts with employers. Consequently the New York longshoremen (as well as other East Coast and Gulf Shore longshoremen) were paid less than their counterparts on the West Coast. As has been shown, beginning in 1945 a series of wildcat strikes broke out along the waterfront as the dockers rejected wages and conditions negotiated by the union leadership. Each time, New York's longshoremen walked out en masse.[10] Local 968 also joined this insurgency. Besides attaching itself to the wildcat strike wave of the late 1940s and early 1950s, Local 968 concentrated its energies on obtaining steady work and combating discrimination. It waged its battle on two fronts: within the union corridors of power and before a New York state agency, the State Commission Against Discrimination.

Local 968 fought hard for control of a pier in Brooklyn to guarantee a modicum of regular employment. Cleophas Jacobs, president of Local 968, charged in 1949 that the "shipping companies . . . in collaboration with various local union officials and the hiring bosses, have an agreement whereby the available work is given to the other nine [white] locals in Brooklyn, to the exclusion of our men." Accentuating the problem was the lack of black representation in the ILA, where not one African American had been appointed organizer even though Local 968 had a membership of a thousand men. Jacobs often complained bitterly to President Joseph Ryan. Ryan "promised to alleviate conditions," according to Jacobs, but "absolutely nothing" had been done "in this direction."[11] Jacobs was also concerned with the loss of members to other Brooklyn locals, charging that these same locals, controlled by Anthony (Tough Tony) Anastasia, were simultaneously creating an "employment pool" for all Brooklyn piers and "inducing" black members to leave 968 and join the white locals. Those black members who joined white locals either worked in mixed gangs or gambled that membership might ensure more steady work. Jacobs attempted to pressure Ryan to redress the situation by getting Local 968 members to picket the ILA's Manhattan headquarters for thirteen weeks in 1949. Ryan unleashed white ethnic members who violently dispersed the picket line. Ryan also took Jacobs to court and ordered a "special election" of Local 968's officers. However, the 1950 election returned Jacobs and his supporters to the leadership of Local 968.[12]

By 1952, Jacobs had become so frustrated with the increasing loss of his members to other ILA locals that he encouraged his men to appeal to Governor Thomas E. Dewey for help. In turn, Dewey handed over the request to the New York State Commission Against Discrimination (SCAD). Modeled on Franklin D. Roosevelt's wartime Fair Employment Practice Committee, SCAD was created to administer New York State's Ives-Quin law in 1945. SCAD was empowered to investigate discrimination by employers, employment agencies, and trade unions. If SCAD found "probable cause" then cease-and-desist orders could theoretically be issued. In practice, however, SCAD relied overwhelmingly on conciliation to correct proven wrongs. Rather than waiting for complainants, however, SCAD went a step further and initiated actions of its own.[13] In 1952, SCAD organized a series of meetings between the officers of Local 968 and Joe Ryan and other top ILA officials. Although careful not to make an official or "verified complaint" to SCAD, Jacobs nonetheless used the meetings to express his anger and resentment toward the ILA hierarchy. He particularly protested the use of hiring clubs on Lennox Avenue in Harlem and on Fulton Street, Brooklyn, which employed casual, "non-union Negro labor." Such activity, Jacobs charged, was "a subtle type of discrimination" because the clubs bypassed union members from Local 968. "The unorganized Negro is thus pitted against the organized Negro for the purpose of driving the organized Negro out of existence," Jacobs argued. Thus by destroying Local 968, the ILA would "deal with the Negro as an individual and not as an organized entity."[14]

Although Local 968 was unable to gain control of a pier, events beyond internal union politics had the potential to rectify the problem of discrimination at the shape-up. As noted earlier, the New York State Crime Commission Hearings in 1952 exposed widespread and systemic corruption within the ILA. The revelations forced state authorities in New York and New Jersey to eradicate the shape-up and to attempt to remove the ILA's criminal elements. Employment centers were created throughout the port to eliminate criminal control. A two-state agency, the Waterfront Commission, was established to oversee the general running of the centers and the registration of longshoremen. Unlike those on the West Coast, however, these centers were not controlled by the union, nor was work rotated among the work gangs or individuals.[15]

Throughout this period many black longshoremen believed that their situation would improve. Employment discrimination persisted, however, as did the use of hiring clubs that employed casual black labor. The thirteen employment centers scattered throughout the port had been established to do away with the evils of the open-air shape-up, but discrimination had only been driven inside. As one black longshoreman lamented, "This just took the shape-up off the piers and put it indoors." The calls for work in the employment centers continued to be driven by either familial connections or kickbacks. Correspondingly, black longshoremen were frequently ignored.[16]

Local 968 fought hard to end discrimination in the employment centers. In its battle, it gained a new ally in the person of Reginald Ingram, industrial secretary for New York's Urban League. During the mid-1950s, Ingram had begun canvassing the port's black longshoremen. By 1956, he had completed an investigation detailing the working lives of the port's black longshoremen. These longshoremen were scattered across the port with regular gangs working in Newark and Jersey City; the "Breakwater" piers in Brooklyn; the Grace Line piers in Chelsea, Manhattan; and the East Side banana piers. But the majority of the longshoremen were relegated to working as "extras" or casual laborers. The plum jobs of watchmen, checkers, forklift drivers, and carpenters continued to be closed to blacks.[17]

Although getting jobs on the "Breakwater," Local 968 continued to lose large numbers of members. Thomas Fauntleroy, business agent of Local 968, testified in 1958 that the membership had dropped to 750 from 1,000 in just a few years. Fauntleroy estimated that while there were eighteen regular gangs (414 men) and three extra-regular gangs (69 men), the majority of the men never worked on a regular basis; many of them often looked elsewhere throughout the port for work. He said that "some of them drift to the westside [Manhattan] . . . or at Greenpoint [Brooklyn]. . . . Some of them go to Staten Island, and we have quite a few who go to Port Newark." Fauntleroy further testified that at "numerous times," Brooklyn employers would "call gangs from other parts of the port before they call our gangs." Correcting the problem proved difficult. Although "we have had hundreds of complaints," when a grievance was made "it didn't get too far. It would stop at the pier."

That is, the white union delegate would be brought in and the company superintendent would simply promise that it "wouldn't happen again."[18]

Later in 1958, Fauntleroy and Local 968's attorney presented a "formal resolution of grievances" to William Bradley, the newly elected president of the ILA, stating that Local 968 was "having its life sapped by a concerted plan of raiding and stealing of its members." Blame was laid at the feet of Anastasia's Brooklyn Local 1814, which was accused of telling Local 968 members that Local 1814 was the "only group that could guarantee work." Anastasia was also accused of conspiring to "malign, slander, and ridicule the officers and leadership of 968."[19]

Local 968 continued to use SCAD as an ally in its fight to stay alive. After prodding by Reginald Ingram, Thomas Fauntleroy met with SCAD officials to outline again Local 968's issue with Local 1814 and to discuss general discrimination on the waterfront. The meeting focused on a plan to encourage black applicants to the Checker's Local 1. Led by Thomas Gleason, Local 1 had a membership of over five thousand men, not one of whom was black. The case went to the heart of discrimination on the waterfront. A checker's job was relatively easy because it entailed no heavy lifting, and checkers were paid more than the regular longshoremen's rate. SCAD informed Fauntleroy it was supporting two longshoremen, James Bey and Albert Miller, in their challenge to gain entry into Local 1. Fauntleroy was not impressed by Bey's application. He explained that Local 968 was "not interested" in Bey but would go along with Miller, who was "loyal to 968."[20]

Bey's candidacy was problematic because he was a member not of 968 but of Anastasia's Local 1814. Fauntleroy therefore perceived Bey as disloyal. Once again a division was evident among the black longshoremen, this time based upon local union allegiance. Bey's recent history of confrontation with the ILA made him an even more discomfiting figure. Bey had angered ILA officials with his successful 1955 suit for back pay as a temporary organizer, wherein he was awarded ten thousand dollars. His religion was also considered problematic. In 1939 "he had embraced the Islam religion" and enthusiastically encouraged other black longshoremen to "seek Allah."[21]

After investigation, SCAD "found probable cause" that both Bey and Miller had been denied entry into Local 1 "because of their race and color." On January 16, 1958, Elmer A. Carter, a SCAD commissioner, met with Teddy Gleason to settle the issue. In a candid exchange, Gleason forcefully pointed out that he considered Bey "a troublemaker and an undesirable person"; Gleason said Bey was "no credit to his people and was just a bad sort." On the candidacy of Miller, Gleason agreed that the "local could not possibly be hurt by Miller if he is admitted." Gleason did argue that his white members were fearful that Miller could be the wedge that other blacks would follow and that they would "take over" the union. Carter convinced Gleason that SCAD would try to issue a cease-and-desist order forcing Local 1 to take Miller. Gleason finally agreed to convince the members "to take in" Miller because SCAD would "force them to take him anyway." By April 1959, Miller was accepted in Local 1; Bey, however, was not.[22]

Emboldened by SCAD's interest, Local 968 encouraged its members to press charges against discriminatory employers. In September 1958, a group of twenty-six Brooklyn black longshoremen brought a case against the hiring boss at the Waterfront Commission Employment Center No. 8. They charged that they were not called for work as extra regulars, while whites with less seniority were employed. SCAD subsequently discovered that eleven white longshoremen hired as extras that day had less claim to the work than did the black longshoremen present. The stevedoring company, Universal Terminal, although agreeing that some irregularity had occurred, attempted to smear Nathaniel Evans, one of the black longshoremen by charging that he "suffered from a disturbance. . . . He is an unstable worker in the sense that he absents himself without warning or advanced notice." It was not the first time, nor the last, that "irritating" longshoremen were labeled as "troublemakers." SCAD was not convinced by Universal's personal attack on Evans and ordered the company to desist from discriminating again and to provide the complainants with monetary compensation.[23]

In the same year a similar case of discrimination was brought by five black longshoremen in Manhattan. It was another case of being overlooked for employment even though seniority should have guaranteed them jobs. The five men insisted they were generally ignored for work, and "only on occasions when white longshoremen were not available" were they employed.[24] The company in question was the Transoceanic Terminal Corporation. The particular case revolved around the hiring of eighty-eight "casual" longshoremen on October 9, 1958. The five black longshoremen alleged they had been passed over for employment. After investigation by a SCAD investigator, it was discovered that these five men had more seniority than twenty-three of the white men hired. This was a clear case of discrimination. The employer argued that the job "required special training" and that it wanted to "retain" its "prerogative to judge who is best qualified to do this work."[25]

In a meeting with company officials, SCAD investigators learned of the daily, almost traditional exclusion of blacks from regular or skilled jobs. Believing his discussion was off the record, Clyde Walters, a pier superintendent, acknowledged "the only jobs available to Negroes . . . are mule jobs in the hold of the ship" and that "Negroes are never selected as dockmen, drivers or checkers." The "hiring agents select 'neighborhood children' in filling all categories of work except for the back-breaking hold jobs." By "neighborhood children" Walters meant the "immediate residential community of white, primarily Irish and Italian" longshoremen. He added that to "buck the 'system'" was to invite "all types of reprisals" by the men. These "reprisals" included "slowdowns, quickie strikes, damaging of equipment, physical violence, etc." SCAD ordered the company to pay the men for the time lost on the job, "to offer to complainants the next regular vacancies that occur," and to provide a "daily record of all casuals" on the affected pier.[26]

These cases could be construed as successful attacks on discrimination by employers who were in cahoots with white union members. However, SCAD was generally reluctant to act aggressively. It took on individual cases but did not seriously challenge systemic racism. Elmer A. Carter justified the tentative approach by arguing, "Discrimination is pandemic in the United States. The only hope for its permanent elimination lies in the extent to which voluntary compliance with the provisions of the law can be achieved." Many cases were also dismissed, leading the *Harvard Law Review* to claim SCAD was "unduly cautious" and its "high rate of dismissal discourages the filing of complaints."[27] SCAD certainly had powerful weapons to fight discrimination on the waterfront; besides issuing cease-and-desist orders, it could subpoena witnesses and records. Its reluctance to act aggressively can be attributed to officials, especially Elmer Carter, who felt more comfortable trying to persuade employers and ILA officials to adhere to the Ives-Quin law. Such timid action could do nothing but encourage men like Arthur McMillon to take what was given.[28]

Elmer Carter's aversion to confronting both employers and union officials was evident in an episode that involved Hispanic longshoremen. On February 29, 1956, Francisco Garcia and twenty other Hispanic longshoremen met with SCAD officials and filed a complaint against a stevedore company, the John W. McGrath Corporation. The men worked in a banana carrier gang and alleged they were being blocked from the higher-paying jobs of banana stackers and general cargo jobs. Garcia separated himself by instituting his own complaint charging that employers had retaliated against him for leading the initial protest; following his complaint he had been dismissed from his gang and ordered by the Waterfront Commission to present himself for work as an extra. These longshoremen also experienced rejection when they went for jobs as extras for handling general cargo. They charged that the hiring boss, Dick McGrath, would ignore them at the Waterfront Commission hiring hall. McGrath would hire white extras with whom "he was unacquainted" rather "than hire complainants or other Spanish-speaking longshoremen."[29]

Edward L. Carter, a SCAD field agent, met with McGrath officials in March 1956. The meetings were initially testy. Carter reported that the officials insisted on written documentation and having a attorney present. Officials contended that they wanted to avoid "'tricky' questioning which would involve them in any legal entanglements." Carter insisted he merely wanted to collect facts about those Hispanics working for the stevedore on Pier 13 on the East River. Dick McGrath (nephew of the owner, John McGrath) informed Carter that both "Negroes" and Puerto Ricans were employed as stackers, thus invalidating the charge of racial discrimination. McGrath argued that the job of stacker was one of "considerable skill" that took "a long period of time" to acquire. Unlike the banana carrier, the stacker was required to load the bananas on the back of the truck without bruising them. Supposedly, stacking had become a skill denied most Hispanic longshoremen.

In a subsequent meeting with Dick McGrath to discuss Francisco Garcia's case, the complainant's mental condition was questioned. McGrath charged that Garcia was "mentally disturbed." Echoing similar labels given to past agitators, the charge of being a malcontent effectively dissuaded others from challenging the system of racial privilege.[30] The charge of mental incapacity was repeated by union officials. Edward Carter met with Fred Fields, secretary-treasurer, and Nicholas Kisberg, director of research and education for Local 856, on June 28, 1956. Carter explained that he was trying to ascertain whether the McGrath Corporation had discriminated against Garcia and others. Fields and Kisberg gave a general account of why banana carriers were paid a different rate than stackers and said that in their opinion no discrimination had occurred. When the discussion moved to Garcia, Fields announced that Garcia was a "troublesome nuisance." Kisberg denied that the union had played any role in keeping Garcia from regular work since he approached SCAD. For Kisberg the issue revolved around Garcia's proclivities as "a rabble rouser and troublemaker."[31]

Elmer Carter was convinced there was no case and determined there was no evidence "to sustain a finding of probable cause." Carter rationalized his decision by pointing to the presence of "some Puerto Rican and Spanish speaking persons among those regularly employed as stackers by the respondent." Although recognizing that discrimination was present throughout the waterfront, which "disadvantaged" Puerto Ricans, Carter insisted it was just a question of racial and ethnic succession: "The pattern of employment in general follows the history of employment of migrant groups—the last arrivals are condemned to the least desirable jobs." Carter did convince the McGrath Corporation to order its superintendents not to discriminate on the basis of "race, creed, color or national origin." He also received a pledge by the company to reinstate Garcia to his gang.[32]

SCAD's decision had a chilling effect on Hispanic longshoremen's work experience. These men had perceived a clear correlation between their ethnicity and their inability to obtain better-paying dock work. When the SCAD cases collapsed, the men were left adrift. There was no other place to turn for redress. Both the employer's and union's arguments had carried the day; Hispanic longshoremen would have to wait their turn. Elmer Carter, however, saw a victory. The company had promised not to discriminate in the future, and Garcia had his job back. Carter was so enthusiastic over the outcome that he heaped praise on John McGrath in a letter explaining SCAD's decision. The rags-to-riches story of McGrath impressed Carter immensely. As Carter put it, "His story is the story which exemplifies the finest aspects of American democracy." Carter hoped that the same "initiative" and "courage" would be recognized in Hispanic longshoremen, enabling them to rise up into the stacker and general cargo gangs.[33]

The SCAD cases provided the backdrop for an extraordinary rapprochement between Local 968 and the dominant Local 1814. Throughout 1958–59, as the SCAD cases progressed, the respective leaderships sparred over the issues of pier jurisdiction and raiding.[34] In an attempt to quiet the calls for change and the SCAD investigations, "Tough Tony" Anastasia tried to argue that to give Local 968 a pier "would be immoral because it would only serve to foster and perpetuate segregation." Clifford Robinson, the new president of Local 968, gave a stinging public reply to Anastasia in March 1959: "Your remarks about Negroes reveal a hypocrisy equaled only by your own dedication to keeping the Negro in a position apart, with diminished rights and responsibilities." Robinson charged that Anastasia's Local 1814 treated its black longshoremen as a "second class membership" and that "Local 968 will survive to demonstrate that you will not do the same to its men."[35]

The jousting between Locals 968 and 1814 came to an abrupt end in the same year. In May 1959, discussions began about merging Local 968 with the much larger Local 1814. Spurring on these talks were two important factors: the continuing loss of Local 968 members to Local 1814, and Anastasia's attempt to become president of the ILA. By June, negotiators had hammered out a tentative agreement. Local 968 officers would be given leadership positions within Local 1814 and in the New York District, ILA; in return they would provide support for Anastasia's presidential hopes. Prior to the merger vote, Clifford Robinson spelled out his reasoning for supporting the merger. Robinson recognized that "Tough Tony" was "the big man in Brooklyn" and that there was "no support [for 968] from the international." Robinson felt it was also important to forestall further defections from Local 968 to Local 1814: "We figure that if we merge now, before we lose any more of our members, we can get the best possible deal for our people." For their support of the merger, Robinson and Fauntleroy would "become organizers and delegates of Local 1814." Other Local 968 officers were guaranteed official positions in Local 1814 and on the District Council, while the remaining individuals would sit on the "international's wage-scale committee, the first New York Negroes to serve in that capacity." In all, twelve officers of Local 968 would be rewarded with union positions.[36]

Bringing in Local 968, Anastasia hoped to attract support from southern ILA locals that had large black memberships and leaders. As the *New York Times* reported, attracting "the support of southern delegates would make him politically the strongest single man in the union." Even if he failed to win the presidency, Anastasia would rule the Brooklyn docks, the "busiest freight dock of the port."[37] Besides guaranteeing positions for Local 968 officers, the agreement also provided something for the members. An organization was to be established within Local 1814 "to insure and promote the rights and interests of Negro longshoremen." Local 1814 also promised to create positions for blacks as shop stewards (two), dock bosses (five), maintenance men, and safety men. If a new pier was opened up, black gangs would be given work "to overcome the present inequality of employment." On June 27, Local 968 members voted by a margin of two to one to accept the agreement. "This will give us about 2,000 Negro members," Anastasia gleefully remarked, "we already have 1,400 or 1,500 in [our] 9,000 member unit."[38]

Livingston Wingate, the black attorney representing Local 968 in the negotiations, was happy with the new arrangement. The merger ensured "complete equality of Negro longshoremen in all categories on the Brooklyn waterfront," he concluded. Some New York City civil rights leaders were also satisfied with the merger. Joe Overton, president of the New York City chapter of the NAACP, joyfully described the merger "as a step forward in the labor movement that places Anastasia in the forefront of labor leaders who recognize the practicality of one for all and all for one."[39] But the *New York Times* was more cautious in its appraisal. It stated that the merger "rules out any serious danger of new complaints of anti-Negro job discrimination, which is illegal in New York State."[40]

For all the celebration and self-congratulations, the merger did not end discrimination on the New York docks. The extinguishing of Local 968 had removed any serious internal or institutional threat to the ILA. Indeed, Local 1814 never ratified the agreement, leaving black longshoremen in Brooklyn rudderless. In effect, Local 968 leaders had given away what little power they had on the promise of future protection. After joining Local 1814, black longshoremen lacked leaders. Once again, they were left to pick up the crumbs left to them by white hiring bosses and their union allies.

Black longshoremen continued to protest discriminatory treatment on the docks, however, appealing to SCAD for redress. In the early 1960s, new alliances within and outside the ILA confronted entrenched power that reserved plum jobs for whites. A. Philip Randolph joined the cause when he attacked the AFL-CIO's decision to readmit the ILA into the fold in 1959.[41] For his actions Randolph was rewarded with the infamous response by George Meany, "Who the Hell hired you as guardian of all Negro members in America?" In a telling rebuke, the *Amsterdam News* editorialized: "Nobody has appointed Mr. A. Philip Randolph as the 'guardian' of all Negroes in America. . . . But we would like Mr. Meany to understand, that A. Philip Randolph speaks for a damn sight more Negroes on this issue that anyone else in America."[42]

Randolph also came to the defense of rank-and-file longshoremen who formed a Unity Ticket within Local 1814. The Unity Ticket appealed to Randolph's newly formed Negro American Labor Council (NALC) for support in October 1959. The Unity Ticket came under violent attack. Tony Anastasia, along with twenty-five henchmen, had attempted to break up a Unity meeting at the home of a longshoreman, Clyde Blue. After hearing Unity's charges and complaints, Randolph insisted to reporters, "The crisis has reached a head and is subject to explode" unless responsible parties eradicated discrimination on the waterfront.[43] The Unity ticket of black and white longshoremen continued to run its slate of candidates and enjoy the active support of the Negro American Labor Council throughout the 1960s. Randolph allowed longshoremen to use the NALC as a springboard for agitation purposes, while simultaneously using his vice-presidency in the AFL-CIO to appeal to Meany and the AFL-CIO Executive Council to force the recently readmitted ILA to clean up its act.[44]

In Brooklyn, battles would continue over job sharing and political control of Local 1814. Local 968 was gone, however. One of the oldest locals in the New York port, it was unable to control a pier and stanch a flow of members to the larger Local 1814, which made for an agreement that signaled its death. Using the services of SCAD, it had at least been recognized as a voice for black longshoremen in Brooklyn and throughout the port. Now the fight for equal rights would take place within one giant local. The general failure of Local 968 to obtain permanent work did influence strategy during the 1960s. As one black activist longshoreman stated in 1962: "We don't need [a] black local—We need work—We need jobs."[45]

Experiencing daily discrimination, black longshoremen adopted different but complementary tactics to survive. When institutional power was available, especially in the guise of Local 968, they adopted open confrontation. They also made alliances with sympathetic allies, whether the New York Urban League or SCAD. If isolated, then some longshoremen employed the stance of making themselves readily available for work, hoping that such action would lead to acceptance, and, ultimately, regular work. The struggle for acceptance on the waterfront had pitted black longshoremen against both employers and trade union officials. Only when strategically necessary were these longshoremen courted by union officers. Such qualified acceptance was fleeting, dependent upon pressure from below or from outside forces. Black and Hispanic longshoremen took different paths to guarantee a semblance of control. The results were mixed, but at least the varied experiences offered the hope that discrimination on the waterfront could be effectively challenged.

Notes

1. The relationship between race and the trade union is a topic that has attracted the attention of social, urban, and labor historians, and recently it has been energized by new approaches that utilize notions of social construction and group interdependence. For literature on construction see David Roediger, *The Wages of Whiteness: Race and the Making of the American Working Class* (New York: Verso, 1991); Kenneth Durr, "When Southern Politics Came North: The Roots of White Working-Class Conservatism in Baltimore, 1940–1964," *Labor History* 37 (Summer 1996): 309–31; Noel Ignatiev, *How the Irish Became White* (New York: Routledge, 1995); Theodore W. Allen, *The Invention of the White Race*, vol. 1, *Racial Oppression and Social Control* (New York: Verso, 1994). Much of the discussion regarding exclusionary trade union practices and African Americans has revolved around the argument by Herbert Hill that such organizations became white fiefdoms. See Herbert Hill, "The Importance of Race in American Labor History," *International Journal of Politics, Culture, and Society* 9 (1995): 317–43; idem, "The Problem of Race in American Labor History," *Reviews in American History* 24 (1996): 180–208. The labeling of trade unions as exclusionary is discussed by Bruce Nelson, "Organized Labor and the Struggle for Black Equality in Mobile during World War II," *Journal of American History* 80 (December 1993): 952–88; Henry M. McKiven, *Iron and Steel: Class, Race, and Community in Birmingham, Alabama, 1875–1920* (Chapel Hill: University of North Carolina Press, 1995); Robert J. Norrell, "Caste in Steel: Jim Crow Careers in Birmingham, Alabama," *Journal of American History* 73 (December 1986): 669–94. In reaction to Hill's contention, a large number of studies have argued that the picture is not so simply drawn. These authors have shown that the trade union experience of blacks has been multidimensional and has changed over time. See Rick Halpern, *Down on the Killing Floor: Black and White Workers in Chicago's Packinghouses, 1904–1954* (Urbana: University of Illinois Press, 1997); Dan Letwin, *The Challenge of Interracial Unionism: Alabama Coal Miners, 1878–1921* (Chapel Hill: University of North Carolina Press, 1998); Eric Arnesen, *Waterfront Workers of New Orleans: Race, Class, and Politics, 1863–1923* (Urbana:

University of Illinois Press, 1994); idem, "'Like Banquo's Ghost, It Will Not Down': The Race Question and the American Railroad Brotherhoods, 1880–1920," *American Historical Review* 99 (December 1994): 1601–33; Alex Lichtenstein, "Racial Conflict and Racial Solidarity in the Alabama Coal Strike in 1894: New Evidence in the Gutman-Hill Debate," *Labor History* 36 (Winter 1995): 63–76; Brian Kelly, "Policing the 'Negro Eden': Racial Paternalism in the Alabama Coalfields, 1906–1922," *Alabama Review* 51 (July 1998): 163–83. For studies that factor in employer action, see Venus Green, "The 'Lady' Telephone Operator: Gendering Whiteness in the Bell System," in *Racializing Class, Classifying Race: Labor and Difference in Britain, the USA and Africa,* ed. Peter Alexander and Rick Halpern (New York: St. Martin's, 2000); Thomas J. Sugrue, "Segmented Work, Race-Conscious Workers: Structure, Agency and Division in the CIO Era," *International Review of Social History* 41 (December 1996): 389–406.

2. *New York Post,* September 20, 1961, 23.

3. See Arnesen, *Waterfront Workers of New Orleans.*

4. Lester Rubin, *The Negro in the Longshore Industry—The Racial Policies of American Industry, Report No. 29* (Philadelphia: University of Pennsylvania Press, 1974), 51–70. Other studies that have examined black longshoremen include Herbert Northrup, *Organized Labor and the Negro* (New York: Harper, 1971), 137–44; Sterling D. Spero and Abram L. Harris, *The Black Worker: The Negro and the Labor Movement* (New York: Columbia University Press, 1931), 198–205; Calvin Winslow, "On the Waterfront: Black, Italian and Irish Longshoremen in the New York Harbor Strike of 1919," in *Protest and Survival: Essays for E. P. Thompson,* ed. John Rule and Robert Malcolmson (New York: Norton, 1993), 365–81.

5. "Urban League of Greater New York Memorandum on the Status of Minority Group Workers on the New York–New Jersey Waterfront, 1956," Vernon Jensen Papers, box 1–4067, Kheel Center, Cornell University. There were five African American international vice presidents but they all represented southern ports.

6. *New York Post,* September 20, 1961, 23.

7. Arthur McMillon, interview by author, March 12, 1999.

8. Howard Kimeldorf, *Reds or Rackets: The Making of Radical and Conservative Unions on the Waterfront* (Berkeley: University of California Press, 1992), 144–48. See also Arnesen, *Waterfront Workers of New Orleans.*

9. For an excellent discussion of biracial unionism among longshoremen see Arnesen, *Waterfront Workers of New Orleans.* For the mix of ethnic and racial groups, see Winslow, "On the Waterfront."

10. Kimeldorf, *Reds or Rackets,* 154–55; Colin J. Davis, "'All I Got's a Hook': New York Longshoremen and the 1948 Dock Strike," in *Waterfront Workers: New Perspectives on Race and Class,* ed. Calvin Winslow (Urbana: University of Illinois Press, 1998), 131–54.

11. "Testimony of Cleophas Jacobs," Senate Committee on Labor and Public Welfare, *To Clarify the Overtime Provisions of the Fair Labor Standards Act of 1938, As Amended,* 81st Cong., 1st sess., 1949, 488–91.

12. *New York Times,* January 19, 1952, 9.

13. Morroe Berger, "The New York State Law against Discrimination: Operation and Administration," *Cornell Law Quarterly* 35 (Summer 1950): 747–96; Elmer A. Carter, "Practical Considerations of Anti-Discrimination Legislation—Experience under the New York Law Against Discrimination," *Cornell Law Quarterly* 40 (Fall 1954): 40–59.

14. Report of Conference with the Officers of the International Longshoremen's As-

sociation and the Officers of Local No. 968, ILA, March 19, 1952, Jensen Papers, box-4067. For Local 968's overtures to Governor Dewey and SCAD, see *New York Times*, January 28, 1952, 37, and February 7, 1952, 55.

15. Peter B. Levy, "The Waterfront Commission of the Port of New York: A History and Appraisal," *Industrial and Labor Relations Review* 42 (July 1989): 508–23; Charles P. Larrowe, *Shape-Up and Hiring Hall: A Comparison of Hiring Methods on the New York and Seattle Waterfronts* (Berkeley: University of California Press, 1955), 41–48; Vernon Jensen, "Hiring Practices and Employment Experience of Longshoremen in the Port of New York," *International Labor Review* 77 (April 1958): 342–53.

16. "Jim Crow Stalks the Waterfront," *Our World*, August, 1955, 21.

17. "Urban League of Greater New York Memorandum on the Status of Minority Group Workers on the New York–New Jersey Waterfront, 1956," Jensen Papers, box 1-4067.

18. "Testimony of Thomas Fauntleroy, in the Matter of Arbitration between ILA-Independent, and Its Affiliated Locals in the Port of New York, and the New York Shipping Association," September 29, 1958, Jensen Papers, box 5–4096.

19. *New York Amsterdam News*, November 22, 1958, 11.

20. Memorandum of Meeting with Thomas Fauntleroy, Business Agent, Local 968, August 23, 1957, series 10409–83, box 17, State Commission Against Discrimination, State of New York, New York State Archives (hereafter SCAD-NYSA).

21. Memorandum to Philip Partnow, Director of Investigations from Jean D. Brown, Field Representative, April 10, 1957, series 10409–83, box 17, SCAD-NYSA.

22. Memorandum of Meeting, Elmer Carter, Commissioner, SCAD, and Thomas Gleason, President, Local 1, ILA, January 16, 1958, and letter to Elmer Carter from Thomas Gleason, April 27, 1959, both in series 10409–83, box 17, SCAD-NYSA.

23. Memorandum to Philip Partnow from Mathew Foner, Field Representative, September 10, 1958, letter to Harry G. Liese, Attorney representing Universal Terminal and Stevedoring Corporation, from Elmer Carter, March 26, 1959 (quote), and letter to Elmer Carter from Harry G. Liese, April 7, 1959, all in series 10409–83, box 22, SCAD-NYSA.

24. Memorandum to Philip Partnow from I. R. Kornbliet, Field Representative, October 10, 1958, series 10409–83, box 22, SCAD-NYSA.

25. Letter to Elmer A. Carter from J. J. Marbler, Treasurer, Transoceanic Terminal Corporation, October 2, 1959, series 10409–83, box 22, SCAD-NYSA.

26. Memorandum to Elmer A. Carter from Reginald K. Ingram, February 4, 1959 (Walters quotes), and letter to J. J. Marbler from Elmer A. Carter, February 26, 1960 (final quote), both in series 10409–83, box 22, SCAD-NYSA.

27. "The Operation of State Fair Employment Practices Commissions," *Harvard Law Review* 68 (February 1955): 694. For a more sympathetic appraisal of SCAD see Frieda Wunderlich, "New York's Antidiscrimination Law," *Social Research* 17 (June 1950): 219–47.

28. Judith Stein identified and analyzed similar bureaucratic timidity with the EEOC in her book *Running Steel, Running America: Race, Economic Policy, and the Decline of Liberalism* (Chapel Hill: University of North Carolina Press, 1998).

29. Edward L. Carter, Memorandum Accompanying Complaint, March 2, 1956.

30. Memorandum to Elmer A. Carter from Edward L. Carter, April 25, 1956, and Memorandum, Jacob Wittner, Field Representative, August 8, 1956, both in series 10409–83, box 13, SCAD-NYSA.

31. Memorandum to Elmer A. Carter from Edward L. Carter, June 28, 1956, series 10409–83, box 13, SCAD-NYSA. Edward Carter's first meeting with Kisberg was an explosive one. Carter reported that Kisberg "began swearing and implying that our real interest had to do with alleged acceptance of bribes." Memorandum to Elmer A. Carter from Edward L. Carter, June 8, 1956, series 10409–83, box 13, SCAD-NYSA.

32. "Determination after Investigation and Conference—Julio Concepcion et al. vs. John W. McGrath Corporation," December 17, 1956 (quotes), and "Determination after Investigation and Conference—Francisco Garcia vs. McGrath Corporation," December 17, 1956, both in series 10409–83, box 13, SCAD-NYSA.

33. Letter to Archibald E. McGrath, Treasurer and General Counsel, McGrath Corporation, from Elmer A. Carter, December 17, 1956, series 10409–83, box 13, SCAD-NYSA.

34. For reports of the increasing pressure on the ILA to end discrimination on the waterfront in this period, see *New York Amsterdam News,* October, 1958, 29, November 22, 1958, 1, 11, May 2, 1959; *New York World Telegram,* January 30, 1959, 4, February 4, 1959, 3; *New York World Telegram,* February 5, 1959, 4.

35. *New York Times,* March 26, 1959.

36. Ibid., June 23, 1959, 1, 20 (quotes).

37. Ibid.

38. "Agreement made this 25th day of June, 1959 by and between Local 968 and Local 1814," box 3, folder 12, James Haughton Papers, Schomburg Center for Research in Black Culture, New York Public Library; *New York Times,* June 28, 1959, 52 (quotes).

39. *New York Amsterdam News,* July 4, 1959, 2 (first quote); *Pittsburgh Courier,* July 11, 1959, 3 (second quote).

40. *New York Times,* June 28, 1959, 52.

41. The AFL-CIO did not give the ILA a completely clean bill of health, but said only that it enjoyed "substantial compliance with the directives of the AFL." Report and Recommendations of AFL-CIO Executive Council Committee Respecting Application of the International Longshoremen's Association (Independent) for Affiliation with the AFL-CIO, series 5541, box 8, Philip Taft Papers, Kheel Archive, Cornell University.

42. *New York Amsterdam News,* October 3, 1959, 10.

43. *Pittsburgh Courier,* October 14, 1959, 3.

44. Letter to George Meany, president AFL-CIO, from A. Philip Randolph, vice-president, AFL-CIO, October 9, 1961, box 3, Haughton Papers; *New York Amsterdam News,* October 7, 1961, 30.

45. Minutes of Meeting, Longshore Committee for Equal Opportunity, August 26, 1962, box 3, Haughton Papers.

CONCLUSION

The oppositional movements by dockworkers in New York City and London were explosive forces during the post–World War II era. They represented a new form of rebellion against union hierarchies and local and central governments. Although separated by the Atlantic Ocean, these men shared intense resentments against their union leaders, albeit for different reasons. Estrangement in turn led to confrontation and to intense questioning of union principles and direction. When these workers rebelled they took on not just their union leaders, but also their respective governments.

In the case of New York City, an indifferent and corrupt union hierarchy ignited the oppositional movement. The backdrop was a casual system of hiring (the shape-up) where longshoremen daily lined up for work and paid kickbacks to be picked out of the waiting crowd. The fact that their union was gangster ridden made most longshoremen yearn for a better deal, one that ensured fair access to the work and better wages and conditions. Most of all, they wanted stronger control in the ILA. Also nurturing the rank-and-file challenge during the postwar period were labor priests and Communist agitators. These two groups used existing labor law to encourage docker militancy. The federal government in turn used legal and conciliatory machinery either to stall strike action or to negotiate a return to work. By not challenging the corrupt and staunchly anti-Communist union leadership, the government further alienated the rank and file, leading to wildcat strikes well into the 1950s. It was left to New York State officials to assume the mantle of reform. They were acutely aware of the damaging financial effects that the corrupt union and wildcat strikes had on shipping operations in the port of New York. A powerful combination of labor mediation board representatives and Governor Thomas E. Dewey eventually supported the oppositional movement's calls for cleansing the union and ridding the docks of gangster control.

Belatedly, the American Federation of Labor joined the chorus for reform, leaving in its wake an isolated but unrepentant ILA.

In the London case, the government played an even larger role. Quasi-governmental dock labor boards were established in 1947 to oversee working conditions and grievances. The dockers' union leadership pledged to the new Labour government industrial peace in exchange for a voice in the country's economic decision making. The rank and file, however, resented such bureaucratic restraint and rebelled against it. Paradoxically, the dockers' militancy was framed by the prewar casual era where protection of jobs was based upon the clarion call "one out, all out." Again, a Communist presence played a catalytic role, resulting in a series of strikes and work stoppages in the postwar era. Industrial action threatened a weakened economy and a population still surviving on food rations. Consequently, the Labour government was far more rigorous than its United States counterpart in dispatching troops between 1948 and 1951 to unload food stuffs and targeting strike leaders for punishment. The clash between the striker movement and the union and government was far more inflammable.

The rank-and-file battles along the waterfronts of London and New York City contained strong elements of insurrection. Each set of workers exhibited subversive tendencies. In London, dockworkers created alternative port-wide organizations that threatened the existing union structure. In New York, longshoremen initially allied themselves with sympathetic lawyers to contest pay inequities. The back-pay committees were symbolic of their resentment, and yet many longshoremen did not join the suits for back-pay. So there were distinct differences in dockworker action in the two countries. London dockworkers were far more synchronized in their struggle against union hierarchies and governments. London union leaders more commonly perceived strike action as disloyal and, at worst, treacherous.

The British and U.S. governments shared antagonistic feelings toward unofficial or wildcat strikes, which they regarded as potentially wrecking the capitalist economies as a whole. This was particularly the case in London. With the nation continuing to exist on food rations, any threat to the movement of such cargo was treated with the utmost seriousness. The British Labour government was trying to rescue a sagging economy, mired in debt. Any danger to the balance of payments—of which trade was so vital a piece—was regarded with dread. Dock strikes were therefore seen as distinct threats to the revitalization of the economy. Thus states of emergency were declared, and troops were dispatched to load and unload perishable foodstuffs and other critical cargoes.

Framed by the cold war, the contest for power also ushered in the notion of Communist conspiracy. The Communist label was applied by established union leaders to smear the strike leaders. Such a tactic had limited effect on the trajectory of the oppositional movements in both cities. Only in London did the issue take hold as the Labour government and the press joined in using Red-scare language and posturing. But even this tactic had little bearing on the rank-and-file movement. Even though substantial sections of the rank-and-file leaders were Communist Party members, this was not of much concern for the members as a whole. As long as the insurgent leaders fought for concrete issues such as discipline, overtime, and the firing of older workers, the majority of dockworkers went along with the rebellion.

There remained critical differences between the two dockworker movements, however. The issue of race in New York created an additional movement alongside the wildcat strike effort. Race continued to determine access to jobs and union offices. African American and Hispanic longshoremen confronted clear barriers to regular work and advancement along the waterfront. Employers and white ethnics argued it was merely a case of getting in line. But many of the black and Hispanic workers had a long tradition of dock work. Even recent arrivals justifiably argued that it was race that precluded their getting dock work. In some ways the black and Hispanic dockworkers' method of redress—looking for help from outside supporters or agencies—reflected what many of their white workers were also forced to do. Unable to gain a hearing from established union elites, the New York longshoremen turned to outside allies for succor. To a large extent this is what distinguished New York longshoremen from their transatlantic cousins. While the movement in London was mainly self-directed, in New York the reliance on outside allies weakened a more uniform response and opened up such allies to criticism as "outsiders."

The elements that unified the two groups were far more important than those that separated them. Their actions were undergirded by a common frustration with union elites. No longer willing to go along with union prerogatives, these men openly challenged established union expectations. Standing up to union leaders was a risky venture. It could result in the loss of a job or provoke an acrimonious response from union leaders. The charged circumstances of the postwar period encouraged such rebellious behavior. The job, and its attendant group identification, nurtured and encouraged resistance. The war experience also played its role. Young men returning from the war were no longer necessarily ready to accept control from trade union officialdom. In sum, the two work forces, British and American, simultaneously demanded democracy in the union. This ensured that conflict on the waterfront would be both ongoing and explosive.

Dignity became the watchword for these dockworkers; they demanded recognition as workers, union members, and human beings. Their struggle was fraught with peril, yet it was grounded in the notion that they were fighting for justice. The dockers shared a strong belief that they mattered, that they were more than mere unskilled workers. These men took on the role of rebels or militants, which says much for their courage and tenacity. Above all, rather than fatalistically accepting their lot they fought long and hard against their unjust treatment both within their respective union organizations and on the job. Their multiple experiences bring into sharp focus the complexity of working life. Ultimately, the unofficial leaders and the rank and file shared a deep-seated antagonism toward union leaders. Whether they wanted to reform or dismiss these union leaders was not the critical point. Rather, the goal was to be heard and recognized as workers and above all as union members.

By rejecting union and government calls for compliance, these dockworkers expressly challenged the emerging cold-war calls for conformity. They could not fail to recognize the irony of a situation where governments constantly berated other regimes for their totalitarianism but tolerated repression within established dockworker unions. While union leaders and governments failed to recognize, or take seriously, the dockworkers' demands for democracy, the men gambled on a policy of confrontation. It was the effect of World War II that energized these men and enabled them to overcome calls for obedience to cold-war exigencies. Although the accusation of Communist manipulation was taken very seriously by the men, it could not extinguish their burning sense of injustice and betrayal. More was expected from their union officers in this era of established union recognition and power.

But dockworkers remained apart from the beginnings of a transformation of working-class life in the second half of the twentieth century. Here were men who literally moved the goods of the postwar consumer revolution but whose alienation isolated them from full participation in that revolution. Experiences such as their being turned away from public transportation because of their dirty clothes reinforced this sense of separation from established norms of behavior. When they were chastised by union leaders, employers, and governments for their irresponsible strike activity, it merely confirmed their identity as "other." They believed they could rely only on one another. In certain circumstances they would accept support from outsiders, whether Communist agitators or labor priests, but they knew they were alone. It was only the work gang, and by extension the portwide labor force, that could be trusted. It was their solidarity that gave them the power and courage to take on forces determined to control them. That in some cases the men prevailed says much about their common values of dignity and their commitment to struggle.

INDEX

COLIN J. DAVIS is Professor of History at the University of Alabama, Birmingham. He is the author of *Power at Odds: The 1922 National Railroad Shopmen's Strike* and co-editor of *A Comparative International History of Dock Labour, 1780–1970* and *It Is Union and Liberty: A History of Alabama Coal Miners.*

THE WORKING CLASS IN AMERICAN HISTORY

Worker City, Company Town: Iron and Cotton-Worker Protest in Troy and Cohoes, New York, 1855–84 *Daniel J. Walkowitz*

Life, Work, and Rebellion in the Coal Fields: The Southern West Virginia Miners, 1880–1922 *David Alan Corbin*

Women and American Socialism, 1870–1920 *Mari Jo Buhle*

Lives of Their Own: Blacks, Italians, and Poles in Pittsburgh, 1900–1960 *John Bodnar, Roger Simon, and Michael P. Weber*

Working-Class America: Essays on Labor, Community, and American Society *Edited by Michael H. Frisch and Daniel J. Walkowitz*

Eugene V. Debs: Citizen and Socialist *Nick Salvatore*

American Labor and Immigration History, 1877–1920s: Recent European Research *Edited by Dirk Hoerder*

Workingmen's Democracy: The Knights of Labor and American Politics *Leon Fink*

The Electrical Workers: A History of Labor at General Electric and Westinghouse, 1923–60 *Ronald W. Schatz*

The Mechanics of Baltimore: Workers and Politics in the Age of Revolution, 1763–1812 *Charles G. Steffen*

The Practice of Solidarity: American Hat Finishers in the Nineteenth Century *David Bensman*

The Labor History Reader *Edited by Daniel J. Leab*

Solidarity and Fragmentation: Working People and Class Consciousness in Detroit, 1875–1900 *Richard Oestreicher*

Counter Cultures: Saleswomen, Managers, and Customers in American Department Stores, 1890–1940 *Susan Porter Benson*

The New England Working Class and the New Labor History *Edited by Herbert G. Gutman and Donald H. Bell*

Labor Leaders in America *Edited by Melvyn Dubofsky and Warren Van Tine*

Barons of Labor: The San Francisco Building Trades and Union Power in the Progressive Era *Michael Kazin*

Gender at Work: The Dynamics of Job Segregation by Sex during World War II *Ruth Milkman*

Once a Cigar Maker: Men, Women, and Work Culture in American Cigar Factories, 1900–1919 *Patricia A. Cooper*

A Generation of Boomers: The Pattern of Railroad Labor Conflict in Nineteenth-Century America *Shelton Stromquist*

Work and Community in the Jungle: Chicago's Packinghouse Workers, 1894–1922 *James R. Barrett*

Workers, Managers, and Welfare Capitalism: The Shoeworkers and Tanners of Endicott Johnson, 1890–1950 *Gerald Zahavi*

Men, Women, and Work: Class, Gender, and Protest in the New England Shoe Industry, 1780–1910 *Mary Blewett*

Workers on the Waterfront: Seamen, Longshoremen, and Unionism in the 1930s *Bruce Nelson*

German Workers in Chicago: A Documentary History of Working-Class Culture from 1850 to World War I *Edited by Hartmut Keil and John B. Jentz*

On the Line: Essays in the History of Auto Work *Edited by Nelson Lichtenstein and Stephen Meyer III*

Upheaval in the Quiet Zone: A History of Hospital Workers' Union, Local 1199 *Leon Fink and Brian Greenberg*

Labor's Flaming Youth: Telephone Operators and Worker Militancy, 1878–1923 *Stephen H. Norwood*

Another Civil War: Labor, Capital, and the State in the Anthracite Regions of Pennsylvania, 1840–68 *Grace Palladino*

Coal, Class, and Color: Blacks in Southern West Virginia, 1915–32 *Joe William Trotter, Jr.*

For Democracy, Workers, and God: Labor Song-Poems and Labor Protest, 1865–95 *Clark D. Halker*

Dishing It Out: Waitresses and Their Unions in the Twentieth Century *Dorothy Sue Cobble*

The Spirit of 1848: German Immigrants, Labor Conflict, and the Coming of the Civil War *Bruce Levine*

Working Women of Collar City: Gender, Class, and Community in Troy, New York, 1864–86 *Carole Turbin*

Southern Labor and Black Civil Rights: Organizing Memphis Workers *Michael K. Honey*

Radicals of the Worst Sort: Laboring Women in Lawrence, Massachusetts, 1860–1912 *Ardis Cameron*

Producers, Proletarians, and Politicians: Workers and Party Politics in Evansville and New Albany, Indiana, 1850–87 *Lawrence M. Lipin*

The New Left and Labor in the 1960s *Peter B. Levy*

The Making of Western Labor Radicalism: Denver's Organized Workers, 1878–1905 *David Brundage*

In Search of the Working Class: Essays in American Labor History and Political Culture *Leon Fink*

Lawyers against Labor: From Individual Rights to Corporate Liberalism *Daniel R. Ernst*

"We Are All Leaders": The Alternative Unionism of the Early 1930s *Edited by Staughton Lynd*

The Female Economy: The Millinery and Dressmaking Trades, 1860–1930 *Wendy Gamber*

"Negro and White, Unite and Fight!": A Social History of Industrial Unionism in Meatpacking, 1930–90 *Roger Horowitz*

Power at Odds: The 1922 National Railroad Shopmen's Strike *Colin J. Davis*

The Common Ground of Womanhood: Class, Gender, and Working Girls' Clubs, 1884–1928 *Priscilla Murolo*

Marching Together: Women of the Brotherhood of Sleeping Car Porters *Melinda Chateauvert*

Down on the Killing Floor: Black and White Workers in Chicago's Packinghouses, 1904–54 *Rick Halpern*

Labor and Urban Politics: Class Conflict and the Origins of Modern Liberalism in Chicago, 1864–97 *Richard Schneirov*

All That Glitters: Class, Conflict, and Community in Cripple Creek *Elizabeth Jameson*

Waterfront Workers: New Perspectives on Race and Class *Edited by Calvin Winslow*

Labor Histories: Class, Politics, and the Working-Class Experience *Edited by Eric Arnesen, Julie Greene, and Bruce Laurie*

The Pullman Strike and the Crisis of the 1890s: Essays on Labor and Politics *Edited by Richard Schneirov, Shelton Stromquist, and Nick Salvatore*

AlabamaNorth: African-American Migrants, Community, and Working-Class Activism in Cleveland, 1914–45 *Kimberley L. Phillips*

Imagining Internationalism in American and British Labor, 1939–49 *Victor Silverman*

William Z. Foster and the Tragedy of American Radicalism *James R. Barrett*

Colliers across the Sea: A Comparative Study of Class Formation in Scotland and the American Midwest, 1830–1924 *John H. M. Laslett*

"Rights, Not Roses": Unions and the Rise of Working-Class Feminism, 1945–80 *Dennis A. Deslippe*

Testing the New Deal: The General Textile Strike of 1934 in the American South *Janet Irons*

Hard Work: The Making of Labor History *Melvyn Dubofsky*

Southern Workers and the Search for Community: Spartanburg County, South Carolina *G. C. Waldrep III*

We Shall Be All: A History of the Industrial Workers of the World (abridged edition) *Melvyn Dubofsky, ed. Joseph A. McCartin*

Race, Class, and Power in the Alabama Coalfields, 1908–21 *Brian Kelly*

Duquesne and the Rise of Steel Unionism *James D. Rose*

Anaconda: Labor, Community, and Culture in Montana's Smelter City *Laurie Mercier*

Bridgeport's Socialist New Deal, 1915–36 *Cecelia Bucki*

Indispensable Outcasts: Hobo Workers and Community in the American Midwest, 1880–1930 *Frank Tobias Higbie*

After the Strike: A Century of Labor Struggle at Pullman *Susan Eleanor Hirsch*

Corruption and Reform in the Teamsters Union *David Witwer*

Waterfront Revolts: New York and London Dockworkers, 1946–61 *Colin J. Davis*

The University of Illinois Press
is a founding member of the
Association of American University Presses.

Composed in 9/13 ITC Stone Serif
with ITC Stone Sans display
by Barbara Evans
at the University of Illinois Press
Designed by Paula Newcomb
Manufactured by Sheridan Press

University of Illinois Press
1325 South Oak Street
Champaign, IL 61820-6903
www.press.uillinois.edu